D0206347

JOHN ARDEN & MARGARETTA D'ARCY

AWKWARD CORNERS

methuen

Awkward Corners

John Arden was born in Barnsley, Yorkshire, in 1930. While studying archi-tecture at Cambridge and Edinburgh universities, he began to write plays, four of which have been produced at the Royal Court Theatre: *The Waters of Babylon, Live Like Pigs, Serjeant Musgrave's Dance* and *The Happy Haven;* while a fifth, *The Workhouse Donkey*, was produced at the Festival Theatre, Chichester. For a year he held an Annual Fellowship in Playwriting at Bristol University, and Bristol Old Vic produced *Ironhand*, his free adaptation of Goethe's *Goetz von Berlichingen. Armstrong's Last Goodnight* was first produced at the Glasgow Citizens' Theatre and later at the National Theatre.*Left-Handed Liberty* was specially commissioned by the Corpor-ation of London to commemorate the 750th Anniversary of Magna Carta and was produced at the Mermaid Theatre. He is married to Margaretta D'Arcy with whom he has collaborated on several plays. Arden's first novel, *Silence Among the Weapons* (1982), was short-listed for the Booker-McConnell Prize for Fiction.

Margaretta D'Arcy is Irish and has worked with improvisational and theatre techniques since the fifties. *Everything* (1987) is an account of her impris-onment in Armagh Gaol. She is a member of Aosdána, the Irish Artists' Association, and receives from it a grant to explore alternatives to Judaeo-Christian patriarchal culture, in pursuit of which she has organized an auton-omous women's group, the Galway Women's Entertainment. Her work with Arden includes *The Business of Good Government* (1960), *The Happy Haven* (1960), *Ars Longa, Vita Brevis* (1963), *Friday's Hiding* (1965), *The Royal Pardon* (1966), *Muggins is a Martyr* (1968), *The Hero Rises Up* (1968), *The Ballygombeen Bequest* (1972), *The Island of the Mighty* (1972), *Keep the People Moving* (for radio, 1972), *The Non-Stop Connolly Show* (1975), *Vandaleur's Folly* (1978) and *The Little Gray Home in the West* (1978). Her play *A Pinprick of History* was performed at the Almost Free Theatre, London in 1977.

Plays by John Arden

Serjeant Musgrave's Dance
The Waters of Babylon
Live Like Pigs
The Happy Haven
The Workhouse Donkey
Ironhand (adapted from Goethe's
Goetz von Berlichingen)
Left-Handed Liberty
Armstrong's Last Goodnight
Soldier, Soldier and Other Plays
Two Autobiographical Plays

**Plays by John Arden
and Margaretta D'Arcy**

The Business of Good Government
The Hero Rises Up
The Island of the Mighty
The Royal Pardon

**Plays by Margaretta D'Arcy
and John Arden**

The Little Gray Home in the West
The Non-Stop Connolly Show
Vandaleur's Folly

John Arden & Margaretta D'Arcy

Awkward Corners

Essays, papers, fragments
selected, with commentaries,
by the authors

A Methuen Paperback

A Methuen Dramabook

First published in 1988 by Methuen London Ltd
11 New Fetter Lane, London EC4P 4EE
and in the United States of America
by Methuen Inc., 29 West 35th Street, New York, NY 10001
Copyright © 1988 by John Arden & Margaretta D'Arcy

British Library Cataloguing in Publication Data

Arden, John
Awkward corners: essays, papers, fragments.
1. Theatre
I. Title   II. D'Arcy, Margaretta
792   PN2037
ISBN 0-413-40340-8

Printed in Great Britain by Cox & Wyman Ltd, Reading

Contents

Manifesto for les Invisibles

It's not what you know, or even
Who you know that counts, it's
What you know about who!
Just as a millstone grinds . . .
Slowly but surely . . .
So we are Big Brother, Big Sister,
Big big big big, and we know
Who's watching who!
We also know
CHAINED EXPRESSION IS NO EXPRESSION!
If you want to be anything,
You must be your true self,
So make up your mind,
Be natural and real
Be just as you are
Be the total you feel
And know that we mean
CHAINED EXPRESSION IS NO EXPRESSION!
Life-force is a living pulse,
And we're all the people,
The greatest institution in the world.
Government is the body politic, meant to
Be shrewdly judicious in support of an aim,
To help and enhance in the world,
And we're all the people who know
CHAINED EXPRESSION IS NO EXPRESSION!

Mutual understanding, with cake that
Goes right round, that's the deal!
CHAINED EXPRESSION IS NO EXPRESSION!
CHAINED EXPRESSION IS NO EXPRESSION!
CHAINED EXPRESSION IS NO EXPRESSION!
CHAINED EXPRESSION IS NO EXPRESSION!
CHAINED EXPRESSION IS NO EXPRESSION!

PART ONE

ARDEN

Introduction: by J.A.

In 1977 Methuen published my first collection of essays and occasional pieces, *To Present The Pretence*. It contained two essays written in collaboration with Margaretta D'Arcy. One of these dealt at length with *The Non-Stop Connolly Show*, which we had produced in Dublin in 1975, our most comprehensive practical attempt at incorporating our theatrical experience and theories with what I then termed 'The Matter of Ireland'. The other one, 'Playwrights On Picket', was an account of our dispute with the Royal Shakespeare Company in 1972, which ended in our going on official strike (as members of the trade-union-affiliated Society of Irish Playwrights) against the working conditions imposed on us during the production of *The Island of the Mighty* trilogy. *Awkward Corners* is largely a follow-through of these two previous themes, Ireland on the one hand, artists' roles in a gathering climate of repression on the other.

That RSC dispute has never been settled: and although we are no longer huddled with our placards outside the stage door of the Aldwych Theatre, we regard ourselves and our labour as still being 'withdrawn' from the RSC and from any other theatre company that maintains the same invidious and overweening management practices. It was a very awkward corner in that back-alley off Drury Lane: all sorts of people, theatrical and other, came to support and sustain us, but others came to revile, and the wind (it was in the early winter of 1972) was extremely cold, and the newspapers that reported our defiance did so, on the whole, with exactly the same insidious distortions and innuendo they were later to apply to much more celebrated industrial actions.

Further on in this book, D'Arcy writes of 'the international art hypermarket'. In *To Present The Pretence* I referred to 'the meaningless foam-rubber of the jumbo-jet culture'. The two phrases describe the same phenomenon. The RSC was but part of it: and still is. Last night I paused from writing this to watch them on TV receiving a Tony award for *Les Misérables* . . . 'degradations of old French poverty, how are yeh?' – as they say in Ireland. The base complacent traffic has extended itself considerably during the past ten years, like one of those alien fungoids in a late-night horror film, and it may seem there is little that can be done to stop it except to howl 'Arrgh, the THING!!' – and to hope hopelessly for the 'inherent flaw-factor in its molecular generative-cycle' to show up before the film comes to an end in total defeat for the 'human race as we now know it'.

But I do not think the hope is really quite as hopeless as all that. There *is* an inherent flaw: and it can only be perceived by understanding that the human-race-as-we-now-know-it is (despite everything) the same human race that we always knew. It has always contained individuals who actually *thrive* upon being driven into awkward corners: and in every individual making up what may appear a solid soggy mass (already incorporated, one might say, into the THING) there are always one or two personal awkward corners (like woody turnip-chunks in a broth) never entirely capable of being fully digested. Jonah in the belly of the whale was able nonetheless to pull together his poetic faculties and compose a psalm so passionate yet so well worked-out that it persuaded the Lord*

---

* Unless it was the goddess Rahab, to whom the great sea-beasts gave allegiance; and whose story was appropriated by Jahve, like so many others.

(against His own worse nature) that the hitherto unsteadfast prophet should not be written-off as a permanent bad debt. And in Kipling's *Just So Story* the seaman in exactly the same predicament made an even more telling assertion of his awkward human nature, he jumped and bumped around so painfully that the whale's interior became more awkward for the whale than it was for himself, and so he secured his release.

There is, in consequence, a certain amount of bumping and jumping among my essays: the times seem to demand it. And, within the jumping and bumping, there is some attempt at thinking out a few new psalms.

The first piece, *Drawing Blood in Galway*, is a reminder that the man not long ago described as 'the most popular president the United States has ever had' was not altogether foisted on the Irish people quite so easily as the Irish Government (his clients as well as Mrs Thatcher's) expected. And this despite the fact that, in the tourist season, nearly every hotel and bed-and-breakfast in the west of Ireland flies the Stars and Stripes, and Irish TV and radio constantly throb with whingeing pleas to America to solve Ireland's incredibly ill-handled economy by allowing more and more desperate emigrants to follow their forebears of the Great Famine across the Atlantic.

Shift of Perspective is 'Matter of Ireland' from a more personal standpoint than I have previously written: and deals *en passant* with an English writer whose life I am presently trying to encompass in a novel – John Bale, a very awkward customer in a series of awkward historical corners.

The long essay on O'Casey is – in a sense – out of place in this volume, as it was written in 1975, the year of *The Non-Stop Connolly Show*, and expresses some notions that were fed into that production. It was excluded from *To Present The Pretence* only because of its length. I publish it now as a kind of farewell to old assumptions – in particular the assumption under which I wrote it – that the regular professionals of the regular professional theatre might, if they set their mind to it, find a proper understanding of the spirit and intentions of Sean O'Casey without radically altering their own preconceptions of their trade's nature and purposes.

Shift of Discipline is a show of biting the hand that feeds, without malice, just to show I can still do it. It is also a cry of relief at my finding the broken chains of theatre no longer hurting my wrists: they haven't fallen completely off; but, gathered in the fist, they still make a useful flail.

Prayers at Ennis was commissioned by a Sunday newspaper to make one of a series of travel articles either delighting-in or detesting some particular place. The editor asked for something 'genuinely personal'. I had, not long before, 'gone over the top' with solidarity and appreciation in the article on Nicaragua, so I thought I would prefer to detest for a few pages. The Nicaraguan piece itself (*Nicaraguan Comparisons*) is, I am afraid, unashamedly enthusiastic: it puts me so clearly in a partisan camp – I would rather call it the camp of human decency – that the *Listener* (who had originally requested it) declined to publish. They had hoped, someone told me, awkwardly enough, over the telephone, for a more balanced weighing-up of pro against con. I felt angrily positive that the only *con* requiring mention at that time was spelt C·O·N·T·R·A, was paid for by the CIA, and was also cognate with 'con' in the sense of *confidence-trick* (as the current Congressional Committee of Investigation is now finding out): it was far too evil to be beguilingly diminished by what D'Arcy in her Introduction (page 123) describes as 'little bridges'. After the *Listener*'s rejection I had an enquiry from *Granta* and sent them the piece, enlarging it to include rather more about Ireland. I never heard about it again, not even an acknowledgement that it had arrived. They were casual, I had been careless. Whose loss? I then had an enquiry from the *New Statesman*. As I recollect, I was very busy at the time and unable to locate my carbon of the article, so I referred them to *Granta*, not knowing indeed whether or no *Granta* was accepting or rejecting – I still don't know: although after more than two years I am forced to assume the latter. I never heard again from the *New Statesman*, not even an acknowledgement. I don't think the article is out-of-date yet, if anything it is more pertinent than it was. For I notice from the literary reviews that it is now quite 'upmarket' to write debunking material about Nicaragua: so perhaps my naïvety (if that's what it is) has some value with some readers. The Nicaraguans are too hard-nosed to be worried that their revolution and its defence against continuously brutal counter-attack has had time to become fashionable and now, again, unfashionable in our fungoid grab-it-all sub-culture, and is settling down comfortably as an atmospheric background for some pretty fellow's pseudo-documentary novel or screen-play of how he *found himself* in Managua, or failed to find himself; or didn't even try to look, either for himself or for anyone else . . . They have an awkward determination to be their own country:*so let them be their own, always.*

The large chunk called *Autobiography* is really nothing of the sort: but it was so commissioned by an American publisher who was bringing out a series of such pieces by contemporary writers, and I wrote it because I felt I needed to set down a number of things about my early life before I forgot them. As it is, I think much of it is probably misremembered: it is neither more nor less 'autobiographical' than the short story about an Englishman living in Ireland (as I do) on a lake island (as I once did). As far as the 'supernatural' part of it goes, *The Fork in the Head* is based upon a County Galway folk-tale, recorded in the Irish folklore commission's archives; the rest of it relates more closely to the *Shift of Perspective* essay: as indeed did the book in which it first appeared, a collection of stories written in Ireland on Irish themes by resident foreigners. I don't think it sold well and the Irish critics seem to have ignored it on the whole ... queering their pitch, I suppose. The two principal characters in my story however are not writers but purveyors of hypermarket commercial art, so in any case their perspective is a sizeable shift away from my own.

Drawing Blood In Galway

published in *Theatre Ireland*, 1985

Guerrilla-theatre – part-satire, part-protest, part-demo, a bit of all of them and yet not quite any of them. (Let me say, not a form I have ever participated in myself.) It is intended to draw blood without warning. If it is tolerated, it has failed. A comedian called Datus once sang a pop-song 'Goodbye Father, goodbye Mother', illustrating it with drinking and swimming gestures. The Emperor, Nero, supposed to have poisoned his father and tried to drown his mother, did not kill the bold Datus:

> 'he may merely have pretended not to care, for fear of encouraging others to be equally witty.' (Suetonius)

Not so the President of University College, Galway, recently, when Ronald Reagan was due there for an honorary doctorate in Law, only a few weeks after his agents had brazenly breached international law by the piratical mining of the Nicaraguan ports. Two severe-looking mature gentlemen in academic robes were to be found up and down the Galway streets, offering for sale ('price 10p, before the documents are rendered totally worthless by the forthcoming ceremony') facsimiles of doctorates, all correctly drawn up in Latin and endorsed as awarded for such recondite fields of study as *'anti-imperialismus'*. Passers-by were stopped, and, if willing, subjected to an abrupt verbal test, hectoring Alice-in-Wonderland questions, all calling for an absurd answer, and then – 'That must be the most ignorant reply we've had yet – of course it deserves a doctorate!' A brisk bit of schools' Latin, the paper handed over, and so to the next candidate.

I was one of the first to be examined and there was some verbal fumbling: but as the day wore on the questions got sharper and the act became more and more authoritative. A later confrontation (seen on RTE's *Today Tonight*), with a flushed mooncalf of a youth, produced an inimitable one-liner: 'What is your name, sir?' – helpless giggles and utter inability to speak – 'Good God here's a man so stupid he doesn't even know his own name! Give him the paper!' The very fact the whole exchange was presented in full on the TV showed how much professionalism this piece of street-theatre had achieved in so short a time: it was as vivid and clear-cut as any rehearsed studio sketch.

And it did draw blood. The President of UCG went on the air over Galway's Community Radio to denounce it with *gravitas* and deep offence. It had brought the university into *disrepute*, he declared . . . If he had possessed the powers of Nero, one felt, wild beasts in the arena would have been too merciful a chastisement.

The point was, the two gowned examiners (Pat Sheeran and Des Johnson) were not actors pretending to be dons: they were genuine doctors of the university, wearing the authentic robes to which they had an unimpeachable right. But they were wearing them *in the wrong place*, carrying their real-life roles into an unexpected direction of public subversion with which their employer could not cope, having neither the experience nor the necessary mastery of the social structure of town-gown relationships in Galway. The success of the act also depended on the highly ambivalent attitude of the non-university Galwegians to the Reagan visit – some welcomed it, but a far greater number were even more ready to welcome a satire upon it; and those in the street who approved of Ronald

Reagan would surely be dumbfounded and disarmed by the strong pedagogic style of the examiners' descent upon them.

And yet at the same time there was 'acting' involved: the pretence of an examination in an absurd context, subjective self-satire as well as the objective satire of public affairs. It could not have been done without a degree of theatrical awareness: both doctors had in fact been members of the Galway Theatre Workshop (not the current one, but its forebear with the same name set up by Margaretta D'Arcy in the mid-70s) and had there acquired those rudiments of street-theatre technique which they were to put to such effective use.

A laugh for the population, a diversion for the media, a vigorous encouragement for the anti-Reagan faction, an embarrassment for the Reagan organizers, an annoyance for the city fathers, and an acute knife-in-the-gut for UCG's pomposity (the whole university being anyway angrily divided about 50/50 on the political issue of the honorary doctorate) – it was, I suggest, a classic piece of guerrilla-theatre: technically skilful, unexpected, real, it hurt where it hit, it did not finish where it apparently ended, as will surely be shown the next time a Taoiseach blithely asks his client-professors to award a visiting head-of-state an inappropriate scholastic honour.

Similar events which come to mind: a crude and grinning Norman knight in his battle-gear dumping himself down on the Byzantine Emperor's momentarily-vacated jewel-encrusted throne at a Constantinople crusading conference in 1098 (thereby predicting the East-West history of the next two centuries); Margaretta D'Arcy, during a poetry-reading, carefully, seriously, embellishing the Ulster Museum with a framed 'H-block' logo at a time when that museum was censoring political paintings and H-block marches were being banned, (and the Long Kesh hunger-strikes were still two years in the future); the American colonials, dressed as Iroquois braves, emblematically emptying King George's

VAT-rated tea-chests into Boston Harbour (R. Reagan owes himself to that one).

It doesn't always work: the Carsonesque mountain-climb of Ian Paisley with a cohort of Loyalists waving what might have been gun-licences, or TV licences, or even market-gardeners' invoices, fell somewhat short on reality, whatever the rhetoric. Moreover, he had no audience, except the media. The exact moment must be caught; the exact tone must be achieved, relating the act to the environment (political, social, cultural – great intuitive skill is called for): and there *must* be an immediate audience of involved persons to provide all the reverberations, hostile, friendly, indifferent.

It can never be totally planned for, no rehearsal can be definitive and you cannot get together with friends saying, 'Let's set up a group to do guerrilla-theatre': rather must some friends without premeditation find themselves together saying, 'This situation is god-awful, why don't we go out now and make some sense of its nonsense . . .?'

Shift of Perspective

published in *The Connacht Tribune*, 1985

Awkward enough, the general notion of myself as mere English coming to live in this country with another playwright (female, Irish, catholic by upbringing, whereas I was cradle-protestant of the deepest inculcation), and seriously proposing to continue an artistic collaboration which had begun among the English on the themes of the English, for the audiences of England.

Mind you, these English themes, presented most frequently at the London Royal Court Theatre, were not altogether without an Irish admixture. Basically they dealt with the social and historical hinterlands of my own country, from a loosely left-wing point of view, although I was really more of a radical-liberal than anything very strictly doctrinaire. But from the very beginning I had a strong attraction towards the Celtic elements of the British tradition: I had shared digs with Tom Austin, an architect from Dublin, who introduced me to D'Arcy; before that, I had lived in Scotland where I met many Irish people from both north and south; and I nearly always found myself inserting some of this influence into my writing. I was not really aware of it at the time: but looking back I see a decided injection of Irish vitality into practically everything I wrote. From D'Arcy, of course, I learned, consciously, a great deal about this country, its facts and attitudes. But these cannot be *theoretically* ingested by a foreigner, particularly an English foreigner: they have to be experienced.

The actual fact of dwelling a step outwards from Britain away from Europe and towards America impels one to see Britain and the British mentality from a unique viewpoint, that of the first permanent landfall made by British imperial expansion. Some very heavy feet were set into Ireland over a long period of history; and for me to follow such feet without, as it were, finding myself fitting into their shoes, was an extremely disturbing circumstance.

When I came here in 1962 I largely refrained from deliberately handling Irish material – I still kept the country at arm's length – regarding myself as a cautious visitor who made use of the landscape (and the people as part of the landscape) for writing that was still psychologically centred in my earlier experiences. I had yet to adjust my view of England so that it became a view *from* Ireland. I had yet to adjust myself to any serious view *of* Ireland at all.

Some other English writers had lived here before I did. Some of them continued to write, as I was doing, for the English, others attempted to attract an Irish public as well. These precedents were often far from auspicious. One need only take a quick glance at the sixteenth century – that glorious time, for the English, of poetry, pageant, and romantic buccaneering seafarers, which has fixed itself into our educational and literary tradition (and by 'our' I deliberately include the English-speaking Irish) as the generative seedbed of all the excellence that is said to have followed. Two major poets were domiciled here during the period, Edmund Spenser and Sir Walter Ralegh, neither of them at all interested in an Irish readership. They share the signal distinction of having both taken an active part in a famous military atrocity, the massacre of the garrison of Dún-an-óir, the 'golden fort', at Smerwick, Co. Kerry, 1580.

Over six hundred soldiers, Irish, Spanish, and Italian, together with their womenfolk, were killed out of hand after the fort had been surrendered on terms. Spenser, as the Lord Deputy's secretary, seems to have signed the chit: Ralegh, as orderly-officer, commanded the execution-party. Spenser devoted an entire canto of his *Faerie Queene* to justifying the deed against the allegorical monsters, *Envy* and *Detraction*, who clearly stand for some sort of 'Troops Out of Ireland' movement active at the time but passed over by the standard history-books. Ralegh does not seem to have written on the subject afterwards, but it has been suggested that a certain dark pessimism running through his work may have its origin in the experience. Spenser's defence of the Lord Deputy (whom he represents as the Just Knight, *Sir Artegall*) did not convince the local people near his Co. Cork castle of Kilcolman: they burnt him out and he died in a matter of months.

Before this calamity he had written his *View of the Present State of Ireland*, a tract advocating genocide as the final solution to the Irish Question. And yet he had a high opinion of Ireland, as a piece of geography: the scenery inspired him. His list of Irish rivers in the *Faerie Queene* is charming:

> . . . the gentle Shure that making way
> By sweet Clonmell, adornes rich Waterford;
> The next, the stubborne Newre, whose waters gray
> By faire Kilkenny and Rosseponte boord,
> The third, the goodly Barrow, which doth hoord
> Great heapes of Salmons in his deepe bosome . . . *etc*

If only so lovely a country had a more convenient set of inhabitants – an opinion that has been echoed over and over in succeeding centuries by residents, not all of them foreigners, who have endeavoured to accommodate themselves to the actualities of Irish life, as opposed to the Bord Failte images, particularly in the west. It has something to do, I suppose, with the 'pathetic fallacy' – a serene dreamlike landscape ought, it is felt, to be peopled with equally serene human beings, who are not going to trouble one with high prices, inadequate public services, unfair systems of wealth-distribution, political repressions, censorship and corruption; or, worse, by complaints about them: or, worse still, by agitation and activism arising from the failure of those in power to give an ear to the complaints. Thus, from original 'love-at-first-sight', the newcomer's view of the 'present state' of the society can turn to unease, and then distaste, and then at last to rancorous hatred, which naturally tends to return as good as it gets.

I have no doubt that when Spenser moved in with his books and furniture, to Kilcolman, he surveyed the landscape in front of his windows and said to himself something like: 'My goodness, what a rake of first-class verse I can write in a place like this!' The Dún-an-óir bloodbath, seven years previously, must have seemed part of another world altogether – rebellion apparently over and done with, he would be able to reflect at leisure and in comparative comfort upon the problems of colonial government. In contrast to emergency action on a beleaguered Kerry peninsula, the destruction of a whole population was not to be considered in hysterical haste. He felt himself indeed sufficiently secure in the locality to court and marry an Anglo-Irish lady who must have really made him believe he had his 'stake in the country', that *sine qua non* of Irish acceptability.

He had time and atmosphere enough to establish for all posterity his unassailable place in Eng. Lit. And the greater part of his subject-matter was the enhancing of England, English religion, English law, which alone among all alternatives seemed to him the only possible inheritors of the beauties of his adopted land. *Sir Artegall*, in his allegory, rescues Ireland from the giant of popish nationalism – an alien doctrine introduced by evil Spain, just as alien doctrines (from Cuba, yes?) are today said to be still coming in on the ocean wave . . . Spenser really did believe he was serving Ireland's better interests. 'We destroyed this town in order to save it', said an American general in Vietnam: he, too, was surely sincere.

Spenser's Anglocentricity had been shared by an immediate predecessor of his in the colonial government – John Bale, Bishop of Ossory at the beginning here of the protestant reformation (1553). Bale was sent expressly to help restructure the English-speaking sector of the Irish Church in line with the new doctrines. He had already made his name as a deeply-committed politico-religious dramatist in London. His plays in fact are the crucial protestant link between the medieval catholic morality-drama and the new secular theatre of Marlowe and Shakespeare. The archaism of his language and, let us face it, the lumbering quality of his verse have caused his revolutionary theatrical skills to be undeservedly forgotten. His best-known piece, *King John*, was an emblematic rewriting of English history in search of the roots of nationalist protestantism. Without it the entire cycle of Elizabethan chronicle-plays might never have come to fruition. He wrote, one might say, in combat: catholic playwrights were also putting their ideas at the same time onto the stage, and English theatre between 1530 and 1558 was a battlefield of opposed philosophies. Exactly the sort of theatre that we at the Royal Court in the 1960s thought we might possibly be inaugurating (there is no doubt we were a conceited crowd: but the times seemed very lively).

On arrival in Kilkenny, Bale discovered that the Anglo-Irish congregations had hardly even heard of protestantism. If they presented plays at all, they would have been old-fashioned affirmations of orthodox catholicism which took no account of any serious intellectual dissent; people would have thought that heretics were heretics and the less said about their notions in detail the better. Bale was having none of this. Not only did he immediately introduce a traumatic brand-new liturgy, to the dismay of his diocesan clergy: but he extended it to the market-place with the production of some of his most outspoken and aggressive drama. His English audience had been delighted to see their anti-papal opinions reinforced by stage-production: in Ireland the same plays appeared no more than crude and brutal insults.

When they objected – physically – Bale called in the security-forces. Kilkenny had previously been a quiet district where the people were neither 'the King's Irish Rebels' nor the outlawed 'Wild Irish', to use the legalisms of the time. The situation resembled that in Downpatrick recently after an innovatory Orange March. The security-forces were unable to cope; and Bale (after a futile plea for help from Dublin, where the Cathedral and Castle authorities were appalled at his insensitivity) fled the country. He never came back. In later days, in England, Queen Elizabeth imposed prohibitions on any drama likely to stir public disorder by topical political or religious content: Bale's theatre-of-controversy became a dead letter even in the island of its origin. His courage and commitment are to be admired: his political intelligence, and his sense of humane intercourse, are not.

Both he and Spenser, as writers, were overt practitioners of cultural colonialism, at a time when this was the natural reflection of an actual and avowed political colonialism, in the service of which they both drew salaries. It might be thought – *I* used to think – that such examples were no longer relevant. I have come to see, in the years since 1969, that they are not only relevant but immediately so. Cultural colonialism does not necessarily come solely from the ruling class of the colonizing country. If Ireland has been most obviously oppressed by the British Establishment, this has only been made possible by a general (often unconscious) acquiescence from the rest of the population, even from those who, in theory, oppose all such things. John Bale, after all, had been extremely progressive against the feudal tyrannies that obstructed liberty in England. Transported to Kilkenny, and sanctioned in principle by government, his enlightenment became in itself a tyranny that he was not able to recognize.

So, today, the British 'left' can look westward and regard Ireland as little more than a backward extension of their own society to which their own rules and priorities continue to apply. A few years ago, at a symposium on Anglo-Irish affairs in the left-orientated Half Moon Theatre in London, a member of some socialist party was stung by Irish expressions of historical recrimination, and offered a half-hearted defence of O. Cromwell: 'What else could he do,' he asked, 'if he saw his English revolution threatened by what he took to be Irish reactionaries?' A young man from Belfast answered him with a heated question: 'Do you mean to say that a socialist government in London today would be perfectly entitled to protect itself by having its soldiers kill me and my friends if you don't take the same view as we do of our policies? We cannot guarantee that a free Ireland would be bound to do everything Britain required, because if we did, how could we call ourselves free?' This argument was not resolved on that occasion – nor can it be until it is realized that the dominant perspective from east to west can never be the same as the one from west to east. The onus of realization lies on those looking from east to west . . .

But *my* perspective is an odd one. I have come to see my own country in many ways as an Irish person sees it: but I cannot do the same for Ireland. Nor can I expect the Irish to be totally at ease with my comments upon them. I daresay if I had been brought up in the bosom of the British Establishment, and carried myself here as though there was still a Lord Lieutenant in Phoenix Park, I would achieve a greater degree of acceptance, shot through at times with the necessary bursts of hostility: the people would at least know where they stood with me – in much the same place as they stood with Sir W. Ralegh. But my background is that of the northern English industrial communities, where the Tories are not really regarded as fellow-countryfolk. A wary solidarity with irredentist Irish dissidence comes easier than 'civilized' intercourse with the successors of Daniel O'Connell, or John Redmond. Contrary to some opinions, this is not a romantic attitude. It derives from the discoveries about Ireland and England I have made through my work, and from a gradual confirmation of some prejudices (as well as the repudiation of others). I have experienced a mingling of two national traditions, or rather aspects of two traditions, which in fact turn out to be the one same supra-national tradition: that which is based on a very simple premise – that if we leave the control of our world to those who have already obtained that control, they will make quite sure that we never find out how they obtained it, what they plan to do with it, or even who exactly they are.

In Ireland it seems to me they find this easier to accomplish than in many other places. But also in Ireland there is a concomitant depth of resistance which exceeds that to be found in many other places. This potent contradiction makes this country such a fruitful base for a writer. It also ensures that the writer can never be entirely at ease here. Ireland can no more be *celebrated* by an English artist living here than the food in the pan can celebrate the heat of the stove it sits on. But the dinner nonetheless may prove worth the eating. Censorship, politically-fixed justice, hysteria against 'subversion', the denigration of civil liberties, are all part of a system left in this country by its former occupiers and rulers. The struggle against that system is the same struggle as the one that expelled (to some extent) those rulers. They are still not expelled from the control of Britain. They cannot be got rid of from one side of the water alone. But if the Irish work against them solely in Ireland and the British in Britain, I am sure that complete understanding – and hence co-operation – can never be achieved.

Ecce Hobo Sapiens: O'Casey's Theatre

(published in *Sean O'Casey*, ed: Thomas Kilroy, Prentice-Hall Inc., 1975)

Three quotations from O'Casey's autobiography, *Inishfallen, Fare Thee Well:*

Morning star, hope of the people, shine on us! Star of power, may thy rays soon destroy the things that err, things that are foolish, and the power of man to use his brother for profit so as to lay up treasure for himself where moth and rust doth corrupt, and where thieves break through and steal. Red Mirror of Wisdom, turning the labour in factory, field, and workshop into the dignity of a fine song; Red Health of the sick, Red Refuge of the afflicted, shine on us all . . . The sign of Labour's shield, the symbol on the people's banner; Red Star, shine on us all!

There opposite was the Pro-Cathedreal, the Church of the Immaculate Conception. An ugly sight. A dowdy, squat-looking imitation of some Italian church, done up in a back-handed Greco style; a cheaply-fashioned souvenir of Rome. No indication that this was Dublin, and that an Irish church . . . not a sign of the Book of Kells, nor that of Lismore; or ever a peal from St.Patrick's Bell; or even a painted symbol of the Cross of Cong. All of it imitation, silly, slavish . . . a cheap and distressing vase for the madonna lily of the slums.

Here at this church Matt Talbot, a Dublin labourer, full-up of sanctity . . . crawled up the steps on his belly to the big door closed against him, waiting prone on the stones till it opened to let him join in the first Mass, so that he might go merry to work . . . *A model workman and a model Catholic . . . and his life points out the only path to true peace for all who labour, a life of self-discipline lived in perfect agreement with the law of God and His Church. Ecce hobo sapiens.* Blow, crumpeter, blow! So, workers of Dublin, and the world, you know now what you have to do. Follow Matt Talbot up to heaven. You've nothing to lose but the world, and you've the holy chains to gain. Read . . . Glynn's *Life of Matt Talbot*, then read Stalin's *Life of Lenin*; and take your choice. Make the world safe for the bosses. If you do, you're sure to get to Heaven when you die.

At first sight it might appear that O'Casey in these passages – which in the original are all part of one longer passage – is setting up a simple contrast: on the one hand Religion, which is only a deceit and a weapon of the ruling classes, and on the other Socialism (as defined by Stalin) which is the ultimate hope of the world. The superficial effect is one of sloganizing agit-prop, which you can either take or leave according to your prejudice. A good deal of O'Casey criticism has in fact accepted this premise, particularly in regard to the autobiographical books. But let us look at the quotations a little more closely. A number of contradictions begin to appear. The first is concerned with the style of the invocation to the Red Star. This is obviously modelled upon, if not almost a burlesque of, a Christian, more specifically a Catholic litany. We are reminded of the identification of the Virgin Mary with the Star of the Sea, which in its turn is a much older poetic conceit originally applicable to various manifestations of pre-Christian goddesses. It is not the ordinary way in which a Marxist might be expected to demonstrate the historical necessity for the Dictatorship of the Proletariat. Compare it, for instance, with a passage of verse from a recent Chinese play *On the Docks*:

> *Now in our new society,*
> *Thanks to the Party and chairman Mao,*
> *We dockers have risen, we are now*
> *Proud masters of our country, cared for*
> *And insured against illness and death.*

Admittedly this Chinese quotation has been taken from a pretty stodgy translation, and therefore, reads tritely; but in the original play it is intended to be *sung* and the context implies a degree of ecstasy in the execution. But the ecstasy is achieved by the use of concrete and practical images – health insurance among people whose history has been filled with famine and exploitation is a very solid good indeed and can be vouched for in the personal experience of everyone in the audience.

O'Casey, however, prefers to remind his readers of a different sort of experience – that of their literary and religious sub-conscious memories. If the 'Morning Star, hope of the people, shine on us' bit reflects the Catholic liturgy, the Protestant tradition (O'Casey's own background) is not forgotten: there is a positive reminiscence of the King James Bible in 'Lay up treasure for himself where moth and rust doth corrupt.' Incidentally, who are O'Casey's readers supposed to be? His book has been criticized and analyzed and evaluated, of course, by the international academic literary dramatic bourgeois establishments all over the world, and has been dismissed in many quarters for its pretentions and its bigotry. Vulgar jokes like 'ecce hobo sapiens, blow, crumpeter, blow' do not appeal to sophisticates. 'Sub-Joyce' is the pigeon-hole into which that class of thing can be patronizingly put. When Joyce makes such a pun it comes upon the reader with innumerable sub-texts clustered round it out of medieval schoolmen and all the rest of the apparatus which a Jesuit college can so easily provide. O'Casey's humour is much more direct: it derives from the building-site at a lunch-break or even a primary-school playground. He *might* have been attempting to imitate Joyce: it is much more probable that he was just making satirical jokes in the way he had always made them or heard them made. Surely at the back of his mind as he wrote he must have had a vague idea of his book being *spoken aloud to* (rather than read by) a group of Dublin workmen? True, this has not, as far as we know, happened: but the autobiography is now out in paper-back, and its readership is bound to be much larger and less socially-exclusive than in 1949, when *Inishfallen* ... was first published. The Chinese play, of course, was specifically produced for the benefit of 'workers, peasants, and soldiers' and its style and content have been carefully prepared to appeal as strongly as possible to such an audience.

What are we to make of O'Casey's views on twentieth-century Irish church-furnishing? He attacks the pietism of those who would praise Matt Talbot's indifference to the reality of the class-struggle: and in so doing he implies that Christianity as a whole is responsible for the failure of the working-class to combine successfully against its masters. But he also seems to suggest that if the Archbishop of Dublin had allowed a genuine native tradition to inform the artists responsible for the interior of the Pro-Cathedral, then the Church would be fulfilling its mission in the slums so much more effectively. But if the Church were to fulfil its mission more effectively, presumably there would be more Matt Talbot and less Lenin, and the Revolution would be delayed even further? But I don't really think that this apparent muddle is a fair interpretation of what O'Casey is trying to say. *If*, he would argue, the decoration of modern churches were to be *truly* impregnated with the spirit of the Book of Kells or the Cross of Cong, then the religion thus illustrated would be an altogether different thing from what is at present peddled in Ireland. Lenin (and even Stalin) would in fact have become part of it, and it would actively *include* all the revolutionary fervour which overturned the Russian state in 1917. He sees the religion of St Patrick and Columbkill as a dynamic historical movement which, in its own day, and in the context of that time, did indeed 'put down the mighty from their seats and exalt them of low degree.' Its twentieth-century equivalent is Socialism – which has, of course, dispensed with the Divine Guidance – a significant variation: but one which O'Casey never chooses to emphasize.

It is not at all clear what O'Casey's precise view on God may have been ... at times he seems almost to accept the objective reality of the persons of Christian myth. 'A cheap home for Our Lady of Eblana,' is another of his descriptions of the Pro-Cathedral – as though there really were a Blessed Lady whom a more sumptuous home would gratify – but then he tends to cancel out such an impression by remarks like 'You've nothing to lose but the world, and you've the holy chains to gain.' Perhaps he didn't have any precise views on God. There are not very many people who do. Professional theologians occupy themselves with the setting-up of divine superstructures, and dogmatic atheists denounce their theories as pure illusion. But in between there are the majority of 'Christendom' (a word which now-a-days must be taken as including all those countries beyond the 'Iron Curtain' which were once formally Christian communities and today still retain great areas of religious belief and practice) whose notions of divinity are pleasantly confused with the creations of the poetic imagination. Christ, the Blessed Virgin, King Arthur, Cinderella, Venus, Cuchulain, Mickey Mouse, Superman, or King Billy-of-Glorious-Memory all inhabit the same intangible, but nonetheless potent, mental landscape. Marx and Lenin frequently belong there also. In his lifetime an attempt was made to add Stalin to the company: but there are dangers when the personage is still alive. Russians who were prepared to accept their leader as a myth could not help comparing the myth with the reality whenever their friends or relatives were hauled off by the secret police, and the resulting confusion between the allegorical personification of the Forces of the Revolution and the vindictive bureaucrats of the Kremlin inevitably led to the Khrushchev denunciation and the desecration of the Red Square mausoleum. Mao is in a rather similar situation at the moment. The author of *On the Docks* makes use of the great name as a stock image in the passage quoted – he does not perhaps mean Mao-the-fallible-man so much as Maoism-the-political-theory – but it is quite possible that Madame Mao herself actually attended script-conferences or rehearsals of *On the Docks*: and the dividing line between reality and imagination is therefore very shaky. If, in the near future, Mao dies and his politics become re-pudiated, there can be no doubt that *On the Docks* will have to be revised in this respect. Though the *overall* message of the play would not presumably need to be changed – it says, by and large, that the work of Chinese stevedores is of dignity and importance and requires constant vigilance if it is to be done properly and the country's socialist economy benefited.

O'Casey was a 'realist': his plays and his prose works present a picture of life as he saw it, with the exploited working class engaged in constant struggle not only against their capitalist and imperialist masters but also against their own human weaknesses and petty meannesses. But he was not a 'naturalist'. His realistic picture is constantly modified by the introduction of allegorical or mythological characters and incidents. Because the culture he writes about is Christian and largely Catholic, many of these 'imaginary' elements take the form of, or are presented in language derived from, the Christian religious iconography. Because he was a socialist he mod-ifies this imagery with various Marxist notions. Because he was an Irishman (who had in his youth been a keen member of the Gaelic Revival movement) he also reflects the prevailing divine machinery of the pre-Christian Gaelic legends.

In *Purple Dust* – a play about two English businessmen who

acquire an old Irish mansion, try to revive a discredited squirarchal mode of life, and are eventually forced to leave by a disastrous flood (which prefigures the collapse of the British Empire – 'Your Tudors have had their day, and they are gone: an' th' little heap o' purple dust they left behind them will vanish away in th' flow of the river,' says O'Killigain, 'a foreman stonemason') – the flood itself appears as a Figure who 'is dressed from head to foot in gleaming black oilskins, hooded over his head, just giving a glimpse of a blue mask, all illuminated by the rays of flickering lightning, so that the Figure seems to look like the spirit of the turbulent waters of the rising river.' 'In a deep voice' this allegorical creature pronounces:

> The river has broken her banks and is rising high; high enough to come tumbling in on top of you. Cattle, sheep, and swine are moaning in the whirling flood. Trees of an ancient heritage, that looked down on all below them, are torn from the power of the place they were born in, and are tossing about in the foaming energy of the waters. Those who have lifted their eyes unto the hills are firm of foot, for in the hills is safety; but a trembling perch in the highest place on the highest house shall be the portion of those who dwell in the valley below!

Here again is O'Casey's Biblical reminiscence: 'I will lift up mine eyes to the hills from whence cometh my help' etcetera . . . and also 'Then let them which be in Judaea flee into the mountains: let him which is on the housetop not come down to take anything out of his house . . . for then shall be great tribulation, such as was not since the beginning of the world to this time, no, nor ever shall be.' The proletarian revolution is thus implicitly compared to the destruction of Jerusalem and/or the end of the world as prophesied by Christ. But the description of the Figure in the stage-directions has a precise heraldic practicality which resembles the descriptions of supernatural beings in the old Irish sagas. Lug mac Ethnenn, Cuchulain's divine father, appears to aid the hero in the *Táin Bó Cuailnge* and is seen by the poet in these terms: 'A tall, broad, fair-seeming man. His close-cropped hair is blond and curled. A green cloak is wrapped about him, held at his breast by a bright silver brooch. He wears a knee-length tunic of kingly silk, red-embroidered in red gold, girded against his white skin . . . yet no one is taking any notice of him and he heeds no one: it is as though they cannot see him.'

It might be objected that O'Casey's stage-directions are not evidence – that the designer of the play needs some note of the sort of costume he is expected to provide, and that O'Casey is simply supplying this for him. But the point surely is that the description makes it quite clear that the costume is to be a concrete three-dimensional arrangement, with no pseudo-mystical nonsense about it, emblematic in exactly the same vigorously real way that the vision of Lug is seen in the *Táin*. The designer is not asked to mess about with gauzes or fancy lighting effects to obtain a suggestion of mystery (the *rays of lightning* are the simplest and most immediately dramatic device available in the theatre, and need involve no more than a dark stage and one or two quick flashes). O'Casey has already prepared for this by a direction so obvious as to be almost laughable: 'The room has darkened still more, and *Poges tugs the string that puts on the light* . . . the light in the room flickers.' It is the equivalent in stagecraft of 'blow, crumpeter, blow,' and would serve in the nursery to frighten one's younger brother. In the same way a practicable Cock in *Cock-a-Doodle Dandy* is allowed to dance around the stage like a figure from Uncle Remus (or Chaucer's *Nun's Priest's Tale*) before presiding over a whole series of pantomime effects with lit-up bottles, shaking casements, and firecrackers. In the battlefield scene from *The Silver Tassie* two soldiers open their parcels from home. One contains a prayer-book – 'in a green plush cover with a golden cross' and another 'a red and yellow coloured ball.' These are not just any old props, introduced so that the dialogue can make a verbal point: but carefully selected emblematic objects like the articles of equipment carried by the heroes of the *Táin* – 'There is a knob of light gold on his black shield . . . they have gold-hilted swords at their waists . . . scabbards with tassles of speckled gold hang down to their feet.'

It will be noticed that I have taken these examples from the later plays. In the earlier works O'Casey uses such devices far less obviously, and nearly always verbally rather than visually. But the shadow of the orator in *The Plough and the Stars* (a tall dark figure silhouetted against the window) belongs to the same class of theatrical vocabulary: and when he quotes Pearse's speech from the funeral of O'Donovan Rossa against a foreground of boozy arguments in 'a commodious public-house,' both the apparition and the words are part of the role of a deus-ex-machina. In the same scene, incidentally, the Young Covey is given lines which deliberately indicate O'Casey's opinion of the barrenness of Marxist thought when unconnected with the mythological landscape of popular imagery. 'There's only one freedom for th' working' man: control o' the means o' production, rates of exchange, an' th' means of distribution . . . Look here, comrade, I'll leave here to-morrow night for you a copy of Jenersky's *Thesis on the Origin, Development, an' Consolidation of the Evolutionary Idea of the Proletariat*,' he tells Rosie, who immediately shows 'an exemplified glad neck, which reveals a good deal of white bosom.' (N. B. *Exemplified* glad neck – another 'emblematic' stage direction.) The Covey reacts with: 'None o' that, now; none o' that. I've something else to do besides shinannickin' afther Judies!' Nothing in O'Casey's work anywhere leads us to believe that he did not accept the 'conthrol o' th' means o' production,' as a valid political goal. There is no question here that he is trying to debunk socialism. His own view of 1916 in fact was that Connolly betrayed the cause of the workers by joining in with the nationalist insurrection, which is more or less the attitude of The Covey ('If they were fightin' for anything worthwhile, I wouldn't mind,' he says later, during the rising itself). But intellectual Marxist theorizing without a comprehension that the proletariat (or, for that matter, the bourgeoisie) is made up of three-dimensional flesh-and-blood human beings who do not necessarily run according to predictable rules is seen by O'Casey as tragi-comic futility: and as belonging in the same contemptible box as religious chicanery – useless pilgrimages to Lourdes, invocations to 'The Blessed St Frigid,' or Orange hooliganism . . . 'Eh, you, aren't you goin' to stay an' put tustimony to the fullness o' th' Protestan' feth? . . . th' Pope's bullies with hard stones have smitten us sore . . .'

Throughout his work O'Casey introduces his popular emblematic imagery as though he can never see a human scene without also seeing in it (or over it) a number of brightly coloured additional actors and props who do not so much direct the action as increase its human intensity and provide it with a historical and moral context. It has been said that his increasing use of such devices illustrates, one, his detachment from his 'roots' after his departure from Ireland – as though in England he was unable to portray Irish life without stylizing it out of all recognition: and two, the influence on his work of fashionable German expressionism. I doubt if either of these two notions has much truth in it. It is probable that, living in England and obtaining his information about Ireland from a continuous reading of the Irish newspapers sent by post, he found himself interpreting the national scene rather as though he was observing it through a telescope . . . colours seem heightened, perspectives diminished, and small gestures take on an exaggerated importance: but the essential accuracy of the observation is not impaired. And although German expressionist writers certainly did make use of similar techniques, there is a much older and more immediate source of them in the old British theatrical tradition. As there was not an old Irish theatrical tradition, this was naturally the chief professional *root* from which O'Casey's work grew: and it is interesting that his first exposure to it was through the plays of Boucicault, whose melodramas were, like most nineteenth-century romantic drama, founded upon a debased and sentimentalized view of Shakespeare.

Now Shakespeare, it is generally recognized, was greatly influenced by the theatre of the period shortly before he was born – that is to say, the age of the Morality Play, when individual characters in the fictional story were inextricably mixed-up with a whole range of Vices and Virtues and other emblematic figures. The greatest morality play of the time (which more than any other assimilated the technique into a consistent and concrete unity of style and content) was Lindsay's *Three Estates*. Here the hero is called Humanity, which means that the struggle waged between Chastity and Sensuality for his patronage represents the war between good and evil going on in every Christian soul, and therefore the whole story may be taken as being set within one typical psychology. But Humanity is also a King: and the Vices who assail him are put to flight by, among others, a sturdy work-ingman called John the Commonweal. So clearly the action is also political, and the stage represents the kingdom of contemporary Scotland as well as the interior of one Christian. At the same time the sinister activities of a man dressed as a Bishop and called Spirituality, who endeavours to protect the King from a Bible written in English, demonstrate that the setting of the play has been broadened once again to include the whole of Europe in the throes of the Reformation. The plot is tied up at the end by the intervention of Divine Correction, who is conveniently able to control all three levels of meaning, as it were *ex officio*. It is doubtful if, after *The Three Estates*, the morality form could have developed any further without falling into tiresome abstractions (of the sort employed in the conversation of the Young Covey): but the situation was saved by Shakespeare and the other Elizabethans – most notably in the huge series of English historical plays that begins with the anonymous *Woodstock* and ends with *Richard III* (Shakespeare himself seems to have written about 80% of this cycle). The Vices are retained, but humanized into people with names like Bushy, Bagot, Pistol, Falstaff, or La Pucelle. The Virtues become John of Gaunt, the Lord Chief Justice, or Duke Humphrey. Divine Correction is 'exemplified' in the House of Tudor, as represented by Henry VII. And King Humanity is partitioned off into a whole series of Plantagenets: but also bits of him, mixed up with John the Commonweal, recur throughout the plays in the persons of such characters as the Soldiers before Agincourt, the Carriers in the Rochester Inn, Alexander Iden (A Kentish Gentleman), and so on. Of the old allegorical types, we are left with Rumour painted full of tongues to introduce *Henry IV, Part 2*; and Chorus for *Henry V*.

After the Puritan revolution in Britain the theatres were shut down and this sort of large-scale dramatic treatment of history, politics and sociology became physically impossible: but the tradition remained, and was carried directly into *The Pilgrim's Progress* – a sort of hybrid between the religious tract, the novel, and the play. As Shaw pointed out, Bunyan's dialogue was more suited to the stage than any so-called theatrical re-writing of it could ever hope to be: and was in fact in many ways more functionally efficient for acting purposes than much of Shakespeare. Bunyan was read in working-class Protestant homes for nearly three centuries – you can probably still find copies, in regular use, in the Shankill Road today – and thus became an integral part of the literary and imagistic background of a man like O'Casey. In *The Pilgrim's Progress* the expedition of Christian represents at the same time the quest of the religious man in search of salvation and also the difficulties of the virtuous Puritan artisan in Restoration England. Vanity Fair, for instance, is of course a state of sin wherein we are all liable to fall: but it is also London with its theatres and brothels and taverns: and it is clearly presided over by a roaring Tory junta with Judge Jeffries on the bench.

The dungeons of Giant Despair are a theological condition: they are also Bedford Gaol. The whole landscape of the book can be taken both as the location of an imaginary journey from this world into the next, and as a historical diagram of how the Puritan revolution nearly succeeded in the 1640's and how, with God's help and human effort, it would once again prevail in the near future.

If, as I believe, it was this type of dramatic structure which was at all times in O'Casey's mind as a pattern of how social and political theatre should be made, then the reasons for the apparent lapse into schematic expressionism in his later works becomes evident. There was in fact no lapse: rather he was compelled to work his way by degrees from out of the conventions of late nineteenth-century naturalism before he eventually found the fluent technique that he was always seeking. Boucicault, after all, had seemed in 1920 to be an anachronistic mentor for a new dramatist who hoped to contribute to a lively young national theatre, and there must have been times when O'Casey, reading and hearing his critics, began to wonder if he wasn't altogether too uneducated in contemporary theatrecraft ever to become a really respectable artist. The high-flown burblings of Yeats, for instance, on the 'symbolic values of the Japanese *Noh*' must have been very daunting. We can now recognize that Yeats' objections to naturalism were not very far removed from O'Casey's own more intuitive reactions: but he couched his theories in such unnecessarily exotic jargon that O'Casey can be excused for retreating from such pretension into an insistence upon an almost pedantic Zolaism in the stage-directions of the early plays.

Rosie's 'exemplified glad neck' and Pearse's emblematic silhouette in *The Plough and the Stars* are tentative intrusions upon the overall concept of the scene. Look how it is introduced: 'It is the south corner of the public-house that is visible to the audience. The counter, beginning at Back about one-fourth of the width of the middle of the space shown, comes across two-thirds of the length of the stage, and, taking a circular sweep, passes out of sight to Left. . . . On the shelves can be seen the end (or the beginning) of rows of bottles . . .' The whole thing is much longer than that, and is in fact quite unnecessary. If O'Casey had simply written 'A commodious public-house in Dublin' any competent designer should have been able to get it right. None of the details add anything particular to the meaning of the scene. But compare it with a stage direction from *Red Roses For Me*:

> Part of the grounds surrounding the Protestant church of St Burnupus. The grounds aren't very beautiful, for they are in the midst of a poor and smoky district; but they are trim, and considering the surroundings, they make a fair show. An iron railing running along the back is almost hidden by a green and gold hedge, except where, towards the centre, a fairly wide wooden gate gives admittance to the grounds. Beyond this gateway on the pathway outside, is a street lamp. Shrubs grow here and there, and in the left corner, close to the hedge, are lilac and laburnum trees in bloom . . . a rowan tree, also in blossom, its white flowers contrasting richly with the gay yellow of the laburnum and the royal purple of the lilac. The rest of the grounds are laid out in grass . . . the Rector is wearing a thick black cassock lined with red cloth . . . a square black skull-cap covers his head.

Now with one or two exeptions (the wooden gate and the street lamp) everything that is mentioned in this lengthy catalogue is given a precise heraldic colour, even to the lining of the Rector's cassock. If O'Casey had chosen merely to write 'Part of the grounds surrounding the Protestant church of St Burnupus – The Rector is seated near the porch' no stage designer could possibly have guessed the elaborate visual pattern that was in his mind. It is not a naturalistic pattern – the trees and flowers are described as though they were the background of a medieval manuscript illumination, with their colours given full chromatic value: and perspective or chiaroscuro deliberately avoided. By the time he came to write this play it was no longer necessary for O'Casey to protect his realism by means of naturalism. It was accepted that he dealt with the realities of Irish life (or at least it should have been: though Dublin provincialism and arrogant snobbery were doing their best to create an opposite impression) and the German expressionists had done this much for him – they had rendered a certain stylization of theatrical effect respectable among audiences and critics brought up upon Galsworthy or Somerset Maugham.

How important is all this? Would *Red Roses For Me*, for instance, be diminished in production if the author's careful colour-scheme were to be ignored? There are, of course, many ways in which a good play can be produced, and they do not all have to be specified by the playwright. But I saw this particular piece presented at the Lyric Theatre, Belfast, in 1972, at a time when the themes of the play – working-class militancy, Orange reaction, police brutality, street violence, were all in full flow throughout the city in very dangerous earnest. The Lyric Theatre is situated in a comparatively quiet, middle-class part of town. Thus the interior of the theatre appeared a civilized oasis where for a couple of hours all the turbulence could be forgotten. And so it was. The play was acted very competently, and the audience applauded very gratefully, and then we all went out to the hazards once more of the beleaguered capital. If the play had been *Love's Labour's Lost* or *French Without Tears* it would all have been very nice. But surely *Red Roses For Me*, in Belfast, at such a time, should have had some more positive effect upon its public? Not even the gross caricature of the two orange buffoons who jump upon the Cross (because it's a Popish symbol – 'Ichabod!') drew more than a casual titter. Yet only a day or two before Craig and his Vanguard ruffians had staged an enormous rally and a general 24-hour strike which had upset the entire province. There must have been someone in that theatre who actually had views on whether or not it was a good thing that the Orange Order has spent the past hundred years diverting the grievances of Protestant working men into anti-Catholic rowdyism (which is what O'Casey is talking about in the scene in question)? There must, in fact, have been many in that theatre whose ability to pay for a ticket in a comfortable carpeted playhouse purveying 'culture' was directly due to the cumulative effect of such Orange traditions. Yet the scene made no impact whatever beyond the immediate appreciation of its superficial buffoonery.

It would be unfair to say that this was due entirely to the failure of the stage-designer to follow O'Casey's directions to the letter – the general style of the acting, for example, was muted and seemed a little nervous, as though the cast knew that they were playing with fire, and , understandably, did not want to get burnt. But the whole play was placed in one of those non-committal multiple sets (which really are part of 'the heritage of German expressionism' but which are nearly always used because they are cheap rather than for their artistic appropriateness), and this consisted of a group of non-committal arches, some non-committal curtains across the back, and a few non-committal steps which led nowhere and said nothing. The director had recognized that the play was by no means 'naturalistic': and that the proper way to achieve the sense of realism was to present it in the bold, bright, clear, iconographic way that the author laid down. It looked non-committal: and in the end it was non-committal. Maybe if it hadn't been, some one would have blown up the Lyric. Maybe in troubled times theatres ought not to put their premises and personnel in jeopardy by presenting committed plays: but there is no justification for first taking the risk of selecting such a script and then emasculating it.

Perhaps the best models to bear in mind when reading O'Casey's plays and considering how they should be put on the stage would be the Penny-plain-twopence-coloured dramas of the Victorian Toy Theatre. These were the domestic versions of the drama of Boucicault and his colleagues: their principal characteristics are firm outlines, gaudy and by no means natural colours, striking postures for the people, conventional picturesqueness for the scenes. A wood in the Toy Theatre is always bosky, a castle always impregnable, a cottage always rose-bowered, a tavern always snug. Sailors are free and jovial, murderers black-visaged, rustic heroines buxom, genteel heroines delicate, and comic characters have either big bellies and red faces or spindly legs, hunched backs, and long noses. Is all this then no more than to say that O'Casey was an uncouth primitive, a sort of Grandma Moses of the theatre? If so, his work would remain attractive and indeed touching, but one would not perhaps feel much need to take it very seriously. But I am not talking so much of the actual matter of the plays as of their essential framework. The simpler the elements of scaffolding, the greater the variety of the permutations to which the structure may be put. O'Casey constructs an entire world, seen in primary colours and arranged in long-established traditional images, in order to present a new analysis of society. He uses the theological emblems of Lindsay or Bunyan combined with their social and political ones for the purpose of re-ordering their God-centred world into the shape of Marxian materialism.

There is a certain danger in this. If religious emblems no longer represent theological abstractions, then what do they represent? O'Casey seems to use them to denote the essential, and sub-conscious poetic core of humanity – a concept in itself so abstract and vague that only the most easily-acceptable images can in fact convey it to a public audience. Thus a Cock stands for virility and fertility (so it does, in the lowest contexts): a Flood stands for a social and political cataclysm (so it does, in the pages of the shoddiest journalism): a Rose stands for love and a Lily stands for sacrifice (Valentine-cards and political agitators at Easter-time in Ireland carry precisely the same notations). But when it comes to a more complex literary requirement – a concise explanation, for instance, of what the Russian revolution meant to a disappointed Dublin socialist who had seen all his hopes for the Citizen Army go up in the smoke of 1916, then the use of a church litany in close juxtaposition to the name of Joseph Stalin creates – in hindsight – an appreciable discomfort.

Except in Maoist circles it is today accepted throughout the left that Stalin distorted the potential of the new Soviet state until he all but destroyed it. The Moscow Purge trials of the 1930's began to sicken many communists and socialists: later Russian activities in Spain, Hungary, Czechoslovakia all added to this disillusion. But the degree of disillusion has varied: some people adopted the doctrines of Trotsky, others shifted towards anarchism, others became embittered anti-communists. O'Casey however remained loyal to Soviet communism – in a letter to his son he defended the Soviet actions in Hungary (1956) by explaining the reactionary nature of men like Mindszenty – who at that time was held up as a hero in the western press – and implying that a middle road between the Prince Bishop and the Commissar was not a practical possibility. He never forgot his first reactions to the Russian Revolution, as described in his autobiography: 'In the spirit, Sean stood with these children, with these workers, with these Red Army men, pushing away with them the ruin they were rising from, the ruin from which all the people would one day rise, sharing the firmness of their unafraid hearts, adding his cheer to the cheers of the Soviet People. The terrible beauty had been born there, and not in Ireland . . .' Disloyalty to Stalin and his heirs would have seemed to him to be a betrayal of the working class, for whom in his youth he had worked as a political organizer, and for whom and about whom he had written his plays. By the time Stalin's oppressions became manifest O'Casey was no longer in active politics, so his attitude did not do anyone any harm: nor has it damaged the essential truth of his plays.

We can, after all, appreciate Bunyan without having to repudiate Shakespeare, even though Bunyan's Vanity Fair was the direct consequence of the strong centralized monarchy which Shakespeare and his theatre so consistently lauded. And one of the consequences of Bunyan's dramatic vigour has been the blue-nosed anti-art intolerance of modern Protestant communities, which results in the prosecution in such places as the American Bible Belt of incautious theatre companies, musicians or itinerant poets. A writer who establishes a quasi-religious framework for his narrative is always liable to confound the imaginary with the real – or, if he does not, his audience might. Once one hails the Socialist revolution as a 'Morning star, red health of the sick, red refuge of the afflicted, red mirror of wisdom' one is not very far from hailing the temporary administrator of that revolution as 'our great leader and teacher, redeemer of the oppressed masses' and all the rest of it. O'Casey did not in fact indulge in such servilities: but he remained sufficiently close to those who did and therefore allowed an element of equivocation and structural weakness to creep into his more direct non-dramatic political statements.

It is also possible that his association with Stalinism weakened his work in another way. During his years in England he was, as we have seen, developing and consolidating his dramatic iconography in a firm and consistent manner. But the productions of his plays do not appear to have brought this out very clearly to the public and critics. (If they had, it would by now be thoroughly understood and I would not need to be writing this essay.) Apart from one production at Unity Theatre (then a largely Communist-inspired organization) he generally had his work done on various commercial stages in London and America. Now by their very nature such theatres would not be able to accommodate their normal methods of work to the precise requirements of O'Casey's stage-directions and highly-patterned language. Why did he never make any serious attempt to break free from this system and find somewhere to work where his own ideas could be really precisely adhered to? During the thirties there were all sorts of experimental theatre groups in operation and it is not altogether an impossible thought. A number of explanations suggest themselves. One, O'Casey was not rich and he preferred not to take risks that might involve him in artistic and/or financial messes. True enough: but his commercial productions were not all that successful – and he had a great deal of trouble with many of them. He tells, in his autobiography, an appalling story of his encounter with a blatant beast of a stage-designer (during rehearsals of *Within the Gates*) that should make the blood of any playwright run cold. Two, his theatrical friends (and his wife) were members of the West End/Broadway world and he did not really know his way around anywhere else. But his plays were uncompromising political statements of a nature not at all adapted to the boulevard atmosphere and both he and his friends must have been aware of this. There is a third possibility. If he had had a theatre of his own, or in some way under his artistic control, it would have had to have expressed some sort of Marxist ideology. The Communist Party – although, as at Unity, it has at various times made use of the drama as part of its overall cultural activity – has always kept very aloof from experiment, either technical or thematic. The principal exception to this was the development of the Living Newspaper style of agit-prop play, which was not really as experimental as it sounds, because a newspaper, after all, is a fundamental propaganda instrument, and the plays were really only features from *The Daily Worker* presented through actors rather than newsprint. Such work can be submitted to editorial control in the same way as regular journalism. But plays like O'Casey's, involving, as we have seen, an entire world of the author's own creation, would have been a very different matter indeed. Who, in the political area, would have been able to evaluate such an outpouring of inter-related images, characters, and action? A quotation from an article by Françoise Kourilsky in a recent number of the magazine *Performance* may illustrate the point:

After the rupture of the Old and New Left in May 1968, the Communist Party (in France) came out vigorously against the theatre people's pretensions about political theatre. The working-class, it argued, has no need of lessons, politics is a party's concern. Each to his own speciality. This position resulted in insidious forms of self-censorship among theatre producers based in Communist areas, with the result that certain theatres around Paris now have given up 'serious' theatre in order to concentrate on 'pure' entertainment; and the classics will come next: let's cultivate the masses, transmit to them their national patrimony, and long live the Comédie Francaise which at least is sticking to its mission. The French Communist Party, which recommends a policy of popular front on the left and conciliation of the middle classes, is attached to the myth of single culture, indivisible, for all. Anyone who maintains that a person subjected to an 'assembly line' belongs to a world which has nothing to do with theatre, or who thinks that in present-day society, the intellectual's culture and the worker's don't coincide . . . is immediately charged with 'workerism.'

Now if the cultural basis of O'Casey's work is, as I have suggested, a combination of medieval morality-play, Shakespeare, Bunyan, and Victorian popular melodrama, it cannot be said that he shares the normal literary equipment of the modern bourgeois intellectual. The latter will no doubt be familiar with all of these writings, but it would be surprising if three-fourths of them at least (which three-fourths would depend upon which intellectual) were not purely marginal to his or her personal preoccupations. Add to the amalgam the jokes and word-play of the building-site, the street-ballad (as understood in the street rather than the college library), the pictures and phraseology of popular religion, and the heroic tales of bronze-age Ireland: and one ends with a creative imagination which is so out-of-the-ordinary as to be positively cranky. 'Workerism' is an inappropriate label for it: but certainly it would not fit into any recognizable Marxist-bureaucratic pigeon-hole. O'Casey as an orthodox socialist-realist would never have been *reliable*, and it would have been hard to see how anyone* in leftist circles in England in the thirties could have been any more adaptable to his inspirations than the managers of the West End. The Abbey Theatre as well, of course, never had a clue.

O'Casey's plays as social documents have not yet become out-of-date: as poetic creations they have not even begun to be realized. The theatre has changed a lot since his heyday – we have had the example of Brecht (who did have a theatre of his own, under a Stalinist government, and subjected by that government to continual niggling) to show us that the kind of emblematic precision that O'Casey required can in fact be attained on a stage, but only as the result of the coming-together of a series of fortuitous conditions in post-war Germany which no-one could have predicted. Brecht brought into the drama an apparently new vocabulary which was in fact a very old vocabulary revitalized: he took up at a different point the same tradition that O'Casey adopted: his discoveries are now part of every producer's stock-in-trade. If it has been done once it can surely be done again?

---

* Jack Lindsay is one Marxist writer who understood O'Casey. But I never heard he ever had anything to do with the practical theatre.

Shift of Discipline

published in *The Author*, 1984

At the beginning of 1981 I had reached the age of fifty and had hardly any money: I did not just need an income, I needed a large chunk of it all in one go. I had lost interest in writing stage-plays. The inability of the playwright to control his or her material in the face of financially-pressed, hence timid and intransigent, managements – timid towards the outer world, intransigent towards writers' wishes and intentions – had finally worn me out. I had 'a good connection' with BBC Radio: but commissioned plays for the wireless do not provide one with the requisite *chunk*. The publisher of my play-scripts had suggested, some time before, that he would be agreeable to commissioning a novel. He was talking in terms of four figures. If I could get £3000 in advance it would all disappear in a week, but at least my immediate necessity would be relieved, whatever happened later. The only problem was, I had never written a long piece of narrative prose, and was not quite sure how to do it. I had, a year or two previously, been commissioned out of the blue to write a short story for a collection edited in Ireland by David Marcus of the *Irish Press*: I had accepted this challenge and had found myself moderately pleased with the tale that resulted. Maybe a full-length piece would not be impossible. I was, however, very nervous at the prospect of thinking up enough description and incident to fill 300 pages, rather than enough dialogue to fill two hours' stage-time.

My fears inhibited me for some months: it was in the end sheer competitive jealousy that enabled me to break the block. Margaretta had been coincidentally commissioned (by another publisher) to write a narrative account of three months she had spent in Armagh Gaol. The task was as new to her as it was to me. She went into a private room, sat down with pen and notebook, and actually began to write – at a steady rate of so many words per day. This obsessive process, going on in my own home, infuriated me. I went into another room: opened the typewriter – handwriting, which I normally use for the first drafts of plays, seemed out of the question – and began likewise. I did not approach the publisher until I had shaped a few chapters – sufficient for me to know that the story was in fact a practicable one. He read these chapters, and my synopsis – and agreed to the commission. Even, after some shabby-genteel Wilkins Micawber pleas, to the £3000: though he did warn me of the deleterious effect this would have upon subsequent royalties. When the contract arrived I signed it all in a rush and sent it straight back. Only afterwards did I remember that *The Author* is regularly filled with horror-stories of novelists who had failed to read the small print: I found myself madly searching through all my back-numbers, failing to find what I wanted, and then failing to find my own copy of the contract to check against them . . . In this case, with this firm, I don't *think* I committed myself un-wisely.

The actual writing of the book became a period of great personal liberation. Liberation, that is to say, from the con-stant playwright's worries as to how the script will eventually be realized upon the stage. There was nothing between me and my public but the publisher's final judgement: and that, during the creation of the work, remains an entirely speculative shadow upon one's dream. I could live totally within the world of my own free imagination.

There was one external tiresomeness that intruded itself, though the publisher was more irritated by it than I was – the

Arts Council about this time offered some sort of grant or bursary to assist the completion and publication of deserving new novels by writers whose merits were already known. Samples of the novels had to be submitted: my samples were considered insufficient for the AC to come to any decision as to the prospective 'excellence' of the complete work (nowadays the AC goes on and on about *excelling* – it must have something to do with the Falklands Factor and the SAS – 'who dares, wins': as though artists were all compelled to some commando-style competitive assault-course, with live ammunition). As I had not written a novel before, how could they judge me on my past form? My career as a playwright, it seemed, did not count. Shifting from one discipline to another distressed the bureaucracy and created demarcation-disputes. My application had to be shelved.

When, at last, I emerged with a finished first draft of *Silence Among The Weapons*, from my self-indulgent self-absorption, I showed it to one of my sons: and found my conceit sorely deflated. 'Boring beginning,' he said, 'there's no action in the first chapter.'

'What about the second chapter?' I asked.

He said, 'Sorry – I couldn't get through to it.'

I naturally put this down to the ignorance and apathy of modern youth and waited for the publisher's verdict. On the whole it was not a bad one: but, 'The beginning is confusing', he informed me, 'the book doesn't seem to start till the second chapter.'

I would have been quite happy to put this down to the ignorance and conservatism of modern publishers, had not most of his other criticisms hit on exactly those parts of the book about which I felt the least confidence. I must pay tribute here to the extreme care with which he went through my manuscript – a degree of minute questioning of meaning, intention, grammar, and style which I had not looked for: all manner of acute queries and suggestions – eg: 'page 145, line 8, perhaps 'old sod' would be better here than 'silly bugger', you have 'silly bugger' already on line 5?' That sort of thing – extremely useful to a far-from-secure writer. Nit-picking, however apparently comical, is exactly what one needs.

He also suggested that I alter my awkward first chapter (I was still preferring to call it my *controversial* first chapter), and then use it as my *last* one: a cardinal change of structure, which I believe in retrospect to have been absolutely correct.

I was amused to discover, by the way, that I had to give approval to the jacket design at a very early stage. It seemed that advance orders from booksellers are solicited almost entirely on the basis of the jacket (as though booking a theatre company into touring venues by means of the poster and programme layouts: an odd notion).

When the novel at length came out I was very nervous about reviews. The publisher hinted that all these were written by members of some mysterious novelists' mafia: they would all gang up together to keep out any interloper who trailed with him bacteria from the coarse performing-arts. But in fact these alleged self-protective exquisites proved very kind – with a single exception: a man who wrote, most gratuitously, that no playwright can be expected to turn out a proper novel, and that the idea of one by *John Osborne* would be even more appalling. I thought this was a professional impropriety: I only wish Mr Osborne *would* write a novel and thoroughly show the fellow up with it.

I had to go from my home in Ireland to London, at a certain cost in peace of mind and general equilibrium, for something alcoholic known as 'the launching'. This was well over before most of the reviews appeared: and was, altogether, not nearly so distressing as a theatre first-night, when you can actually *see* the wary faces of the public and, worse, the critics, and *hear* them shift in their seats, coughing and muttering. I was interviewed for some papers and radio programmes: which was good for my vanity. When it was all over, I returned home, pulled myself together, and buckled down with Margaretta, to a long-standing radio-play commission, which had slipped far beyond our deadline and simply would *not* resolve itself.

The novel was out, the reviews were out, radio-plays were your only man: and then suddenly, quite by accident, I heard over the wireless – or *thought* I heard – could I believe it? – that *Silence Among The Weapons* was on the short-list for the Booker Prize.

Had this been followed by by an immediate confirmation, I would no doubt have gone bounding across to London for the prize-giving dinner and all the trimmings: but, as it was, the vagaries of the cack-handed Irish telecom system meant that it was two weeks before I was in actual touch with my publisher. During this period I was beginning to behave, all at the one same time, (a) as if I had won the £10,000 already, and (b) as though the whole thing had been a dreadful mishearing. Under the influence of (a) I worried and worried what I should do with the money – I had visions of begging-letter writers, hortatory political fund-raisers, my own friends and family, all battening like vultures and turning me into Scrooge or Shylock spitting miserly defiance; (b) could only be banished from my mind by intense re-application to the radio-play, which, despite all, continued to progress.

When I did speak with the publisher, he let me know they all expected me to come to the dinner as a matter of course: he seemed to think, as I did in my dafter moments, that the prize was already mine. I said, 'what happens if I don't win?' (the radio-play was not in so good a state as to be interrupted unscathed: I was forced to consider the horrid concomitants of Aer Lingus or Sealink as winter encroached). He said I would at least get the dinner. I asked for more details about the Booker Prize, who gave it, out of what funds, had there not been high-principled political rows about it now and then? I knew little about it, as a playwright I had never found it *impinged*. He said he would send these details, but somehow they never came. What did come, eventually, was an invitation-card from Booker McConnell (I still do not know quite who they are) stating 'dress: dinner-jacket' – what about female short-listers? Anyway I have always thought, ever since the Army, that compulsory dress regulations are an affront.

By this time I was in a very bad state. All that dreadful journey to London, simply to eat a dinner for which I would have no appetite at all, not knowing whether or not I had won: and yet it was supposed to be the consolation-prize? One might as well honour writers by drawing them on a hurdle to the pillory, I thought. So, late enough in the day, I wrote to my publisher, excusing myself from attendance. He wrote back, horrified: a letter like a house-master's note. I lacked the team-spirit, I was letting down the house (publishing, not school, but even so . . .), they had never had a Booker short-lister before, I really *must* reconsider.

But I did not. My London-based son, an up-and-coming jobbing-builder, went to the dinner instead, in his first-time hired dinner-jacket, a far more debonair figure than ever I could have been. He enjoyed himself, I hope, not getting the prize on my behalf. There *was* another consolation-prize – a beautifully-bound copy, all bright cordwain and gilding, of – *my own book*. I would seriously have preferred buckshee copies of each of the other short-listed works: I could have read them, not just gloated over them. Afterwards my publisher admitted I had probably been right to stay in Ireland. A purely commercial and media affair, he implied – the diners even had to finish up extra quick because the TV demanded it! My son told me that the short-listed writers were not even given seats together; and everyone was dreadfully on edge; except for a number of heavy capitalists out of one of Brecht's more diagrammatic plays – it seemed to be their evening. He also said that the dress-regulations were strictly enforced, nearly excluding an essential TV crewman in an anorak. (Surely *everyone* knows TV-persons *must* wear anoraks everywhere, what century were we in?) My publisher, claimed my son, was more on edge than anyone; my son had felt very protective towards him, practically held his hand, I gathered.

All in all, the Booker Prize, and similar commotions, for which my novel has *not* been short-listed, seem to me to be, for writers, more of a stomach-churning inhibitory hazard than anything else: of course they must be good for publishing, otherwise publishers would not encourage them, and if they are good for publishing – doesn't the argument run? – writers in the long run will get the benefit. Certainly Thomas Keneally, the 1982 winner, did get the benefit – and moreover he deserved it, he'd been short-listed, I think, four times. I only wonder how he managed to write any more novels after the first time . . . By the way, I laid a bet on him: I made £2.00 out of his victory.

But what would be wrong with a small social gathering, *after* the announcement of the prize itself, where the writers involved could really meet one another, have a nice dinner, quietly, at Booker McConnell's generous expense, dressed how they liked, with most of the tensions already eliminated? I am sure most novelists are privately aware that these prizes anyway have less to do with competitive merit than luck of the stars – how else could it be when so many new books are published every year? *I* wouldn't know how to choose between them. And what would be wrong with a slightly smaller main prize combined with, say, half-a-dozen consolation prizes of reasonably chunky cash? This is what would be wrong with it: it would deprive the publicity-persons of a downright knock-out romanesque circus, all the macho cut-throat Russian-roulette element would be missing – why would any self-respecting journalist publish a word about it? Falklands Factor all the way . . .

Prayers At Ennis

published in *The Mail on Sunday* colour-supplement, 1986

Ennis, Co. Clare, is a small and pretty country-town in the west of Ireland. It has a cathedral (RC), a ruined friary, and a most comfortable hotel where they serve delicious teas. The 'only modern building of note' (according to the *Shell Guide*) is the Victorian court-house. A political miracle once took place in Ennis.

1829: the decisive Clare by-election, whereby Daniel O'Connell won political rights for Catholics. During the turbulent polling, an O'Connellite priest harangued the crowd. 'A Catholic,' he shouted, 'had voted against his country' (ie: for O'Connell's opponent). Wild cries of rage and despair changed at once to a patter of prayers, as the priest went on to say that the man in question had immediately fallen down dead in the polling-booth. Gone straight to hell in the very midst of the sin of bribery. Were the prayers grateful, or were they compassionate? Even those who offered them were not, I'd guess, entirely sure . . .

When I, in the most miserable depth of last winter, had occasion to visit Ennis, I too felt tempted to improvise a prayer. Without ambiguity. It would have been an orison of solemn commination, to curse head, body, bowels and bones of all who administered the Irish State Transport system (CIE). I had to travel, hurriedly, from Galway to London: my plane left from Shannon airport, and the CIE bus timetable told me of thirty minutes' wait, between local bus and airport bus, at Ennis Railway Station.

It didn't sound too bad. A railway station; perhaps the lounge of the station hotel, perhaps only a buffet – but the cup of coffee, the excitement of trains coming and going, the vitality of all the ages and sizes of country people with their picturesque baggage – and then: the businesslike international atmosphere of the 'Airport Bus', brisk executives with briefcases, Joan Collins-type jet-culture women-of-glamour, exotic Russians and Cubans making the Aeroflot connection . . . And I could always curb my fear of flying by playing a private game of 'spot-the-potential-hijacker' . . .

The intensity of the cold must have addled my brain. I forgot there had been no trains into Ennis since – when? 1940? I forgot that the station was a mile out of town among a dismal dribble of tentative semi-detachment advancing slowly towards Limerick. I forgot that the 'Airport Bus' was in fact the ordinary route through the vast housing-schemes of Shannon Industrial Estate, and, as such, stopped every hundred yards and had no upholstery left unvandalized on its rudimentary seats. That sort of bus in Ireland knows nothing of airport schedules, and is as likely to be early as late. Therefore you have to be ready for it. The public house across the road, even if it proved to be open so soon in the day (it was just after most people's breakfast-time), did not command a view of the windswept tarmac where the buses waited: so if I dared go for a drink and a warm, I risked losing all.

I should have known that what looked like the road into town was nothing of the sort, but a road *around* town through winter-bound market gardens and little sheds, with nobody about except one sad old man spitting phlegm beside a gatepost. The sole picturesque item: a historic steam locomotive, relic of the West Clare Railway (about which Percy French had once written a song), on a snow-encrusted pedestal. I abandoned my unwise walk through the market-gardens and returned to examine this trophy. Its jaunty green paint was pitted with rust-holes; a rural felt-tip artist had written on the cab-side, 'Ennis Bootboys Rule OK'. Had not someone once told me that Ennis was the home of a most vigorous Gaelic culture, musical, poetic . . .? Ah, but that was in summer. This day it was appallingly clear there would never be summer ever again, in Ennis.

Oh, I should have known that the stone dungeon called a 'waiting-room' would be even colder than the blackened frozen slush of the unprotected forecourt.

Someone else had told me, I now ominously remembered, that Ennis was also the location of a grim county mental hospital, notorious as the place to which disorientated foreign travellers, found 'behaving oddly' in Shannon Airport, were remorselessly and frequently consigned by the Aer Lingus security-staff. If they had had to reach the airport via a bus-change at Ennis, I was not altogether surprised. I was beginning some fairly odd behaviour myself.

Did I say there was no one, but absolutely no one, waiting for a bus at the railway station, apart from me: and, by all the signs, no buses whatever to wait for, in this species of a County Clare open-gulag? In half-an-hour, forty minutes, fifty minutes, sixty, I had become so cold that I could no longer even jump up and down (in front of the old green tank-engine) without agony through every limb.

The bus, when it finally came, was not only late, but unheated, and the door would not shut, and the seat, on which I sat, collapsed and bit my buttock. Oh yes, I caught the plane. Just.

To 'vote against one's country' is a terrible thing indeed. To vote to put paid to a dreadful mendacious bus-service is a democratic right and a duty: but where is the candidate who can both promise it and carry it out . . .?

Autobiography, 1930 – ?

published in *Contemporary Authors, vol 4*:
Gale Research Co, Chicago, 1986

I am far too young to write an autobiography. Ideally, it ought to be written ten years after my death: then I could put all my life into it, plus a fierce rebuttal of the smears and inaccuracies contained in obituary notices and subsequent critical reappraisals ('Arden, an exploded myth': 'Arden, the long decline', and so forth). But early this year my mother died at the age of 89, and in 1979 my father had died aged 88; also this year my youngest son (of 4 sons living) achieved his 21st birthday: so maybe 1985 does represent some sort of watershed. Also, this week Robert Graves died. I never knew him, though I did once get a very friendly letter from him, answering a query I had made to him about an ancient Irish saga he had treated in an essay: and all his work – particularly *The White Goddess* – has always been of immense importance to me ever since I first read *I Claudius* when I was a schoolboy. *His* obituary notices were up to standard, right enough. 'He considered he was one of the very few who knew what poetry was, and such pretensions did not seem justified by the quality of much of his large output' ... 'Anthropologically and mythographically, it (*The White Goddess*) is partially unsound'. . . . As he himself wrote:

> 'To evoke posterity
> Is to weep on your own grave . . .'

I am thinking about Graves particularly because for a crucial space of his life he was living with, writing with, and inseparably (until the separation, if indeed it ever really occurred) connected with, a woman poet, Laura Riding. In 1955 I met Margaretta D'Arcy, an actress from Dublin. She was the first professional theatre-person I ever got to know: and through her I met many people without whom my career as a playwright could never have got off the ground. Two years later we were married. She was closely involved with the most progressive aspects of the theatre of that time, aspects which I knew nothing of, with my limited Shakespearian provincial orientation and my academic (and indeed pompous) attitude towards the stage. She gave me a copy of Brecht – a writer I had only heard of: she introduced me to the works of Beckett, Strindberg, Toller, Behan ... Her name now appears sometimes first, sometimes second, together with mine, upon a great deal of published work which nonetheless the male critics, managements, publishers, and broadcasters, will insist upon referring to as 'Arden's'. Or, worse, as 'the Ardens''. It also appears on work of her own, but this did not appear until after the collaborative pieces. It would have been different if I had collaborated with a man called Hiram Hinks, or even with a woman called Evadne Pershore (assuming that she was known already as a professional author and *not* known to be married to, or living with, me). In that case, the *Arden-Hinks opus*, or the *Pershore-Arden* volumes, would be perfectly acceptable concepts, just like Beaumont-and-Fletcher or Hart-and-Hammerstein. Graves's difficulty, like mine, has been that his name was to an extent before the public as a writer before he began publicly to collaborate with his female partner: and the female partner was known to have a personal/ sexual companionship with him – with me – before the artistic one became apparent. D'Arcy was indeed known in theatre before I was, but as a performer, not a playwright. By swopping one discipline for the other, she did not make things easier as far as *recognition* was concerned: though it should not have mattered a damn. What did matter was the nature of the collaborative work, after 1968 anyway. Before then the problem had been but slight: because our plays were fairly conventional in form and content. After 1968 their political dimensions became less and less acceptable to the British cultural establishment, which has its own very decided notions of what liberties may be taken with the Imperial traditions: and can unfortunately influence other peoples abroad to respect these notions as examples of British liberalism and tolerance. (Also, neither in our case, nor in the Graves/Riding case, was the work light-comedy or musical-showbiz, where joint-scripts are so common as to cause no comment).

If it is too early to write a proper autobiography, it is also too early for me to write accurately about my partnership with D'Arcy, which must be taken 'as read' throughout the following pages. It is still very much in progress, and its nature changes from day to day, from sequence to sequence of completed work, and I might as well try to define a rainbow as the clouds move across the sky. But D'Arcy herself has set down some of her thoughts on the subject: her thoughts of what she thinks *my* thoughts might be if I were to write them. I won't either contradict or confirm them. She presents me as it were a character in a play, thus:

ARDEN (*sol*): I think all men must find it difficult to be objective when writing about their partner, especially if it is a woman. We could say it is modesty, or that the woman is so precious to us that we don't want other predatory males stealing her away, or that she is so wonderful that we don't want to appear vulnerable in the eyes of our partners, we don't want to *wear our heart on our sleeve*. There is nothing that belittles one more than the notion that one is 'uxorious'. Ken Tynan, in reviewing a *Macbeth* in London where the actor-manager's wife played Lady M., wrote that the

casting was 'the ultimate in uxorious-miscalculation':
he didn't object, however, to parading with *his* wife,
Elaine Dundy, a known writer in her own right,
through the foyer of the Royal Court theatre on first
nights, like Justinian and Theodora receiving the
homage of the Byzantine eunuchs, while George Devine (who ran the theatre so courageously from one
crisis to another) had to return their nonchalant waves
and hope that between them they could decide on a
review – to be printed under the Tynan name alone –
that would not kill both play and theatre in one swoop.
The Tynan-Dundy double-act on these occasions was
one of the wonders of London theatre in the hothouse
1950s. But somehow the 'obscenity' of working with
one's own wife undermines the whole concept of personal creativity. Firms of solicitors, 'Widgey and
Fellock'; drapery-shops, 'Death and Son'; these are
OK-symbols – heredity, families, patriarchal
amalgamations: but 'Widgey and Mrs Widgey', 'Death
and Wife' . . .? No. Is it the fusing of new blood with
old, the mixing of cultures, or is there something
deeper? Certainly in western culture artist's wives are
fair game for all sorts of offensive innuendo – consider
the cases of D. H. Lawrence, or Thomas Hardy. As far
as D'Arcy and myself are concerned, there seems even
to be a public accusation that I have gone over to the
'enemy'. What enemy? Well, D'Arcy is Irish: and has
expressed herself hostile to British political and
cultural policies. So have I: I have gone so far as to go
and live with her in Ireland itself. But Ireland is not
itself 'the enemy'. There is no state of war between the
British monarchy and the Irish republic. Well, not
really . . . don't all the British know it is only 'the
troublesome Irish quarrelling amongst themselves'?
When I asked Martin Esslin, then head of drama for
BBC radio, if he would commission a radio-play from

me, he specified to my agent that it must be 'genuine Arden'. The meaning was unmistakable, no joint-work with D'Arcy, and nothing about Ireland. Have I broken a very ancient taboo and allowed myself to 'be held in thrall' by the Witch-wife? And thus am in need of rescue, protection? That seems to put me in a very wet, wimpish role. And who are my protectors, then? What are their fantasies? One very blatant critic actually speculated about what we said to each other in bed. Our pillow-talk could not, he deduced, have been very happy, or we would not have written a play which satisfied him so little. The extreme interpretation of this gratuitous comment would be that he, the critic, really wanted to be in bed with me himself. That's it, of course. The post-religious society elevates artists into sacrificial gods, and critics are the new priesthood with their celibate sexuality directed solely towards dreams of the godhead in passionate love. In our regular religions, Christian and Jewish at least, God is not married: and when he was married (Zeus and Hera, Woden and Frija), this was only because he had already conquered the Great Goddess who had once been Mother of All Things, (including himself) and made her subject to his will. I doubt very much if any of this would now be so clear to me if Margaretta D'Arcy had not been so clearly established by so many commentators as the Serpent in my garden. Laura Riding was, let us not forget, an American, a revolted ex-colonist of renegade British stock, (whether her forebears had emigrated from Britain or not, that is what Americans, subliminally, *are* . . .): Yoko Ono was Japanese. The British Empire – cultural rather than political these days, but still an Empire – does not say any 'thank-yous' to those who have said to it 'no thank you' . . .'

I won't write here any more about my present life, indeed about my life as an adult. I prefer to continue with a series of snapshot pictures of those whom I lived with as a child. They are not complete, and do not pretend to be. More like the odd memory which seems to have some relevance to what I am today, and what my work contains. Suggestive rather than precisely narrative. And I will not draw any specific conclusions. Readers who know my work can, if they will, draw their own.

My life began among Aunts. My father had ten sisters and no brothers. My mother had four sisters and only three brothers. At the time of my birth my father's mother and father were living, and my mother's mother was living. My mother's sisters were unmarried (though one was a widow), and of my father's sisters only four of them had husbands. Three of my father's sisters lived with their parents: and all my mother's lived with their mother.

I was an only child. Our small household was therefore little more than an outshut (to use a north-of-England term – it means a small building attached to a greater one, a 'lean-to') for two awe-inspiring lower-middle-bourgeois matriarchal establishments. That one of them contained a grandfather did not make any difference. He thought he was a patriarch, but he wasn't: he was a lazy old man who was kept by his active females in a passive state of indulgent luxury until his time came to surrender his kingdom. Significantly, he died before his wife, as had my maternal grandfather. All three households were, geographically, quite close. All in Yorkshire. My parents lived in Barnsley – a coal-mining, glass-blowing, linen-manufacturing dirty town. My mother's mother (Granny Layland) lived at Otley, 27 miles away: and the Arden Grandparents at Beverley, 52 miles. Yorkshire is an important county, it is more important to be Yorkshire than English. Anyone can be English: to be a Yorkshireman is to have been *chosen*. By whom, and for what? The question is unanswerable. So is the other question: why say Yorkshire*man* when, by all my own experience, the place was ruled by women? These are contradictions which I have never been able to resolve. Subconscious reactionary atavism, but . . .

The Laylands however were not really Yorkshire at all. They came from Lancashire, to the west, less than fifty miles from Otley, but on the far side of the Pennine Hills, which psychologically were mountains, Alps, Rockies, Andes. The Woodhead railway tunnel that pierced them was a structure of gruesome legend, how many lives had it cost to build, how many train-wrecks and murderous falls of rock had taken place in it since its first building? I shuddered to travel through it and had to be calmed with barley-sugar.

So, as the Beverley family were more 'authentic', ethnically, than the Laylands, and as I preferred, for other reasons, to go on visits to Beverley rather than Otley, I'll talk about Beverley first.

Christmas dinner at Beverley. I was the only child present (perhaps four years old). All the Aunts round the long table, Grandfather at one end, Grandmother at the other. Only Auntie Mary, who had had, I think, polio, and could not use an ordinary chair, lay on a couch to one side. Not enough chairs for everyone, so two Aunts, Olive and Florence, Twins, sat on high kitchen stools between me and my Grandmother. At my Grandfather's elbow, Great-Uncle Charlie. My Grandfather had a white beard and I confused him with King George V. Great-Uncle Charlie had gold spectacles and was clean-shaven and plump, I confused him with Mr Pickwick. There was a picture of Mr Pickwick on the wall, among an array of portraits, from the seventeenth century through to the nineteenth, some of them Ardens, some of them other families married in to the Ardens, oil-paint, water-colour, pastel, silhouette, large and small, wigs and cravats, widow's-caps, mob-caps, serious Christian people, very still and ceremonious for the godlike judgement of the provincial face-painter contracted at so many shillings per square inch of human feature.

My Aunts, for digestive reasons, drank warm water with their meal. It was poured out of a special glass jug with a silver cover and spout. There was also wine, which my Grandfather sold for a living. It was not the blood-red wine but the virginal digestive water that caused the strange noises. One by one my Aunts rumbled, as the eating came to its end. I turned my head left and right, following the sound with wide eyes, like a plumber tracking a fault in a pipe. I began to giggle. I *made a comment*. It was a comment upon *personal noises*. It brought about the most dreadful silence. Aunt-eyes, censorious, bore in upon me. My Grandmother's Roman profile turned sharper, even more marmoreal. My Mother, half the height of any of them, attempted desperately to catch my attention before it was too late, she was angry at me and angry in defence of me against her husband's people: and she *was* too late.

My Father was looking worried; my Grandfather was sucking in his red wine, oblivious; Great-Uncle Charlie was the first to speak. He was a lawyer in real life when he wasn't being a courtier (with an indefinably disreputable past) in his sister-in-law's house: and, as he crumbled a portion of dry cheese onto biscuit, his voice was his professional voice, reluctantly concurring with the magistrate's view of the worthlessness of his client. 'Yes, I do think that John is the – worst-behaved boy I have ever – ah – had occasion to observe.' One of the Twins said, 'Yes.' The other Twin said, 'Yes indeed.' Auntie Ruth, the Aunt Whom I loved, said, 'Poor John.' And she took me swiftly out of the room. Across the hall, in the sitting-room, she sat me down with one of my Christmas presents, a book about Ancient Greeks, and launched into a story: King Odysseus and various monsters. Pallas Athene helped Odysseus at all his most dangerous moments: and Auntie Ruth was Pallas Athene – she even looked like the picture in the book.

Beverley was a classic Olde English town, almost a Toytown. It had two shining white limestone Gothic churches, one of them (the Minster) a thirteenth-century pocket-cathedral, more exquisite though less formidable than the much larger real cathedral in nearby York. Dedicated to St John the Evangelist, the Minster contained the tomb of a local saint of the same name, Anglo-Saxon John of Beverley, who had cured deaf-mute children in the Dark Ages, and to whose grave-slab the school-children even nowadays bring annual offerings of daffodils. My father or Auntie Ruth would bring me into the Minster choir to look at the grotesque oak-carvings under the tip-up seats: a hairy devil carrying away to hell the wicked man who cut wood on the Sabbath, or two knights fighting in front of a toy castle full of fair ladies (aunts?) in horned head-dresses, or another devil playing the bagpipes – except that they weren't bagpipes, but a fat little dog held upside-down under the devil's arm, he bit the dog's tail, the dog's four legs stood up in the air like the pipe's drones, and the dog's open mouth howled and squealed. I found it hard to believe that these carvings were five hundred years old. They seemed neither older nor younger than the Wren-style market-cross with its curling baroque roof-dome and its ring of doric columns, or the two conical stumps of windmills on the great greensward common that bounded the entire west of the town (my Grandparents' house opened onto it through a private gate).

Nor did the north gate (the Bar) of Beverley – all that re-mained of the town's fortifications – with its battlements and narrow arch, particularly bring to mind King Henry V, in whose reign it had been built. Double-decker blue buses went through it, and I vaguely thought that the Bar and the buses had been made for each other. In fact the East Yorkshire bus company had designed its double-deckers with special coved roofs to fit the Bar. I found out later that they had done this reluctantly: they had first put all possible pressure on the town council to get the ancient Bar torn down to accommodate their progressive transport business. I think Great-Uncle Charlie, who had been Mayor, was instrumental in resisting this pressure.

A number of old Ardens had been instrumental in various ways in Beverley throughout the nineteenth century. One of them had prohibited the Beverley Football Game, some time towards the end of the life of Thomas Jefferson, or the start of the life of Abraham Lincoln. The Football Game was in fact an annual legalized riot in which every hooligan in the town took part, there was but one goal, the Bar itself, and the hundreds of players divided themselves into those who would kick the ball from the common through the arch and those who would try to keep it out. Whoever won or lost, windows were broken, shops looted, heads cracked, women assaulted, and public-houses wrecked during the evening and night following the Game. When Dr Arden (Mayor no less than nine times) decided this picturesque tradition was only fit to be forgotten, he sent the Town Constable onto the common to seize the ball as soon as it was kicked-off, throw it to a Deputy on horseback, who was then to ride away with it at full speed and deliver it to Dr Arden in the Mayor's Parlour of the Town Hall. There being only one ball, it was assumed that this brilliant strategy (worthy of Captain Queeg of the *USS Caine*) would prevent all football-violence for evermore. It didn't work: the devoted Constable indeed seized the ball, but was immediately himself seized by the infuriated multitude, and dragged through a quickset hedge until his eyes were almost out and the ball was dropped to the ground. Play recommenced, and the riot was far worse than in any preceding year. Next year, Dr Arden, still in the Town Hall, called out the military: and that did work.

Also, the same Dr Arden, nine-times Mayor, refused to give a bull to be baited in the market-place. All the Mayors of Beverley had always given bulls – or paid for bulls, if they were not themselves farmers. How did a man with such disdain for the people's Olde English pleasures get himself elected so many times?

No need to look far for the answer. All inns in those days had political connections, and Dr Arden, who combined liquor-sales with medical practice (he wouldn't be allowed to do it in England today), owned the Beverley Arms, a known Tory house. Inside this inn was an unusual hatchway, between the main entrance and the bar-parlour. It did not open into the back of the bar for quick sales, as might have been thought, but into a small office, only used on election-days. The voters, coming in from different parts of the town and suburbs, and pausing for refreshment before going to their democratic duty, would each in turn insert a hand into the hatchway. When they removed the hand again, it would have a golden sovereign miraculously in it. Nobody saw the bribe given, nobody stated for what it had been given, nobody saw who gave it. But everybody knew that the chief Liberal inn could only provide half-a-sovereign.

Later on, in the full respectability of Queen Victoria's reign, Anthony Trollope was the Liberal parliamentary candidate for Beverley. A good political novelist but an ineffectual politician: he lost his contest of course. His defeat was sufficiently blatant as to cause enquiry to be made. The historical accounts of this enquiry do not mention the Arden family. They were hatchetmen rather than bosses, and great survivors, first-class at closing ranks and keeping the name out of things. But the corruption uncovered *was* undeniable, and for several years disgraced Beverley was forbidden to have a Member of Parliament at all.

Much earlier, before any Ardens lived in Beverley, the local Member had been a man called Topcliffe, chief persecutor of Roman Catholics for Queen Elizabeth. He was a Reagan-Thatcher kind of operator: his torture-chamber in Westminster, was a privatized concern, with some sort of government licence to be sure; but, as torture was illegal, no one could say that he had been officially ordered by the State to perpetrate it. In those days the Ardens lived in Warwickshire, were themselves Catholics, managed to steer clear of Mr Topcliffe's private enterprise: and one, of them, Mary, became the mother of William Shakespeare. There was another Shakespearean connection with Beverley. An ancient knight's helmet hung on a pillar in the Minster. It was said to have belonged to Harry Hotspur.

The old Arden of Trollope's time – I think, my Great-Grandfather – was presented, by a grateful Conservative Party, with a magnificent clock, in token of all his 'years of service'. (I daresay he had been covering up more names than his own.) This clock was a brass fretwork construction about two-and-a-half feet high, representing the front of a twin-towered Gothic church. I always used to think it was Berverley Minster, though in fact it was of German make. On the hour and the quarter-hours little shining hammers visibly rang bells in a gallery between the towers. It stood on the Grandparents' sideboard, and then, after my Grandmother's death, on a table in my Father's house. Every fifteen minutes it sang and chimed away, a most haunting tone, which has remained in my ears ever since.

A brief word about the other old church in Beverley. St Mary's, completed in the reign of Henry VIII. It had a most glorious roof, flat wooden panels, black with age, and then, in the 1930's, amazingly restored. Some of them all blue with silver and gold stars, moons and suns. Others with a series of allegorical portraits of the Kings of England, starting with the legendary Brutus, great-grandson of Aeneas the Trojan refugee, and running through Lear, Cymbeline, William the Conqueror, Edwards and Henrys, up to Henry VI. One of the more mythical ones, whose name proved indecipherable, was repainted as King George VI, who had just come to the throne. His naturalistic clean-shaven features were pale and unimpressive alongside all his farouchely-bearded fore-runners. His presence, though patriotic, did rather spoil the fairy-tale quality of the whole. Constitutional Hanoverian monarchs necessarily look unwilling to cut people's heads off, which is what all the other kings, each with his huge broad-sword, seemed to think was their main *raison d'être*. I was anyway disappointed in George VI: just after the Coronation of 1937, he came on a formal 'progress' around his kingdom. I was at school, in Barnsley, and all the children were marched out of town to a place on the main road where we would see the King in his car arrive. It was a very hot day, we had to walk about three miles, we were all tired and ill-behaved, and the teachers were totally losing patience. And we waited and we waited and we waited. *The King was an hour or two late.* At last, when he came, all we saw was about four black limousines, driving very fast behind motor-cycle police out-riders. In which car was the King? In every car there were men in top-hats and ladies in flowered hats. No doubt the Queen was there too, but she was as invisible as he was. We had gone all that way, sick with loyal excitement, and all for nothing but a sort of speeded-up funeral. So much for constitutional monarchs. One of the Beverley church-roof kings would have come in on a horse with trumpets on either side of him, and we would have known for sure it was him because his varlets would have struck at us with clubs to make no doubt that we knew. It would not have been pleasant: but at least it would have *happened*.

Also in St Mary's was a row of pillars in the nave, each of which had been erected by donors who had their names written up to prove it. 'Thys Pyllar made the Minestrals': the Minstrels' Guild of Beverley, famous throughout Europe: they left behind a carving, painted and gilded, of themselves playing late-medieval instruments and wearing thick gold chains. 'Thys Pyllar made Gode Wyves': the rich ladies of the parish. A man's head, in a Tudor beret, presumably referred to '+ lay and his wyffe' who 'made' – over the next capital – 'these two Pyllars' – and then, over the half-capital abutting on the end wall of the nave – 'and a haffe'. Mr Crossley, solid citizen of the 1530s, was evidently addicted to silly word-play. East Yorkshire jokes have always been fairly rudimentary, like the tale of 'th'owd man as sat near t'door: he nivver spoak in aall his life but th'yah time (*one time*).' You are supposed to ask what it was he said, expecting some great word of wisdom.

'Why, he nobbut towd 'em to shet t'door . . .': pay-off. A solemn pursed mouth and an appreciative grunt will amply repay the comedian. West Yorkshire people (Otley and Barnsley were *West* Yorkshire, there's a deal of difference) speak far more rapidly and raucously, and do expect a noisy response to their one-liners.

When I stayed with Grandmother Arden, St Mary's was the church I was taken to, surrounded by Aunts, for Sunday service. My crippled Auntie Mary, a very sweet-natured person, became confounded in my mind with the dedication of this church. I used to call it *Auntie* Mary's Church, and was rebuked for my profanity.

I must mention the Great-Aunts. They were Sarah and Gertie, my Grandmother's sisters, unmarried: they lived next door to her and shared a front garden, so that to go from one house to the other you did not need to go all the way down the path, out at the gate, and in at the next gate. American readers will not find this strange: in England dividing fences between bourgeois front-gardens are an absolute essential. In England, people *mind their own business*: the Anglo-Saxons came in their pirate ships, fought battles, took root: and immediately built fences round their individual homesteads so that *their own business* could be very severely minded. The Great-Aunts seemed older than the Grandmother. Their name was Stephenson: Stephensons were tall and blonde, Ardens were shorter and darker and had big noses. Their house was a treasure-chest of eighteenth and nineteenth century curios, miniature Chinese gardens, built to the last pagoda and mirror-glass boating-lake in porcelain fruit-bowls; cigarette-boxes made of whitey-brown porcupine quills; carved ivory games of spillikins or chess: and an array of Samurai swords, razor-sharp – 'for heaven's sake, Ruth, keep that child's fingers to himself!' – East Indian blowpipes with real poison on the tips of the darts: and a regular tiger-skin stretched along the wall, with the tiger's head, teeth, and claws, all in place. A male Stephenson had been an engineer of imperialist renown, building railways, bridges and harbour-works all over the Orient.

There was also a mysterious cupboard full of toys dating from the Great-Aunts' own childhood – I guess some time in the 1860s. German toys, mostly: strange puzzles, stereoscopes, little dancing men, and picture-books. I was, under supervision, allowed to play with them. You have to play with toys, even though you risk breaking them. They cannot live, as museum objects. I remember the savage book of *Struwwelpeter*, still in print; though frowned upon by modern child-psychologists, for the cruelty of the fates that befall the naughty children in it. Little Johnny Head-in-Air (me, according to Aunts), who fell in the river and nearly drowned; Fidgety Phil who wouldn't Sit Still (me again), *he* pulled the entire contents of the dinner-table, boiling soup and everything, all over himself by dragging at the cloth; the Suck-a-Thumb boy whose thumbs were gorily cut off by the Great Long-Legged Scissorman (this one did not scare me, thumb-sucking was not my vice): and the very wicked boys who laughed at the black man in the street and were therefore plunged into an inkwell by Tall Agrippa, a sort of schoolmaster, until they themselves were as black as the object of their racialism.

Great-Aunt Sarah became very tremulous. I amused her, and scandalized some younger Aunts, by asking once, as she poured out tea, did she make the stream of tea shake on purpose so that we could all see how clever she was at never spilling it?

Great-Aunt Gertie was given a radio, by her nieces. This was in the early days of broadcasting, but after the crystal-set had become obsolete. The new bakelite box, with all its workings flush inside the smooth moulded envelope, and only the control-knobs, dial, and decorative trellis over the speaker, to break the functional outline, was regarded as a most progressive novelty. Some weeks after the gift, the Aunts asked her was it giving satisfaction? 'Oh yes,' she said, 'but there is far too much interference. It is very difficult to hear the programmes sometimes because of all the crackling and other noises, For instance,' she said, carefully pointing to the bottom left-hand corner of the box, 'there is a wretched little man just *here*, who will keep jabbering away in German whenever I am trying to listen to a symphony concert.' Could she have meant Hitler? He was very much in evidence in those days, interfering with everyone's programmes: a pleasing fancy, that he might have been confined in the bottom of a radio like a genie in an Arabian bottle. But even so, some fool would have let him out.

I mentioned York Minster, larger and coarser version of Beverley's elegant church. York is not a lucky Minster. In 1984, for instance, it was severely burned by lightning. The superstitious (and it's amazing how many of them there are in an allegedly secularized country) attributed this to God's wrath against the consecration there of the new Bishop of Durham, a man of good sense who has been accused of heresy by the 'Moral Majority' – or so they call themselves, stealing an up-to-date mendacious Americanism to dignify their age-old English nonsense. The real problem with the Bishop of Durham has been that he – to an extent – supported the coal-miners against Mrs Thatcher when she compelled them into a year-long strike, but that is by the way . . . The recent York fire, however, was as nothing compared to the one that gutted the building about 160 years ago. It was lit, not by God, but by an arsonist surnamed Martin. He believed indeed that he did the work of God. He had written pamphlets denouncing the 'great height' of the Bishops and their pagan pride, and stating that their palaces and churches must be destroyed, in fulfilment of listed prophecies. When the pamphlets were ignored he broke into the Minster by night, piled the stools, benches, and hymn-books in the middle of the floor, and applied a lucifer-match. His bonfire shot up in flames so high as to enkindle the timber vault. When he was caught, he made no attempt to protest his innocence: and was consigned to the madhouse, from which he continued an uninterrupted flow of pamphlets. He had a brother, almost as mad; but not certifiably so. This was John Martin, an artist, and, for a time, a highly fashionable one. He specialized in enormous canvases of flood, death, battle, destruction, doom, Belshazzar in Babylon, Noah and the Deluge, Moses engulfing the hosts of Pharaoh. His best-known work: a series of highly-excitable engraved illustrations to *Paradise Lost*. Gustave Doré out-dramatized him in the same line of country, and largely replaced him in public esteem. The Martins (there was a third brother, a sailor, also a visionary of sorts, who had *experiences* in ocean storms) were ancestral connections of my Uncle Guy, who married Dorothy, one of the Beverley Aunts. There was a book of John Martin prints, either in his house or my Grandmother's. For a time it strongly affected my view of world history, which I saw as having been broken at irregular intervals by huge and hysterical catastrophes, involving hundreds and thousands of terrified people, earthquakes, electric tempests, and the annihilating rage of a deity out for blood.

When my Mother married my Father she was much smaller than the Arden Aunts, of a different religion (brought up a Methodist, though now confirmed into the Church of England), from a different part of Yorkshire (indeed not really from Yorkshire at all), and from what the Arden Aunts regarded as a slightly lower social class within the bourgeoisie. That is to say, her father had sold insurance and not wine. An important distinction in the north of England. She was a schoolteacher in Barnsley. When she first became employed there, at a primary school where the children were the sons and daughters of 'rough' coal-miners or of embittered and impoverished unemployed, she wore her hair down her back in a tail. Her slight figure, conducting games in the playground, gave rise to protest from the parents; 'That's no right teacher you've got in charge of our Ethel; she's nowt but a schooil-lass hersen: even though we are on t'welfare, we've got an entitlement to a grown-up teacher! I shall complain at t'Town Hall!' She had, not surprisingly, something of an inferiority complex, particularly among what she called the 'bossy' Arden women: she made up for it by a determination to disapprove of rather too many people and institutions; and, after her marriage, and more so during her widowhood, to retain a set of social and domestic standards of cleanliness, taste, and propriety which I always found overstated and needless, though impossible to refute. Any argument, she'd simply set her stubborn mouth: 'No. I've had my say. I say no more . . .'

When she was very young, her father, who was a Liberal activist, busied himself in support of the coalminers from South Wales who were on strike. Two of them came up to Otley to appeal for funds at a public meeting, and he entertained them in his house. My Mother was astonished to hear them talking Welsh to one another: she could not believe this language. She asked one of them to put out his tongue. Surprised and amused, he did so. She touched it with her finger. She could not, she said, get over the fact that it was as wet and red as her own . . . On another occasion, her father brought home a young woman whom he had met at the railway station. She had a little girl with her, about the same age as my Mother; and was exhausted and depressed. She had travelled from the far end of England, following her husband, who had gone to Otley to find work. When she arrived, she discovered that he had failed in his desperate search and had moved on to another town; and if she were to go after him, she would have no money left for a bed that night. My Grandfather Layland invited her home with him. He must have had a winning manner; invitations of that sort, late at night, on railway stations, from strange men, were justly suspect, then as now. But she came: and was given tea by my Grandmother, who served boiled eggs. 'The strange lady' accepted one egg only (the Layland children were all, as usual, helping themselves to two each), and carefully divided it, half for her little girl, half for herself. 'Oh do give the child a whole egg, my dear!' said my Grandmother. And she did. And then, after persuasion, two. But my Mother said she thought about it for years afterwards, only slowly realizing that there were people so poor that they automatically shared eggs, even when eating at someone else's table . . .

She was about twelve when she came under the influence of a new young teacher at the Otley school. This teacher, very vigorous and beautiful, talked to her class about rather more than the prescribed syllabus. My Mother came home and announced in the middle of tea that 'women ought to have the Vote.' Her father was appalled. He beat his fist on the table and asserted that he 'would have no militant suffragette in *this* house!' Given his undoubted Liberalism in politics generally, indeed his *radicalism*, toward certain causes, (for example, opposition to the colonialist Boer War), this may appear to have been an inconsistent aberration, but not so. His political hero was David Lloyd George: Lloyd George was against women's suffrage, partly perhaps because in his own sexual life he was a promiscuous pasha, and partly because his strength in parliament depended on an uncertain coalition of interest-groups. The Women's Lobby was not yet strong enough to take first place: so his meetings became the continual scenes of feminist interruption, disruption, and what the press called 'petticoat hooliganism'. My unwitting Mother was threatening to bring all this into her family home: hence her father's indignation, and the sudden rebuff. After it she tended to keep her political feelings more closely within her own breast. Nonetheless, she was clearly on the Liberal side of the nation – not as far to the left as the newly-formed Labour Party but far enough to incur the unspoken disdain of all those Tory Ardens. On one occasion, at Beverley, there was a cousin of my Father's present who had been living in Egypt. She spoke with enthusiasm of a day of riot in Cairo, when the British colonial authorities had successfully sent British troops into the 'native quarter' to overawe the nominally independent Egyptians. My Mother asked, incautiously, 'But why *should* our troops go in? Isn't it the Egyptians' own country?' This remark was not well received.

Her feminism suffered a diminution in later years, though it was never actually denied by her – she and my Father used to argue good-humouredly about it: did female suffrage in fact come because of the women's militance, or was it a natural constitutional development which (as my father maintained), was only delayed by the militance? She disliked Mrs Thatcher as Prime Minister – not because Mrs Thatcher was a roaring Tory, but because a 'bossy' woman is always a menace, whatever her ideology. She warned me, when I got married, never to lose control of the household. And her vocabulary has caused my cultural subconscious an amount of difficulty now that revived feminism is seeking to change the male-dominated word. One example will suffice: she came back home from the shops one evening during the war, upset because she had been accused unjustly of queue-jumping by a female of obnoxious manners and low social status. My Mother said of her: 'She was standing there swearing at me, a very large and virulent lady – no, not a lady, she was a *woman* – I won't even call her a woman, she was definitely a *person*, and a *most* unpleasant one!' This was not up-to-date speech, even by the standards of West Yorkshire gentility forty-five years ago. I think it really belonged way back in Jane Austen's time: my Mother's mother had been brought up by *her* grandmother, and the entire cultural development of the family was accordingly retarded by the space of a complete generation, in a very interesting, but sometimes embarrassing way.

The Layland household in Otley carried a totally different atmosphere from that of the Beverley Ardens. I don't remember Grandmother Layland very well, she died when I was quite small. I do recollect a kind and gentle old lady, short, just like my Mother, and easily tired. She stayed with us once in Barnsley and took me out shopping. Unwise of her. On the way home I got tired of keeping pace with her small legs, and ran on ahead to play *ambushes*, pretending to be a 'savage', hiding behind gateposts and corners, and leaping out on her just as she came up with me. She endured this with great patience. I became over-ambitious, and ran too far ahead. I waited and waited in my chosen hide-out, behind a corner. But she never came. I could not look round the end of the wall to see how close she was – I feared she would be so close that my ambush would be spoiled of its drama. I concluded, at last, that she had taken an available side-turning and had gone home by the back streets. She would thus be already at my Mother's doorstep, triumphantly waiting to ambush *me*. So I ran for home as fast as I could go. I rang the bell, my mother opened the door, and looked at me in horror. 'But, John, where is Grandma?' 'Hasn't she come? She left me in Victoria Crescent to come the other way and get here first.' 'John, you are not telling the truth: she cannot have left you!' My Mother must have thought that Grandma had been taken ill in the street, she appeared so alarmed. And then, suddenly – 'Oh, there she is!' A small trudging figure in black, with a large black straw hat, bent by the weight of her shopping bags, wearily turning into our road a hundred yards away beside the mailbox corner. 'Naughty naughty boy, and a *lying* boy as well, you ran away from poor Grandma and left her to walk home all by herself, how *could* you be so unkind?' And when Grandma reached us, she was not at all in the spirit of the game: all she could say was how scared she had been when she lost sight of me altogether. She had imagined I don't know what – everything from motor-accidents to kidnappers, I suppose . . .

I had the impression that the Otley ladies were always slightly scared of something. A feeling there of a hostile world full of danger and offence, which was precariously kept out of their house: but which at any time might come insidiously (or violently) in. Methodist preoccupation with Sin had much to do with this. So did the sudden death of Grandfather Layland from heart failure in 1914 when he was still under fifty. His children were all young and not settled in the world. Such unexpected bereavements must always leave the survivors with a sense of general insecurity. I do know that at Beverley I was often made conscious of my capacity for naughtiness: whereas at Otley I tended to feel guilt even when I had not discernibly been naughty. This must have been due to recollections of my Uncle George, whom I never knew, but who was regularly held up to me as having been a very naughty, nay wicked boy, who brought such great disgrace and distress to his parents and all Laylands generally. As a child I was not given details: except the Quarry Story. The Otley house was on a steep hillside, overlooking the narrow gray stone town that clustered with its woollen-mills along the green valley of the River Wharfe. Behind the house reared the Chevin, a long brooding ridge, now wooded, but at one time, I guess, as bare and bleak as Wuthering Heights. There were stone-quarries near the top. My Uncle George, as a schoolboy had once climbed, with some wicked friends, up to the quarry (a forbidden place), and, moreover, on the Sabbath day. They got to playing with a crane, which the off-duty quarrymen had left unattended and unsecured. Somehow the boys managed to wind up the cable, and then, unable to control it, let it run with a load of rock straight onto George, shattering his leg.

His later adventures illustrated even more plausibly the way the Lord pursues Sin (and Sin, alas, pursues the Lord). With a good deal of parental influence, he found employment in a local bank. To be a bank clerk was then the ultimate in middle-class provincial respectability, and you needed as good a character as a Hollywood movie-star in the days of *morals-clauses*. But before long the restless spirit of George was bringing him out at night on the town. It is hard to imagine what exactly was to be found of soul-destroying intensity at night on such a town, but whatever there was, he found. Liquor, for a start. His father was now dead, or you can be sure his stumbling ascent of the bedroom stairs long after everyone else was asleep would not have been put down so easily to 'extra work overtime' and fatigue. His elder brother, a lawyer, knew quite well what was going on, but he did not live in Otley, and he was unable to be at hand when the crisis came. The crisis was the altering, forging, fudging in some way, of a cheque, or bank-statement, or some other paper of trust, to enable George to pay off a gambling debt. Or so at least I understand the story, which I have never heard fully told. My Mother had always been a great raconteur, as indeed was my Father, but the George business was genuinely painful, and was evaded as far as possible in subsequent reminiscence. Anyway, there was no prosecution: but George had to go to Australia, where he died about the end of World War II, having apparently got married out there. I never met his wife and I do not know whether they had any children. The whole tale has a strangely anachronistic flavour.

The Layland Aunts were mostly teachers and tended to treat me like a tiresome pupil. The eldest one, Nessie, was not a teacher, and was a complex person. She had been a real beauty when young. Her photographs recall Burne-Jones's paintings of maidens in Arthurian forests, tied up for dragons to ravage, and awaiting rescue by melancholy but courageous knights. During World War I she married a young soldier who was killed in France immediately after the honeymoon. She was very brave and refused to give way to grief. Instead, she opened at hat shop, to be quite independent of her (fatherless) family, and also to provide for her mother-in-law who was, it seems, penniless. By the 1930s she had soundly established herself: but in so doing had tightened and repressed any outgoing elements of her character – at least, as far as her response to me was concerned. She was invariably kind, but kind in such a way that all the time one was aware she was only doing her duty by me, a melancholy duty, and that lively small boys ought not ideally to have formed part of it. Of course I did not realize she had already had one small boy to deal with, and that she loved him so much that any others were redundant.

This was the youngest Layland, my Uncle Harold. Only a schoolboy when his father died, he had been brought up by his sisters more than his mother. He gained an Oxford scholarship from the Otley grammar school, and at Oxford had been a great academic success. He had also run up a large amount of debt, and Nessie had bailed him out, at considerable personal sacrifice. He then married a young woman from the North of Ireland and went to live in Belfast to teach modern languages at a most illustrious Protestant boys' school there. I saw him but rarely: but my mother was very fond of him, as indeed were all the Laylands, and he was constantly in correspondence. When I was eight he sent me a present, which greatly excited my mind: a book of Irish legends, Cuchulain and the Red Branch Heroes. I knew already the Greek and British (Arthurian) mythologies. But these Gaelic tales were something new. They struck at my heart, with their unpronounceable names; their combination of battlefield butchery with hallucinatory landscapes, druid-haunted bogs, bare mountains, bottomless pale lakes; their alarming women: Morrigan the death-goddess, Scatha the war-goddess, Deirdre the self-willed man-stealer, Maeve of Connacht filled with unslakable rage for the loss of her prize bull. And also the sense of death: Cuchulain reluctantly killing Ferdia his friend in the middle of the river with the one battle-trick Ferdia had never mastered; Cuchulain himself strapped to a pillar-stone so that he would die standing while none of his enemies dared come any closer to his deeply-wounded but still dangerous body. I had of course no notion of the recent Irish rebellion and the relevance of these tales to it: but there was an odd political irony associated with my Uncle's gift. The parcel arrived very late: weeks after his letter saying he had posted it. The reason was an IRA bomb in the Belfast Post Office which had thoroughly disordered the due process of the mails . . .

Uncle Harold was a man of mischief. I remember him, in the 1940s, mildly distressing the strait-laced Nessie by a defence of Charlie Chaplin's sex-life, at that time the subject of salacity in the tabloids. Harold maintained that the 'greatest comic genius since Molière' had been abominably abused by mean-spirited prudes, not because he was really to blame, but as a cover for reactionary American capitalists who were in fear of his radical humanism. To the morality of Methodist Otley these opinions were almost as nerve-racking as they would have been in the US Bible-belt.

He got into trouble in Belfast during the war. As a teacher of German he became well-known among a circle of Bohemian friends for his imitations of Hitler. He also spoke Irish: a language not favoured in the British-ruled North of Ireland, where it immediately suggested Catholic 'Fenian' Nationalism and pro-Nazi gunmen. He could do Hitler in Irish as well as German, he could also do Churchill in both languages. His friends, in so far as they were Ulster Protestants, were drawn from that fast-waning area of true Protestant radicalism which had set afoot the Insurrection of 1798 with all its French-Revolution republican principles. Insofar as they were of Catholic origin, they were determinedly anti-Fascist and would have supported that section of the IRA which sent volunteers to fight against Franco in the Spanish war. Anyway, the police were told that meetings of 'German spies' were taking place in Harold's flat. He and his late-night guests were thereafter followed about by detectives: whom they encouraged by pretending to pass secret messages in public places, scratching their eyebrows at one another, cocking their hat-brims, and generally behaving like B-movie foreign agents. It is a wonder he was not interned . . .

He had a cottage in the Mourne Mountains, just a few miles north of the Irish Border, where the people, mostly Catholic, still spoke Irish as their everyday tongue. Cuchulain's fort had been at Dundalk, in the immediate vicinity, and the area was steeped in ancient history and legend. One day, about seven years after the war, he was staying in this cottage with his wife, daughter, a sister, and a colleague from Belfast. On an impulse he asked his fellow-schoolmaster to go up the mountain with him for a walk before bed. It was a moonlit night, but there was cloud-mist higher up, and the slopes of rock were slippery. Harold lost his footing and, before his friend could catch him, fell to his death hundreds of feet below. I was spending my own summer holidays with my parents on the Isle of Arran, between Scotland and northern Ireland, when the news came. Arran has its own place in the old Gaelic poetry. It seemed appropriate I should have been there to hear of Harold's end: the landscape, common to both isle and mainland, has been well-recorded by a twelfth-century Irish writer:

> 'Arran of the many stags, the sea reaches to its shoulder; island where companies were fed, ridges where blue spears are reddened. Wanton deer upon its peaks, mellow blaeberries on its heaths, cold water in its streams, nuts upon its brown oaks . . .'

Had it not been for Harold, I might never have become acquainted – least not for many years – with that particular aspect of European literature. It is now inseparable from my imagination.

Otley as a town had no great resonance for me, as opposed to the very powerful historical under-currents of Beverley. Probably because the Laylands had anyway only lived there for a half-generation. The Laylands did not on the whole have much to say about their own family story: but my Mother always, and rather irritably, assured me that it was quite as ancient and distinguished as the Arden pedigree. She said that there had been a Layland family-tree, but one of her Aunts had taken it away with her when she got married, and now no one could remember exactly who was in it. John Leyland, topographer and antiquary to King Henry VIII was allegedly included . . . In any event, my Mother was never to be persuaded that the Ardens were in any way a better class of family than the Laylands. Of course, they thought they were, they did have a family-tree, and it ran far back to the days of the Norman Conquest, to before the Norman Conquest, to before even the Anglo-Saxon invasions. They could not claim it ought to be actually *believed*: it had presumably been cooked up for some member of the Arden family in the eighteenth century by an office of the notoriously venal College of Heralds (which is what happened with most Olde English genealogies). But the very fact that an Arden had had sufficient pull to get a Herald to do the cooking for him was in itself suggestive of the worth of the family. Provincial north-country wine-merchants, true: but sometimes one would have thought they entertained a secret claim to be Kings of England.

My mother's personal pride often led her to 'stand no nonsense'. One day, in Barnsley, in appalling winter weather, when the thawing snow had been scooped by the municipal workforce into mounds of black slush completely covering the sidewalks, she found she could not walk into town without getting her short legs soaked to above the knee, and her boots full of snow. The other pedestrians were apparently prepared meekly to submit to this discomfort. But not Mrs Arden. She stepped off the curb into the middle of the road, and marched on into town as though she was heading a parade. Very soon she did head one: a line of motor-traffic, angrily piling up behind her, unable to overtake her either to left or right because of the snow-mounds, and all hooting, honking, and calling out abusive epithets. She led them at her own pace for maybe a mile: her own pace in the slippery conditions being about 2½ m.p.h. After a while, other people followed her example, until the ascendancy of the motor-car (on what was indeed the main throughfare into Barnsley from the north, a very busy highway) was completely demolished. If the police saw her, they wisely decided to take no action. They knew it was neither the time nor place to be partisan in defence of internal combustion.

During World War II she worked as a volunteer in the

Citizens' Advice Bureau: largely concerned with bewildered people who could not understand the ludicrous embellishments of wartime bureaucracy and its tyrannical regulations. As Barnsley was not bombed by the Germans, her work was perhaps lighter than had she been doing it in Liverpool or London, but it was taxing enough. For instance, evacuees had been brought into the town from the blitzed areas. A nervous maiden-lady, elderly, living alone in a small house, would heroically offer to accomodate two persons. The evacuee-billeting-officer leaves six adults and four children on her doorstep. When she states neither she nor the house can cope with such a number, she is shown a docket or chit authorizing her home to accept 12: and told that two more children, without parents, will be arriving the next day. Clearly a clerical error, 12 for 2; but it has passed all sorts of official desks where it has been stamped and countersigned. How to set it right? Undoing such a muddle might well take all day. Meanwhile the ten evacuees will also have turned up at the Advice Bureau, complaining that they have been put to live with a woman who refuses them entry, and the billeting-officer, run off her feet, has abruptly told them it is now *their* problem, and has left them in the street to sort it out for themselves. Finding a roof for them before nightfall has automatically doubled the load ... Barnsley was run by a self-perpetuating mafia of Labour Party Demagogues. Their ideology was humane and excellent (and was to prove itself the genuine choice of the people in the General Election of 1945): but we lived in a pocket of highly complacent local politics, where socialist-jobs-for-the-socialist-boys had been the watchword ever since the failure of the great Coal (and General) Strike of 1926: defensive barriers had been set up against whatever Tory government ruled in Westminster, and a mule-headed obstinacy took the place of intelligent and imaginative administration. The Citizens' Advice Bureau, as a national non-party voluntary organization, was highly suspect to the local ward-heelers in the Town Hall. The Bureau's chairperson was the Church of England Rector, instead of being a trade-union hack: and many of the Bureau workers were thought to vote Tory or Liberal. So, in a dispute like the one I have outlined above, you could be sure that Town Hall would be highly obstructive. My mother always brought these problems home with her and worried about them all week. At the end of the war she received a letter, from the infuriating Town Hall itself, telling her that in view of her sterling war-service, she had been recommended for a national medal. She was enraged: not that she did not think she *deserved* a medal: but it was altogether too much that the King should be giving it to her merely on the say-so of the incompetent halfwits who had done their level best to prevent her sterling service having any sort of practical effect. She replied with what she called 'a strong letter, a snorter', refusing the medal, and explaining why . . .

In their old age my parents moved into the North Yorkshire countryside. They had never owned a car, and were dependent upon the local bus-service (expensive and irregular) or a taxi (expensive) if they wanted to go anywhere outside their village. My Mother was an active member of a church ladies' group. After some years – she would have been in her late 70s – she saw this group being taken over, slowly, by a number of younger members, wives of newcomers to the parish; or, more precisely, of newer-and-wealthier-comers than my Father. There was an amount of ill-feeling, genteely expressed, but no open hostility. Just a self-augmenting undercurrent of Byzantine shiftings of alliance, and a sense of lurking con-frontation. Then suddenly, the occult struggle became overt. A deputation of the younger ladies waited on my Mother. Over her coffee and cakes they temporized like old-fashioned Arab sheiks about to negotiate oasis water-rights. Their event-ual request: would my Mother please make one of her famous trifles for a joint-meeting, the following week, with an affili-ated ladies' group in the parish of M—, twenty miles away. Is *trifle* a dish known in America? In the north of England it is the *sine qua non* of any formal tea. It is made in a large bowl, layers of cake, biscuit, fruit, jam, jelly, custard, cream, pieces of chocolate and so on, and necessarily takes a long time to prepare: each layer must set solid before the next one is added. My Mother spent the next few days planning her masterpiece, special journeys into the market-town to buy the ingredients (returning home by costly taxi because the parcels were more than she could manage on the bus), intermittent worries about what she should wear for the trip to the joint-meeting, and her assured triumph there. It seemed to her the hidden intriguers were at last coming to terms with her status in the group.

On the morning of the great day the great trifle was complete: a vast yellow mixing-bowl. filled to the brim with rich sweetness, almost more than she could lift, covered in plastic film to prevent it slopping over. She would carry it in Mrs B—'s car, balanced upon her knee: she would guard it with her very life. Mrs B— at the door, fur from head to foot, her polished car humming at the garden-gate. In the car, a clump, copse, thicket, of ladies' best church hats. 'Oh, Mrs Arden, what a beautiful trifle! Exactly what we'd expected!' And then: shockingly: 'How are you going to get to M—'?' My Mother was speechless, for was she not going in Mrs B—'s car? She was not. 'I do have a carful, you see: just room for the trifle on the back seat with Mrs C—, but we're so sorry, not for you. We really thought you had your own transport . . .' My Mother could have rung for a cab: expensive, yes, but not impossible. But she disdained the expedient. She stood on her doorstep and watched her trifle carried off in the car, like a little fat princess taken to the ball amidst sycophantic ladies-in-waiting. As far as she was concerned, declaration of hostilities had been unilateral, on *their* part, not *hers*. They must remain unilateral. She gave up all connection with the ladies' group: and evaded all efforts by the clergyman or by other well-wishers to involve her ever again . . .

My Father began his life defeated by women. One son

amongst all those daughters, and his parents always favoured the daughters. They went to college: they received paternal influence if their careers needed it (except for those who did not have careers – the Twins, for instance, must stay at home to do the housekeeping): but my father at Beverley Grammar School was only allowed to stay there till he was sixteen, and then he was told to earn his own living. He was not even groomed for the wine-merchant business. The old Grandfather may or may not have disliked or despised him, I don't know: probably he enjoyed so much deference from his more dependent daughters that he preferred to make the independent ones so finally independent that they would not interfere with his complacence, while a son in the Arden counting-house would only expose his own commercial incompetence. So my Father went to work as a junior clerk in local government: and then went to war, returning home in 1919 as a Sergeant Major, happily unwounded, but with his health severely impaired. His clerkship in the County Hall had not been kept for him – the postwar government did not place veterans' rights high on its political agenda – and he had to look outside Beverley for a new career. He did ask his father, could he not come into the wine-business? This was run from an atmospheric medieval vault, an ancient monument indeed: but the traditional clientèle (East Yorkshire country gentry) had fallen on evil days, and sales were dropping off badly. How to restore the business? My Father made an unwise, though commercially-sound suggestion: diversify, turn the vaults into a regular wine-bar, and establish a restaurant upstairs. But this, to my Grandfather, was *quite out of the question*: it was incredibly vulgar American-style 'hustling', and under no circumstances, this time-honoured family enterprise, under *no* circumstances would he allow, etc etc . . . In fact he understood he could not organize such a development himself and he greatly resented any possibility that his son might be seen to outpace him in Beverley society . . .

So my Father found a place as a trainee-manager in a glass-manufactory in Barnsley. Eventually he became works-manager, and had a perfectly dreadful time. His owners were a family of exceptionally neurotic capitalists, and inept into the bargain. Their approach to labour-relations verged on the permanently hysterical. The worst of them all was an elderly lady known as 'Auntie', who had a controlling interest in the firm without any technical knowledge to support her vehement prejudices. Whenever there was a dispute between the trade-union and the bosses, my Father (who, as manager, was supposed to support management) found himself siding with the employees and their grievances. This in despite of his strongly-felt ancestral Toryism – of course, the authentic old English Tory was always in danger of gravitating towards radical anarchism in defence of human liberty – principles and grass-roots practice became inextricably mixed-up.

There was a traumatic day, just after the end of World War II, when a woman, absolutely distraught, telephoned our house an hour or two before breakfast. She was the wife of one of the glass-blowers, and the police had just completed a dawn-raid on her home, hauling her husband off to jail, and ransacking the whole place. It emerged that a malicious person, never discovered, had sent an anonymous letter to the cops, accusing this man, and several other of the firm's workforce, of theft from the factory. There was, at the time, much press-agitation about a supposed local crime-wave, and the men-in-blue were under pressure for results. They did not check their information, but swooped with macho enthusiasm. In every house they raided, they assembled all the family glassware, and demanded to see the receipts for the purchase of each item. Well, whoever can produce a receipt for a set of beer-glasses bought fifteen years ago? As it happened, the glass-blowers were, by common custom, allowed to take home at nominal cost any items that were found to be *flawed* after cooling. A *flaw* might be a slight bubble in the glass, scarcely visible to the naked eye, but it nonetheless rendered the piece unsuitable for public sale. Our own home was equipped with items of this sort: receipts were never given for them, they were a perquisite of the work and it was all well understood. About half-a-dozen workers, in handcuffs, in the sight of their terrified families, had been imprisoned all in one morning. My Father was furious: I had never seen him so upset. These men could not 'ring for their lawyers', workers in a town like Barnsley simply didn't have any lawyers. *He* rang for one, right away: and − in case the lawyer failed to turn up − went himself, in great haste, down to the courthouse to offer evidence for the defence. As soon as the magistrate had heard what my Father had to say, he stopped the case, refused to let the police-prosecutor add another word, and told the police that their action was a disgrace to Barnsley law-and-order. I suspect there was good luck involved: this particular magistrate was Labour Mayor of the town: and whatever may be said about the Labour Party in unchallenged office, their members on the bench of justice had some thought for the underdog. Had it been a Tory politico, things might have gone badly for the accused . . . Certainly, when my Father got back to the factory, having been missing most of the day, he received an angry tongue-lashing from one of the directors of the firm − 'Good God, Charles, I'd had a conference here this morning, I'd expected you at it, we needed your report; damn it, man, what on earth were you doing *in court*? Auntie was in a terrible rage: she says if those chaps hadn't stolen the glassware, she's damn sure they'd been up to *something*. She's usually right, you know. No smoke without fire. That letter-writer must have known *something*. J— and K— (two of the arrested men) − have always been trouble-makers, you shouldn't be so damn ready to believe everything they try to tell you . . . Are you losing your touch, or what . . . ?'

It is likely that some details in what I have written are not exactly accurate. I have made a point of not checking my memories. And many of the things I have written are known to me only by hearsay. It is not so much a question of what really took place, as what I grew up believing took place. There is no such thing as true history, anyway. We all, individuals, nations, classes, religions, make up our own particular biographies (separate or collective) to suit the needs of what we are doing now, or what we mean to do next. To take a very simple example: Julius Caesar was assassinated by Brutus, Cassius and others, on the Ides of March, 44 BC. It took place before witnesses and is established as a proper historical fact. It is assumed that whatever the reasons for this killing, Caesar was thereby cut off short just before he really got into his stride as the new ruler of Rome: and what he would or would not have done, had he lived, is treated by historians as a matter of consequence. But suppose he would have done nothing, because he could think of nothing to do: and because he could think of nothing to do, he therefore deliberately allowed himself to be murdered? Such an interpretation would not contradict the ascertainable facts. He *is* supposed to have ignored several attempts to warn him, and so forth . . . Reading back from the Ides of March, it is an interpretation that must alter absolutely any view we may have formed of Caesar's career and intentions prior to his taking of power. The point is, one cannot possibly *know*. Assumptions must be made, without verification: and they are made. In the interests of those to whom Roman dictatorship, Roman republican 'democracy', carry political lessons for today.

I do not know why I am who I am, or why I have written what I have written. I don't know, either, whether anyone else can make any better guesses at it than I can, in the long run. But simply to be asked by an editor to think about it prompts a number of recollections, to be added-to or subtracted-from, according to the available space. The space is now filled: and there you are . . .

Nicaraguan Comparisons

1984

About a dozen of us went to Nicaragua for a fortnight this last February – a 'cultural delegation', so-called, writers, artists, actors and so forth, of several European nationalities – we went under the auspices of the Nicaragua Solidarity Campaign, which meant that we had no claim to be *unbiassed*; we were there, at least *I* was there (I ought not to speak for the others), because I had already decided that as Nicaragua was asking for support, I was prepared to give it. I live in the west of Ireland and my decision was to a great degree affected by the information brought back from Central America through many Irish people, mostly connected with the Catholic Church, which had been given much greater prominence in the Irish media than was the case in the UK. The Bishop of Galway, for example, had been a personal friend of the assassinated Archbishop Romero of El Salvador – he had been present at Romero's funeral when the 'security-forces' opened fire upon the crowd of mourners and he had talked and written at large in Ireland about this experience. He also administers Trocaire, the Irish third-world catholic relief organization. I am not a catholic myself: and my solidarity with the Nicaraguan revolution is not based on confessional grounds: I mention all this simply to explain the preconceptions that I took with me on the trip.

If, as a result of our tour, I had come to the conclusion that

Nicaragua is in fact, as the North American administration accuses, an aggressive totalitarian threat to human rights and liberties, I would either have to say so in an Orwellian burst of candid self-reversal, or else keep silence. As it happens, I came to no such conclusion. The revolution in that country, which overthrew the Somoza dictatorship in 1979, has not yet 'gone sour'; it may of course do so, one of these days, because who can say what corruptions and internal conflicts cannot afflict a small country under enormous pressure, military, political, economic, from a powerful neighbour? But one thing seems at present to be certain – the Nicaraguans are as well aware of the danger as anyone else and are determined not to succumb to it. That at least is my opinion, based upon what I saw and heard there.

In July some foreign priests were expelled and the Pope denounced the Sandinistas: Washington immediately gleefully repeated its heretofore unsubstantiated allegations that the Nicaraguan government persecutes Catholics. A week or two later the centre-right opposition withdrew from the elections, agreeing with Washington's prediction that 'conditions for a really free election do not exist'. The State of Emergency in Nicaragua has been extended: press censorship, although it is to be 'eased', will not be abolished, as had been hoped. These are not trivial events. I cannot acclaim them. As a writer I hold a free press, free media generally, to be the *sine qua non* for my profession. It doesn't exist in Britain or Ireland so I have the more sympathy with the Nicaraguans. But, of course, censorship in Britain is not imposed by governmental decree . . . (some of us think that if it were, it would be easier to fight against). I cannot weigh the outrage of *La Prensa*, the sometimes-censored daily paper of the centre-right in Managua, with the outrage of Arthur Scargill against the baronial dictates of the owners of the *Sun*, the *Daily Mail*, the *Daily Express*, as to how the coal strike should be reported. I merely suggest that a comparison exists and that we do not live in so free a 'Free World' that we can afford to be too condemnatory of Nicaraguan expediences. As for the other events: in February it was clear that only by a miracle could they be avoided. N. American policy has been continuously to create them by denouncing them before they occurred: they have now occurred, and the denunciation may to that extent be said to be justified. It is a strategy, as I will soon show, that has been applied before, in a context nearer home.

Let me admit that I don't speak Spanish, that everywhere we went in Nicaragua we were accompanied by an official guide/interpreter, that we received first-class accommodation in a luxurious government hostel administered by a delightful lady who asked us (and meant it) to treat the place as if it were our own home, that our tour was conducted in an air-conditioned mini-bus shielding us from the ferocious Central American sunlight as well as – if you have a suspicious mind – from the putative approaches of local malcontents and dissidents, and that our programme was chosen for us on a basis of what would best serve to fortify our solidarity. This will clearly weaken my argument in the eyes of those who wish it weakened and there is nothing I can write to diminish the fact. So picture, if you will, a clutch of leftish trendies, picking our way in incongruous straw hats with naïve delight among the doctrinaire Sandinistas and their misled masses, clicking cameras, taking notes, failing to observe this that and the other evidence of Marxist-Leninist deceit – Beatrice and Sydney Webb with G.B.S. in Stalin's Russia, perhaps. Why didn't we find out where were the concentration camps, where were the relatives of the death-squad victims, how many of the numerous armed soldiers and militiamen and women we saw around us on every street were about to bring terrorist death-and-destruction to the peaceful democrats of Honduras or El Salvador? There was a reason why we didn't: because we didn't ask. We didn't ask because the questions seemed totally irrelevant, and nobody – not even the Nicaraguan conservatives whom we met – gave us any reason for putting them. The overall atmosphere of the place was simply *wrong*

for such notions. It would have been as though a Latin
American visitor to Britain in 1984 were to enquire, 'If Arthur
Scargill wins his strike, what arrangements have been made for
Mrs Thatcher and her cabinet to take to the hills: and which
hills will she choose? Can we go and see them, please?'

So what *was* the atmosphere? I can offer two, quite
different, areas of comparison. First: it most strikingly resembled what I recollect of England in the summer of 1940. I
was only nine in that year, belonging to a patriotic anti-fascist
(though far from socialist) family, and being educated at a
patriotic anti-fascist school. My critical faculties about the
state of England then were at about the same stage of naïve
acceptance as they were about Nicaragua in February this year
– then I was cut off by immaturity, now I was cut off by
official sponsorship and ignorance of the language. The results
in both cases being the same – I had to take in a general
impression and make my opinions accordingly. My father was
in the Home Guard when it was first formed under the title of
Local Defence Volunteers (he kept a rifle in the umbrella-
stand), my maiden aunts were Air-Raid Wardens (and kept
tin-helmets on the front-hall hatpegs), my mother did
voluntary work in an emergency clinic and in the Citizens'
Advice Bureau. A few years later, in 1944, I was placed,
(without being asked) in the school cadet-corps, and even at
that late date in the war we speculated on the possibilities of
being called in earnest to arms if the Germans tried some
commando-style shock landings. There were air-raid shelters,
often rudimentary slit-trenches, constructed at every convenient corner: parties from school went out to farms in the
plain of York to help each summer with the harvest: at least
one of our teachers began all his lessons (French) with a series
of chanted slogans – 'Vive la France, vive la libération, vive la
victoire, vive le Général de Gaulle!': we used regularly to be
called together to hear Churchill on the radio: and we were
vaguely aware without being surprised at it, that the national
press was censored – at the same time we were also told that

Freedom of Speech was one of our great national War Goals. Elections had been placed under a moratorium ('for the duration'). Strike-action in certain industries had been inhibited. If Hitler won, we were told, the most appalling atrocities would take place, and our (regrettably postponed) democracy would never be resumed, ever. We knew about the Poles, Czechs, Maltese, Jews, Channel Islanders, and all the other refugees and displaced persons up and down the country, enduring their barracks and camps: and we believed what we were told. We know now that we were, on the whole, right to believe it. There are examples of everything listed above to be seen in Nicaragua today.

And Britain, bear in mind, had not entered those years of threat as a result of a widely-based popular revolution overthrowing our own Hitler: the Nicaraguans have actually *experienced* the rule of those who now seek to make their comeback under the protective arms of the United States.

Which brings me to the second – and, in the context of an 'After the Revolution' umbrella-heading, the more crucial comparison. The national politics of the Republic of Ireland, internal and external, are still inextricably involved with the War of Independence (1916–21) and the consequent Civil War (1922). In many respects the Irish Revolution, as conceived by the signatories of the Dublin Proclamation of 1916, was a 'Sandinist' revolution. That is to say, the armed groups who fought against British rule were a coalition of working-class activists with an international socialist ideology (James Connolly's Citizen Army) and middle-class or rural nationalists (Padraic Pearse and the National Volunteers). Both sections subscribed to traditional Irish Republicanism, with its descent from the French Revolution as expressed in the Irish Rebellion of 1798: just as the majority of Central and South American liberation movements incorporate Simon Bolivar into their ancestral Pantheon, so all Irish separatists at some point invoke the memory of the hero of '98, Wolfe Tone.

The first independent Irish Dáil ('illegally' created by the defection from the Westminster Parliament of the successful Sinn Fein coalition candidates who had won an immense majority of Irish seats in the General Election of 1918) contained in its programme so many socialistic items that it was denounced by London – and by many US supporters of Irish independence – as Moscow-inspired. Every effort was made to keep an independent Ireland out of the clutches of international bolshevism and within the sphere of influence of the British Empire. The conservatives among the Irish revolutionists were incited, encouraged, and finally forced, to split from their associates in the coalition: and a new Irish (Free State) Army, commanded by Michael Collins, found itself in arms (arms provided by Britain) against its former comrades of the liberation-front. Collins's operations were seen by the British very much as Pastore and his Contras, operating from Costa Rica, are seen by Washington – the 'reasonable democrats', with whom 'we can do a deal', who have become sickened by the excesses of the revolution and fight to 'restrain' it. A certain equivalent of the Honduras-based Contras (essentially the survivors of Somoza's National Guard) can be found in the overtly-imperialist Ulster-Loyalist forces whom the Anglo-Irish general Sir Henry Wilson was attempting to mobilize in 1921. Wilson's military intervention was in fact never really needed, because Ulster-Loyalism was granted its own partitioned Six County statelet: and he himself was assassinated by Collins's agents, while Pastore was recently subject to a bombing attack by the northern Contras. The details of the situations differ: the rough similarity of the forces involved, and the interests they represent, nevertheless holds good.

In Ireland, the Civil War was won, militarily, by the British-equipped Free State Army. After a few years the political leader of the defeated Republican irredentists, De Valera, came back into the fold, formed the Fianna Fáil party, and eventually secured parliamentary power. In the process he had to shed his 'extremist' colleagues, who continued – and still continue, as a second (or rather third and even fourth) generation of the outlawed IRA – to pursue the same war for the same cause. He also shed those 'extremist' political notions which had led his Free State opponents and his British enemies to label him a Communist. (They had never really been *his* notions: but this is no more than hindsight). Workers' Soviets, enthusiastically embarked upon in the first flush of the British withdrawal in the south of Ireland (notably Limerick) had been speedily demolished on the orders of the victorious Free State military ('General Mulcahy riding into the town on a gun-carriage' as an Irish Republican once graphically described it to me), reinforced by heavy denunciations from the Catholic Church hierarchy. The Bishops were strong partisans of the amenable Free State, but parochial clergy very often supported the Republicans: there is a readily-seen Nicaraguan parallel. De Valera made it his business to woo the hierarchy once he attained power: and even most of the IRA abandoned socialist ideology during the 1930s. Bourgeois-ification of the society extended in all directions. The Irish Labour Movement became marginal, having avoided committing itself to either side in the Civil War.

The role of Irish women in the revolution, which had been very marked in the early days (Countess Markievicz, for instance, who had commanded an echelon of insurrectionary troops – including a female unit – during the 1916 rising and then was the first woman ever elected to Westminster – she became a Minister in the Dáil instead), fell away almost completely, and was replaced by the overt suppression of sexual equality enshrined in De Valera's 1937 Constitution. The cultural outburst of the first decades of the century (W. B. Yeats the poet, Jack Yeats the painter, Synge, O'Casey, Joyce, O'Flaherty, O'Donnell – and all the other talents connected in some way either with national identity or socialist struggle) was speedily subordinated to the exigencies of a clerically-orientated censorship and the respectabilities of middle-class catholic conformism. Women and writers are at the moment leading figures in Nicaraguan life, alongside, and often identical with, revolutionary commandants. Fr Ernesto Cardenal, one of the Jesuit priests in the government, whose existence disturbs North American middle-class catholic conformism (Al Haig and Jeanne Kirkpatrick *et al*) so much, is also a poet: the Minister of the Arts is both a poet and a woman . . .

I could adduce many more details of similarity and potential similarity between Ireland and Nicaragua: the basic one however is simply that both countries were small dependencies of a larger power whose newly-won independence was to be threatened directly by force of arms and indirectly by propaganda, manipulation and infiltration. The Irish revolution was not so much aborted as stunned, the present resurgence of it in the partitioned north exhibiting every possible symptom of a slow, agonizing and embittered awakening from half-a-century of stupefaction. The damage done by such a period of narcotic catalepsy is evident from the increased brutality of the struggle and the vastly increased unwillingness of those involved to accept anything from their enemies on trust. I think the Nicaraguans have incorporated this, and other equivalent experiences from all over the world, into their present consciousness. An important point of difference, however, is the nature of the surrounding societies. In the years after World War I there was no Cuba for the Irish to look to: and the Soviet Union was itself in the throes of its own post-revolutionary civil war. Great-power rivalries were therefore not a factor in the situation. British fears about a successfully-revolutionized Ireland were not quite the same as N. American fears about Nicaragua. They were (a) that internal British social stability would be threatened by an Irish left-wing example, and (b) that Britain would be deprived of an offshore military and naval base in time of war, while a potential enemy might be able to secure one. The United States now claims (in the Kissinger Report, January 1984) that the leaders of 'Central America', including democratic and unarmed Costa Rica . . . express deep foreboding about the impact of a militarized, totalitarian Nicaragua on the peace and security of the region'.

Central American nationalism is unlike Irish nationalism because it is an international nationalism – the entire region is inevitably brought in to any discussion on the subject. The little nations that make up Central America were once all part of one large Spanish colony, the Viceroyalty of Guatemala: and their present frontiers are the ad-hoc arrangements introduced (usually violently) by local ex-colonial grandees during the post-Bolivar ferment in the nineteenth century. They have little or no *raison d'être*, cultural, economic, ethnographic, geographic. Their peoples look forward, eventually, to some sort of federated union of republics stretching from Mexico to Colombia – socialists, naturally, see such a union as being ideologically bonded. Hence the inevitable solidarity expressed by Nicaraguan Sandinistas for Salvadorian guerrillas and the acceptance in Nicaragua of settlements of Guatemalan refugees. If the establishment of such a union is deemed, before it can even happen, to be an act hostile to the USA, then of course the N. American strategic control of the area is threatened: does not the Panama canal run right through the middle? And of course the Soviet Union will take what advantage it can. But surely this is a threat that is self-created by the threatened party? Self-created threats become self-fulfilling ones. N. American blindness to the real self-interests of the USA is as hard to understand as Britain's blindness to its own interests in regard to the Irish. . . .

It should be pointed out that, despite the general cultural unity of the Central Americans, there are indeed divisions in the region: they are not exactly national ones, being those that existed among the Native Americans (Indians) long before the Spaniards came. The revival of the traditions of the Native American peoples (often non-Spanish-speakers – their own languages are of a great diversity) is a part of Central American revolutionary consciousness, though not, as yet, a highly-developed one. The admittedly-mistaken treatment of the Meskitos by the Sandinistas, and the attempt, in the face of damaging US propaganda and manipulation, to remedy this, is a case in point. Probably the problem would not have arisen at all had not the Meskito territories been divided by the factitious border between Honduras and Nicaragua, and had the Meskitos not been originally subjected to British rather than Spanish colonization. The complex difficulties of revolution only mirror the complexities of the previous imperialism. Compare the Anglo-Scottish Protestant plantations in Ulster and the fearful running sore that has resulted from them. But the US government in the role of guardian and guarantor of Native American civil rights is almost laughably incongruous. One would like to seek an opinion from the late Sitting Bull of the Sioux, or from the contemporary Guatemalans who face deliberate genocide from the US-sponsored authorities. But it does make plausible apologetics for liberal audiences, whether in North America or in Europe. There is a long history of Hispanic racism in the region. It will take a long time to root out: and the more the revolution is interfered with from the north the longer it will take.

With reference to this problem: we attended in Managua a cenference-workshop of theatre-groups from all the countries of Central America: a weekend of lectures and rehearsals produced a series of short improvized plays. Each play had to be on the one prescribed theme 'America for the Americans' – a deliberately ambiguous title, offering scope for invention and interpretation. Each acting-group was made up from all the different nationalities at the conference. The directors of the plays each were drawn from a different nationality. All the plays endeavoured in some way to grapple with the same cultural situation – Spanish colonists as a superior oppressive caste dominating Native Americans: dominator and dominated both under threat from the more highly-developed industrial power of N. America. Not so much the 'Third

World against the First', as the 'Third *and* Fourth Worlds struggling to discover their own *inter*dependence' before any sort of genuine *in*dependence could be achieved. Some of the actors were Hispanics, others Native Americans. The discussions between the plays were often acrimonious and highly critical. Interestingly, none of the plays brought in the 'Second World', the Soviet bloc: the latter seems to bulk more largely in State Department and CIA thinking than in the cultural consciousness of Central American artists.

I have compared Nicaragua with both Britain defying the Nazis and Ireland outreached by Britain: neither simulacrum includes the experience of Somoza. Latin-American tyrants are an archetypal image in modern English-speaking popular cultural consciousness – I suppose because we live so far from their Upas-tree deadliness – that their very monstrosity seems to bestow on us a contrasting sense of cosiness: but one has only to think of such films as *The Wild Bunch*, or such comparatively lightweight fiction as C.S. Forester's *The Happy Return* (Capt. Hornblower in the Gulf of Fonseca) or John Masefield's *Sard Harker* and *ODTAA* (British merchant seamen at large in the sugar-republics) to understand how entrenched the stereotype can be. In a sense the Somoza clan – described by the Kissinger Report in a phrase of delusive candour as a *kleptocracy* – was 'only what everyone knows goes on in that part of the world'. The implication of Kissinger was, of course, that it does not go on any longer, and therefore we should expunge the stereotype. D'Aubisson in El Salvador is conveniently forgotten, as are the rulers of Guatemala. Kissinger does not recognize that Nicaragua has indeed expunged the stereotype: the Report slides over this by invoking a new one, 'Latin-American totalitarian marxism': but even so it has to do so by means of a sort of future-conditional tense – '. . . *should* the Sandinista regime now be consolidated as a totalitarian state . . . the existence of a political order on the Cuban model in Nicaragua *would* pose major difficulties in negotiating . . .' etc (my emphases).

The experience of Somoza created Sandinism. I find it amazing that Sandinism is *not* totalitarian-marxism: had it been it would have seemed no more than poetic justice, the one extreme deserving the other, as it were. But history is not necessarily symmetrical. Let me refer to this experience by recalling one of the few loosely-structured and rambling conversations I was able to take part in with a Nicaraguan – time *was* very short, and so many of the people we met were speaking to us ex-officio; serious discourses, under revolving electric fans or against a roar of air-conditioning, from chairpersons, editors, artistic animateurs, politicians and so on, who of necessity began most formally with: 'the problem for Nicaragua may be divided into three parts' (Jesuit education, with a background of J. Caesar and his Latin prose-logic, leading through to St Thomas Aquinas?), 'the political, the economic, the cultural aspects . . .' But one day at lunch, a long lunch in a down-at-heel youth centre that had once perhaps been an attempt at a jazzy nightspot for the unworthy rich of the ancient Spanish-colonial town of Leon, we were able to hear some of the memories of our minibus-driver, a fifty-year-old man called Raoul.

Raoul had been a truck-driver before the revolution., He had had to let his licence lapse, because in the last years of the Somoza dynasty (there were three US-backed dictators from the family over nearly half a century, and the third one was reputed to be trying to found a monarchy) the National Guard were hi-jacking trucks and their crews for service, without appeal or legality, against the guerrillas. They had always extorted tribute from the users of the roads: previously this had only been financial, now it was in kind. Refusal meant arrest, arrest meant torture and death. Raoul went into comparative safety as a handyman of various skills in his local *barrio*, where his papers might not be so frequently called into question as on the open highway. The district where he lived in Managua was not one of the first to be involved in the revolution: but when it was eventually attacked he and his neighbours had to fight against the National Guard with whatever they could lay hands upon – sticks, stones, clubs, petrol-bombs, he said, until they could provide themselves with firearms from defeated Guardsmen. He did not claim to be a war-hero, he had not been an old guerrilla up in the hills where Sandino led his rag-tag army until his murder in 1934, and where some form of resistance had continued ever since. Raoul was one of the thousands who had had heroism forced upon them. Note: he used the passive verb-mood: the people *had been attacked* by Somoza and his guards. The integrity of their lives, (such as it was) had been affronted by their rulers and they could endure it no longer.

Somoza, of course, had virtually owned the country. He was more like a medieval robber-baron than other modern dictators who at least pretend to preside over some sort of political *system*, fascist or whatever. Everything he perpetrated seems to have had a personal dimension. He is believed to have, with his own hands, tortured captives in the basement of his house: and with his own loins personally violated a distinguished woman dissident before turning her over to the gang-rape of his praetorians. These are stories from a schoolboy's horror-book: I suspect he encouraged them, to give himself the aura of a fairy-tale ogre-king (which is not to say they are not true). At the same time, he was to be seen all over the land: visiting his properties – farms, factories, housing-projects – looking into his agents' ledgers and collecting his own dues like any traditional peasant-proprietor, genial and grasping, vindictive in the extreme if all was not up to his very personal scratch. His National Guard (originated and trained by the US Marines who had once occupied the country) were established in menacing hilltop forts to overlook the towns and crossroads like Norman keeps in Saxon England. When the international relief poured in after the devastating Managua earthquake of 1972, Somoza simply pocketed it. Managua today has no centre, all was demolished. It is as though all of London north of the Thames between

Pimlico and Aldgate and as far inland as King's Cross had simply disappeared, leaving a ruined St Paul's, a ruined Mansion House, an unruined Hilton Hotel and an unruined Bucklersbury House (because of the modernity of their structural design). There is in Managua a cathedral, shattered; a large government building, shattered; the Bank of the Americas and the International Hotel, all in a desert of emptiness. Everything that makes a metropolis is contained in the small-scale buildings of the suburbs, shops and offices, public and private, crowded into villas, shacks and shanties. It was this final contempt for his capital city which finally finished Somoza. When he fell, only the National Guard and a few family-associates supported him to the end: the conservative, bourgeois, business-and-landowning-class linked themselves to the revolution.

Today, they are the opposition, and it now seems that they have finally decided to assume the role of the non-participant opposition – eventually perhaps the opposition-in-exile, along with Pastore, if they wish to preserve some rag of democratic respectability, or with the Somozistas if they don't. Their spokesmen talked to us of the marxist-jesuit-pluralist Sandinistas as their British equivalents might talk of Tony Benn – which is to say that the fear-and-loathing appeared not a little factitious. They were unable to supply the atrocity-stories we expected: no secret-police-at-dead-of-night or genteel corpses found at dawn on rubbish-dumps. Merely a long tirade about expropriation of properties which government had declared were not being used to the full benefit of the people. There was one melodramatic account of anti-catholic 'persecution' – a priest being forced to 'do a nude-show on TV'. It turned out that a priest in a provincial town had been having an affair with a married woman whose angry husband called in friends from the local Sandinist militia. They turned the priest out of the woman's bed, naked, into the street; and one of them had fixed it with the TV news to have a reporter and camera-crew ready to record the humiliating event. In no sense could any of it be said to have been the result of government policy. It was on the level of some *News of the World* story about 'Nude Vicar in Scunthorpe love-tussle' or the like: and that was the worst they could tell us. It was so silly it was comic. But it is not wise to laugh.

How many people in Britain seriously maintain that Mr Benn – or Mr Livingstone – if they were a government – even a government that included Mr Scargill – would really be an adequate cause for a North American invasion here? Or at any rate a CIA destabilizing operation? There are certainly some who do: if they were in Nicaragua they would be non-participant opposition, or contra opposition infiltrating from Honduras and Costa Rica. And I am sure that President Reagan, given his holy-roller world-view – 'The Forces of Light v. the Empire of Evil' – would be only too pleased to recognize them as 'the real Britain'. But I believe – I hope – I hope I can believe – that by far the greater part of the British population would, under such a circumstance, feel as unified against such a threat as was the case in 1940 . . . ?

It is not wise to laugh.

Hitler looked like Charlie Chaplin, Somoza looked like Sergeant Bilko on a dirty weekend in Mexico. But both of them, before they were finished, killed multitudes of people and laid waste vast quantities of prosperous land. If the present US administration insists (for its specious reasons of global strategy well-mixed with commercial advantage for a few well-placed corporations) on intervening in Nicaragua to bring down everything that has been so carefully and courageously built up there since 1979, then there will not even be anything left in that country – lives, liberties, houses, factories, farms or produce – for the exploiters to exploit. If they insist on doing this, they must not be backed from Europe. If they are not backed from Europe – and in all Europe, Mrs Thatcher's government is the least likely to refuse support to Washington – they may, just possibly, not insist. While we were in Nicaragua we met many US citizens touring the country like ourselves. They were not, of course, supporters of Reagan or of his policy: and they let us know what had not been very clear from the British or Irish newspapers: the depth of anger that his policies have been arousing in the United States. To what extent this can reverse his expected victory in the forthcoming election is an open question. But they all said the same thing: that European opinion on Central America is far more important than Washington cares to admit and that it must be mobilized. It is indeed Vietnam all over again: but this time the war must be stopped *before* the full destruction is launched. Nicaragua was nearly destroyed before 1979: by earthquake and by revolutionary war. Unimaginably, the country and the people survived. Their survival is our survival. If they cannot be saved, then we are all lost.

The Fork In The Head

A story
published in *Visitors' Book*, Poolbeg Press, Dublin,
1979

Jackson came back to Galway after two weeks in London 'meeting potential clients' – he had not met very many, and had wasted most of his afternoons in the cinema watching insipid films about naked women: but he had succeeded in conducting *some* business, and was able to inform Fionnuala that although progress was rather slow it was nonetheless 'appreciable'. She looked at him sideways and said, 'See any good movies?'

'Oh yes – one, anyway – Japanese. Very sadistic, Samurai: but offbeat. I'd had lunch with Jack Levison, and hadn't anyone else to see that day – Macgregor had cried off. The Academy in Oxford Street. How did you spend your time?' Fionnuala grinned at him, ubiquitous, omniscient: certainly maddeningly superior. 'How do you suppose? There was a meeting in Eyre Square about the Republican Prisoners and I made a speech. O'Reilly and his crowd tried to exclude me from the platform but Maeve Hanratty and the Red Tendency Group insisted that it was a united front or nothing and in the end I had to be accepted. But they wouldn't let me march immediately behind the banner, and Maeve and I ended up at the end of the demo amongst the odds and sods. What's your opinion?'

'Eh . . .? Oh, well, so long as you actually were on the march and you did get to say your bit, I suppose it was okay?'

'It was bloody hell *not* okay, Jackson. There is a definite attempt to manoeuvre the whole Group out of the campaign. What are you going to do about it?'

Jackson did not want to do anything about it. His lady's political alliances, confederations, and country-dance permutations were so fluid and progressive as to be always one move beyond his immediate comprehension. Besides, while he had been in London there had been a tolerably large Irish meeting at Kilburn about the Prisoners, which Fionnuala would have wished him to attend, which he knew he ought to have attended, and from which he had been inexcusably absent – he had in fact been at the Cinecenta off Leicester Square between two-thirty and six, sprawled in front of something French called *Midnight Streets* . . . or had it been *Women of the Night Streets* . . . ? anyway, he had the uneasy feeling that Fionnuala must have read about the Kilburn meeting in one or other of her mail-order news sheets, Republican or Trotskyite, and she would certainly ask him for an account of it. He changed the subject and went into the kitchen to make some more coffee. When he came back into the studio, Fionnuala had his portfolio open, and was prowling through the various drawings he had or had not managed to sell in London, and the conversation became mercifully professional.

Jackson was a 'layout designer' and Fionnuala had been a children's book illustrator. He had originally met her when he was on a visit to Dublin to attend an exhibition of Irish posters and book-jackets. After a year or two's random contact, in and out of Ireland, in and out of bed, and in and out of various emotional absurdities, they had settled down together to produce freelance 'visual motifs'. His alleged business acumen kept them together as a 'firm', while her creative talent was responsible for the actual work. They had gone to live in Galway, where a series of state and semi-state subsidies were always about to come through as a result of drinks bought in lounge bars for enthusiastic but unreliable local politicians. There was some notion of their setting up a weekend school for young graduate designers in connection with UCG. Fionnuala – in Jackson's opinion – did not improve the chances of this project by taking part in so much national-liberationism. Jackson – in Fionnuala's opinion – did not improve the creative quality of their joint work by refusing to recognize his political backwardness.

Their relationship, already under stress from his Britishness and her Irishness, had lately become exceedingly unstable – or so at least it might have seemed to their intimates. But then intimates are rarely as intimate as all that: and in fact the pair of them managed remarkably well. Probably the real reason they still held together was that he loved her drawings; and she loved the way he could adapt and develop her drawings within the context of the industries they served. At all events, they had not seriously quarrelled over anything for very long. Despite her political obsessions – as he regarded it – she was a decent, tolerant, and courageous person; and despite his laziness and egocentricity – as she regarded it – he had never questioned the correctness of the left-republican line on the national issue – and he was a very good cook.

Sexually they were perhaps but moderately compatible. But there is a certain sensuality to be derived from the joint production of even plastic carrier-bag designs: and there is no doubt that they took full advantage of this.

The day after his return from his London fortnight, Jackson said they ought to be going to the island for the good weather. This island was in the middle of the big lake, and had on it one small weatherboarded fishing-cabin. When they had no engagements, but needed peace and quiet to develop a new line of work, they would get into their Volkswagen, drive into the Galway shopping centre, fill up the back of the car with boxes of tinned food and bottles of wine, and then drive about ten miles to the small strand where they kept their boat. Jackson would start to fool about with the outboard motor, while Fionnuala went behind a hedge to urinate. When she had finished, he would abandon the useless motor, and they would row out across to the island, a distance of about half a mile. They would unlock the cabin, collect twigs and dead branches, light a fire on the hearth, cook some sausages, and boil a kettle for coffee or tea. Jackson would eat the sausages. Fionnuala would gather blackberries from the brambles all round the back of the cabin and eat them. She thought that sausages were conducive to fat and eventual cardiac trouble. He thought that the island blackberries were full of worms. It would take them the rest of the day to clean up the cabin and assure themselves that the rats had not damaged their things since the last visit. Usually there was a good deal of nasty rat dung everywhere, and a sour smell. They would lay out poison in little tin can lids under the house, which was supported upon six concrete bollards.

Upon this particular occasion, Fionnuala suddenly remembered something. 'Oh God,' she said, just as Jackson put his last piece of sausage into his mouth. 'I have suddenly remembered something.' It appeared that there was to be another demo, or march, or picket, or whatever, in Galway, the following evening: and she had suddenly remembered it. It was all Jackson's bloody fault she had forgotten it, going on so much about his damned Japanese films. She had promised Maeve that she would be at the Tavern at two o'clock for a preliminary laying-of-plans.

'Let Maeve get up her own riots on her own for a change, for God's sake,' said Jackson. 'If the freedom of Ireland cannot proceed without your personal presence at every damned meeting, then all I can say is that the Irish people at large are not worthy of such liberty. Ha!' Fionnuala replied that Maeve needed all her friends to counteract O'Reilly and his fucking crowd, and that Jackson ought to be there too, by rights. Jackson said that all they were fucking doing was helping to make fucking O'Reilly into the future Irish Hitler;

and he would be buggered if he would do anything to give that sodding hooligan any chance at all to make himself more conspicuous. 'To counteract O'Reilly is exactly what he wants,' he yelled. 'He's bloody using you to advance himself, and in my small opinion he's an agent of the Special Branch!' Fionnuala said that of course O'Reilly was an agent of the Branch: so they had to counteract him. He was ultra-left and infantile: but it had to be recognized that much of what he propounded was nonetheless correct, and therein lay his danger. 'The student element will always go for the O'Reilly line unless someone can expose it. You ought to be in there, Jackson, doing your utmost. You're well enough known, for God's sake, and the young people respect you.'

'Do they fuck! A bloody Englishman, a blow-in, respect hell. God dammit, Fionnuala, I have made myself a monkey far too long in front of those riff-raff students of yours. I am not going to get involved.' And that was that. He rowed her over to the mainland the folling morning, saw her off from the strand in the VW, and then returned to the island in great annoyance and paradoxical relief of mind. He made himself a lunch from the last of the sausages, had a glass or two more red wine than he ought to have drunk at that time of a hot day, and stretched himself out on the grass with a large picture-book of erotic Indian miniatures and his transistor radio. He fell asleep. At about four o'clock he woke up, sweating, a little headachy, and bitten all over by the island's hot-weather insects. He decided to go out in the boat. He took another bottle of wine and a plastic container of some sort of salad compilation which Fionnuala had bought the previous day at Roche's Stores. He stuck a fork in his hip pocket to eat the salad with, and nearly forgot the corkscrew. He left the Indian miniatures behind in the cabin, and brought, instead, the Penguin translation of Petronius's *Satyricon*. He was going to have a thoroughly self-indulgent afternoon.

He rowed out to the northeast, until the boat was floating easily between two round uninhabited islands where sheep moaned crossly over the water at each other. He pulled in his oars, pushed a cushion into the bows of the boat, and lay down in the sunshine with his book and his wine and his salad. There were no insects out on the lake, thank God. Three-quarters of a mile away were a couple of boats with fishing parties in them. The sky was blue and untroubled. He forked away at his salad, dropping bits of it on the flies of his trousers and the pages of his book. This was a nuisance, so he altered his position, put the book on the thwart, and sat properly to finish his snack. He pulled the wine bottle to his mouth – he had forgotten to bring a cup or glass – and swallowed a large quantity. He felt suddenly surprisingly drunk. He spoke aloud to himself: 'I suppose she'll stay in town overnight with that silly Maeve. If she gets in amongst that Lesbian lot, God knows where she'll end up. I don't fucking care. Let her march with O'Reilly or against O'Reilly, on behalf of or in the face of or up the fundament of the bloody Branch. Jackson is drinking his wine.'

He was vaguely aware of a series of quick ripples running towards him across the flat lake. He balanced his bottle on the thwart and balanced his salad box on the gunwale and stooped to pick up the fork which had fallen to the bottom-boards of the boat. He held the salad box in his left hand and executed an over-large manoeuvre with the fork to pierce a piece of pimento. The ripples and the small squall which moved them surged up to the boat. There was a swift heave of the water, a sudden sway of the boat, the sun went in behind a grey cloud; and the fork fell into the lake. For two long slow seconds he looked down and watched it sink, deep deep and glistering like a dream of a fish into the dark green water and the aspiring darkness of the water weeds. Then all of a hurry, he thumped the salad box back inboard, saved the wine bottle, which was rolling off the thwart, grabbed hold of his oars and thrust them onto the rowlocks, and began to row back to the island.

It had become chilly and he had not bothered to bring his shirt. The wind rose as he pulled across the water, and his bare skin shuddered. A few small spikes of rain pricked on to his shoulders. The pages of his book were all spotted with wet brownish circles as it lay, open, in the bottom of the boat. When he landed he discovered that his cushion was quite damp. He did not bother to take it with him as he went up to the cabin and made himself a pot of tea.

That evening the wind continued to rise, blowing from the west, from the mainland onto the island. The rain rattled on the corrugated iron roof of the cabin with an undue amount of noise, as though a shower bath had been inadvertently left on. This cabin, being roofed with metal and walled with a double layer of light plank, had all the properties of a sounding-box – in rough weather it was like living inside a banjo. He listened to the radio as he lay on his bunk and smoked cigarettes. There was a lengthy programme of Irish and English folk song, introduced by a very solemn commentator who talked heavily about ethnic values for five minutes between every two-minute musical item. Jackson enjoyed folk music and even sang it – when there was no one to hear him. He could not indicate the difference between one note and the other, which made it impossible for him to perform for other people's musical pleasure. But he was good at delivering the meaning of the words and could even suggest a certain poetical passion in his renditions. It had been his ability to do this which had originally got him into Fionnuala's bed – or so he believed. He could in fact sing himself into a state of amorous excitement. He ignored the pedantic commentator, and murmured the words and what he took to be the air of *The Red-Haired Man's Wife* until he felt a genital erection inside his trousers.

The programme changed: and the news bulletin began. Still murmuring the song, and stroking his body, he listened with less than half an ear to mutilation in Belfast, villainy in Rhodesia, corruption in Washington, mysterious goings-on amongst the leadership of Fianna Fáil, and some rubbish about the Bishop of Cashel. Then he heard the word 'Galway'.

What – Galway – what was it . . . ? 'After the demonstration, a spokesman for the local Gardaí had stated that the trouble was now contained and the women who had been taken away had since' – had since – *what* . . . ? 'been released . . . ?' Or had they? Jackson hadn't been listening properly. What women? Taken away? What the bloody hell had happened? He jumped up and began to sweat. Should he get in the boat and go ashore to find out? There was a telephone box two miles away up the boreen, but he'd have to walk because Fionnuala of course had taken the car. And the phone was always out of order in that damned box – the drunks out of Feeny's Bar used to jam the slot with bent coins every night trying to call for taxis to get them home, damn the bloody drunks, it was always out of order. And besides, wasn't it bloody rough out there on the lake, and his outboard not working? Besides, it was dark. If she had been released, she'd be back the next morning. But was it her? God knows there were enough women in Galway fit to be 'taken away' by the Guards. God knows some of them needed it. He could make an absolute public monkey out of himself panicking like this. When was the next news bulletin? They had one at the end of the night's programme, didn't they? So he waited, still sweating, till the end of the night's programme. Twice he went and emptied himself – his bowels running like a tap – on the chemical closet round the back of the cabin in the lean-to.

The bulletin again. He put his ear to the radio, and his hands trembled. Belfast, Rhodesia, Washington, the Bishop of Cashel. Fianna Fáil had slipped to fifth place – apparently the rumours about Haughey were unfounded. Then Sport, motor-accidents – but nothing, but nothing at all about Galway. God, he'd imagined it. Hadn't he? Well, even if he hadn't, it couldn't be that important. Surely nothing important could happen in so small a country and RTE not pick it up and enlarge upon it – but they hadn't. He'd go to bed. Yes, bed. God in Heaven, what the hell had that fool of a woman been up to? He knew it, he knew it, he knew it. *O'Reilly* an ultra-leftist? In the name of – of all manner of archaic ridiculous blasphemy – what in the name of *anything* could we call that unbelievable Maeve? He went to bed, growling, maintaining himself wronged. He slept, after more wine: and he dreamed.

He saw the lake, flat, windless, in the middle of the night. It was raining. It was raining so hard that the smooth water was pitted all over like smallpox – he had once seen a child in India in a village infected with smallpox, not a smooth place anywhere upon the poor little brown face, black eruptions on every inch. It was pitch dark and yet he could see everything. Out of the water arose a dark lump, no, not a lump, more like a column, it rose up, it was moving slowly towards the shore. It splashed as it came, growing taller all the time. It was a woman. She was naked, with long black hair streaked all down around her flanks, wet, shining under the clouded sky where there was neither moon nor star to make anything shine. She had two eyes as white as water underneath her black fringe, and a huge mouth wide open with water running out of it. He had a fearsome feeling that there were also two eyes looking out at him from the thick mat of her pubic hair, and the mouth beneath them was also wide open – certainly there was a white stream of water running down between her legs as she walked. She was clear of the lake and coming up the grassy gleaming strand of the island, walking slowly upon tip-toe. In her forehead was a silver fork: stuck deep into the pale brow up to the roots of the prongs.

Then the dark became dark again – how could it be anything else when there were clouds across both moon and stars? He saw the woman no more; and he heard only the continuing rainfall.

He was in the cabin, on his bunk, and the rainfall roared on the roof. He was sitting naked on his bunk, and cold, cold as the lake itself, he was trembling all over and unable even to reach out his arm for his clothes. All his bedding was wet, and there were puddles between the bed and the door, they shone in the moonlight that flooded in at the window – but there were clouds across the moon, so how could there be moonlight? He looked at the puddles. Some of them were near his bed, some of them near the door – but most of them to one side all round the base of the little narrow door that opened into a cupboard where fishing-rods were sometimes kept. Neither Jackson nor Fionnuala fished: but the previous owner of the island had done little else, and the furnishings of the cabin were all for the furtherance of immeasurable murder of trout. This door was about twelve inches wide and six feet tall, and the cupboard could contain whole fasces of rods, standing erect in the shadows, all ready for instant use. Jackson discovered his own phallus in such a condition, though never in his life had he felt less venereal. Was it possible that a man could become tumescent through sheer fear? He had always believed that the opposite should be the case.

What the devil was in that cupboard? There was water leaking out of it, drop drop drop down the low sill onto the boards of the floor. With a strenuous effort he spread his feet upon the floor, took one step, then two, stretched out his arm, and pulled open the cupboard. She was in there, stark naked, with the fork in her head. Her mouth was now closed.

He looked at her, rigid. She looked back at him and there were no pupils to her white eyes. She stood stiffly upright: and he slowly became aware that a greeny-white trickle of what ought to have been blood was coming down from the prongs of the fork, down either side of her flat nose, down her chin, onto her chest. It was not a large trickle, but it was continuous and ran all down her body, between her small breasts, over her belly, down the inside of her thighs, continuous, to seep out of the cupboard, over the doorsill, throughout the whole cabin.

She did not open her mouth; but he was sure he heard her speak. It was as though she spoke between torrents of water. He could hardly distinguish the words, they were so confused with the wet noise. 'It was yourself sank down the fork till it came into the flesh of my head: and I have come to bring it back.'

He returned to his senses – or awoke – or recovered – he could not be certain exactly which it was – the following morning, after daybreak. He was very cold and his body ached all over. He must have been lying on the hard plank floor all night. He had every symptom of a bad hangover. He dressed himself clumsily, unable to remember anything, except that he was on the island and Fionnuala had left him. But what for? And for how long? He could not fix his mind clearly enough to sort it out. He tried to put on his shoes and dropped one of them. He picked it up, and picked up a fork that was lying untidily under the corner of his bunk. He put the fork on the table, put the shoe first on the wrong foot, then on the right one, and went over to the door. He opened it and looked out. It was beautiful weather, though the thorn leaves and the grass were soaking wet as though it had rained all night. The outline of the mountains at the top of the lake was so clear that it might have been painted by a sixteenth-century Indian miniaturist. There was a lot of water in patches around his feet on the floor of the cabin. Of course the roof had always leaked. Then he heard an outboard motor – he must in fact have been hearing it for some time: because even as he noticed it, it cut out. A boat was coming in to land beside his own boat at the island's small pier. It was a strange boat, larger than the standard lake-skiffs, with a bigger outboard than usual, and it was painted an unrelieved black. There were three men in it – one of them in the tweed cap and nondescript jacket of the local boatmen, the other two in dark uniforms. They were Civic Guards. The boat grounded on the strand and the two Guards scrambled out, carefully, taking good care not to get any splashes of water into the tops of their wellingtons.

Jackson remained standing in the doorway of his little house: he watched them as they came solemnly up the green shining slope. The first Guard was a Sergeant, a solid hard professional heavyweight with very sharp blue eyes. He sent these blue eyes in every direction, taking in the cabin, the island, the trees, the birds, the flowers, Jackson's own boat, the tins of rat poison under the joists of the house. The last thing he looked at was Jackson. He said something, at length. 'We endeavoured to take her in for her own protection, d'you see, sir, but there is no doubt the crowd was aroused. Not a matter, d'you see, sir, of convenience to the Guards on duty. And we judged it best at the time to make no statement to the Press or the radio representatives. The blow she was struck could easily have been harmless: but the doctor at the Regional Hospital said something about a vital place, like it might have been oh a chance in two hundred – bedad the man hadn't even screwed his fist into a ball. Being poked as it were with the bend of his knuckles. But the Regional Hospital said internal, a vital place, d'you see, sir. Oh there's no doubt at all, sir, that the Guard who held her is exonerated – how the divil could he know that the only way back to the Barracks would be filled up by certain elements. The poor fellow had no choice but to fetch her, so, through the thick of the crowd, and they hostile. You'll be making your own arrangements about the funeral, I suppose. Would you say now your – your wife – would that be correct sir? Would you say she was a Catholic? There are arrangements fair enough for the Protestants in the Galway cemetery, but if it's not a religious burial, bedad, I've no notion indeed how you'll manage at all at all. . . . Her friend, Miss Hanratty – er – her friend, I forget the full name – the friend was after making the very divil of a hullabaloo; but I think we have her settled by now, if you want to talk to her. Will we give you a lift over?'

The other Guard, who had not yet said anything, was a tall thin bitter young man with a swart pointed face like an eagle. He uttered what seemed – incredibly – to be a screech of laughter. 'Sure he has his own boat. If we took him in ours, wouldn't his own be left on the island for the divil and all his dogs to be coming over to collect afterwards, he'd never get the dispositions right in all the confusion – let him take his own boat, Sergeant, and if he's not fit to row her himself, let

Sean Riordan go with him to see her beached and properly tied-up.' Sean Riordan must have been the civilian in the dark brown tweed jacket.

Silently they climbed into the boats and shoved off. Sean Riordan made no attempt to start Jackson's motor, but set to the oars with the practised skill of a regular lake-dwelling man. Jackson, in the stern, sat as dumb as a fish and stared at him as he pulled. The tweed jacket gaped to the movement. Jackson saw an underarm holster and the butt of an automatic. Sean Riordan was no boatman, but a Branchman in plain clothes, Sean Riordan's voice was hoarse and by no means expressive. He paused between phrases to give himself breath as he rowed. 'Certain elements in these times – oh a terrible deal of difficulty. You'll understand, Mr Jackson, the out-siders in the community have their own place and their own welcome here. When all's said, 'tis a difficult matter. Your – your wife, now: they tell me, in the first place, from Dublin? And you yourself, would it be Birmingham?'

'No,' said Jackson, 'no, I was born in York. As a matter of fact.'

Sean Riordan pulled the oars for another hundred yards or so. Then he showed all his teeth, in what might have been a smile, but was not. 'Don't you think you should go home?' Jackson made a movement towards him – a movement of vehemence, almost of violence. Sean Riordan's hands were off the oars in an instant, and his right hand towards his armpit. But Jackson was still again and the hand stopped in mid-air. There was a noise in Jackson's throat that rose up and was cut away. Maybe the Branchman never understood it, but Jackson had in fact spoken. He had said – or had attempted to say – 'God shut up your mouth, man – I *am* at home!' Then he fell forward from the thwart into the bottom of the boat and slumped down heavily on the sodden cushion which still lay where he had kicked it the previous afternoon.

PART TWO

D'Arcy

Senator David Norris (Dublin): 'There are people in this city who would sell their country for fourpence, and get down on their knees and thank God they have a country to sell.'

The Economist: 'An English businessman settled in Dublin praised "the rich vein of anarchy that runs under everything. It tells me these are nature's capitalists." A gombeen man is after all just an entrepreneur gone bad.'

Introduction: by M. D'A.

I am a third daughter. If I had been the fourth daughter, or the first daughter, or the second daughter, I would not now be having to answer the question put to me by Nick Hern of Methuen, 'Why do certain people find you so obnoxious, Margaretta?' This conversation took place just after the Sunday afternoon symposium, at the Royal Court Theatre, which he had set up for the Methuen list of playwrights in June 1985. I had compared the role of theatre-workers to that of the hare at a coursing-meeting: devotees of both activities swear blind that they are carrying-on a traditional ritual in response to the inherent needs of the human psyche, without which all culture would collapse. Just as the hare is put into the field to be chased till it either escapes or is killed, so we in the 'established' theatre are planted before audiences to entertain or to be destroyed. By their acquiescence, the audiences are perpetuating a principle of cruelty. I was talking about *the formal structure of theatre*, not *the content of plays* – if the cultural forms are cruel, then the society and the state which that culture expresses must also be cruel, and so they are: we live in a world of winners and losers, aggressors and victims, interrogators and suspects, and our vaunted 'arts' are a miniature of it.

I had said I did not want to be a hare, so I left the stage (where I had been placed as part of a 'panel') and invited all who were interested in what I was saying to come with me to another floor of the building where we could create our own space with neither aggressors nor victims. Many people did: but not the critic Michael Billington, who responded in the *Guardian* with a barrage of incoherent personal abuse practically accusing me of terrorism . . . I think he genuinely thought I represented a dangerous minority who wanted to wipe out four hundred years of British cultural tradition. I recognize that I *am* part of a minority: but he should recognize that *he* is too. The majority of the British people do not support the cultural values of the established British theatre. And indeed the British government – responsible for theatre-subsidies – had a majority in parliament based on a *minority* national vote. Neither does the voting pattern show that the majority of British people want radical social change. At both ends of the spectrum are embattled minorities: and they are fighting for control of the middle ground.

In my own country, Ireland, a recent referendum on a very important issue – ratification of the Single European Act – was passed 'yes' upon a total vote of only 44% of the electorate. The 'no-voters' interpretation of the SEA – that we as a nation were being railroaded into abandoning our right to an independent foreign policy in return for more loot for the rich – was slammed in the European Parliament by an Irish Member, who stated that all the main political parties supported the Act and that the opposition to it were a rag-tag of wreckers, spoilers, and cranks who could not even muster 5% in the polls: in fact we got 30% of the votes cast, and all the others with their triumphant 70% had convinced no more than three-tenths of the enfranchised population to mark their ballots in favour . . .

For the time being I am quite happy to be on the losing side: and that is what really annoys my attackers.

Which brings me back to my position (in pre-pubertal childhood) as third daughter. Number Three is always on the losing side. Two is company, three is a crowd: Number One and Number Two stick together, and isolate Number Three. Number Three could adhere to Number Four, but that would mean that Number Four would be isolated from One and Two: and Three and Four together would only become a second-class One-and-Two, the one family thus splitting into a dualism of continued power-struggle. But what would we be struggling for? To present a front of social acceptability outside the family: which means *toeing-the-line*. Who drew the line, and what for? *They* didn't know. So *I* wouldn't. I let One and Two make their own arrangements with Number Four . . . So I became the one who was always breaking down the imposed 'good order': and when, in later life, I was attacked for the same offence, I was already well used to it.

But I also understood the fragility of hierarchical structures, which can only hold together by the minority in power imposing its will upon everyone else, whether they know what they are doing there or not. Those outside the structure must be made ridiculous and their opinions devalued so that to those inside the necessity and correctness of the hierarchy's traditions are confirmed by the continual object-lesson. This applies to all structures, whether of the establishment or the opposition, of the right or the left. There is always a 'Number Three' to reject the regular dualism. In geopolitics it is known as the Third World. Among the orthodox left or in the feminist movement those who reject structures are labelled 'ego-trippers'. In communist countries we recognize them as 'dissidents', and praise them: but here in the West . . . ?

In the West one is only permitted to express dissidence by means of a vocabulary of little bridges of apologetic hesitation – tentative adverbs, conjunctions, mitigating phrases: 'perhaps', 'maybe', 'rather', 'in so far as', 'with all due respect', 'it could be argued that . . .' suggesting that one might be quite wrong, and that one is always open to conversion and submersion, a verbal cap-doffing that proves you know your place, and legitimizes the minority in power. Little bridges are linguistic manipulation: I refuse them, so therefore I cannot be wooed or seduced, I am obnoxious.

The pieces that follow have been written over the past ten

years. The one on Censorship in Ireland was delivered to the
Norwegian Writers' Union, in 1978, at an international conference they held on Censorship in general. A Czech dissident
writer was present, and his speech was the main theme of the
gathering. My paper, with its references to British cultural
colonialism rather than Soviet, was emotionally interrupted by
a British delegate, the then editor of *Index On Censorship*, who
accused me of nationalist paranoia, and wanted the conference
to stop me reading it. It so happened that one of the Norwegian
writers there was Felix Thorson, who had lived in Ireland in the
late 1940s. He supported me: and the committee agreed I was to
continue my analysis of censorship without being censored. At
that time it must have been rare for Irish voices to be heard at
these conferences openly pointing out Britain's role, because
my interruptor was truly startled by what I had said – he
obviously had expected me to take the same line on Irish
censorship that he would have followed – i.e. that it is all to do
with the inherited backwardness of the Irish . . . I, too, was
equally startled by his lack of understanding.

I had gone to Norway during a break in rehearsals of
Vandaleur's Folly, by the 7/84 Company, a play in which
Arden and myself contrast the activities of revolution and
reform. The production was invited to the Queen's University
Festival in Belfast, and Arden and I were asked to give lectures
there during the company's visit. I wrote *Theatre in an Age of
Reform* for this occasion, but I could not deliver it personally
because I was in Armagh Gaol. (Arden explains why in his
essay *Drawing Blood In Galway*, page 11.) It was hardly likely
that immediately after my talking to the Norwegians about
censorship I would cheerfully acquiesce in *toeing-the-line* in
Belfast simply because I was an invited guest. When I requested
the poets Michael Longley and Paul Muldoon to give evidence
on my behalf, they refused: one of them on the grounds that he
was a civil servant . . . 7/84 also did nothing: I was no longer a
'member of the company', as my contract as co-director of the
play had lapsed once the actors' collective went on tour. As

playwrights we were never deemed members of the collective. This episode – as I lay in Armagh – made me seriously question the stance of the theatre towards either revolution *or* reform.

Breaking Chains and *Lift The Taboo* are both explorations towards a use of theatre where women can develop themselves instead of *line-toeing* for the patriarchy, a field of thought which in turn made it easier to find a more open format for the radio-plays on Christianity, *Whose is the Kingdom?*, which have an essay all of their own.

The Aosdána fragments cover a struggle within that organization which continued from 1983 to 1986 and is still simmering on and off the boil. Once again, back to Michael Billington: the structures we have as artists must be looked at in relation to society as a whole, just as we look at any other social or political structure. The arts should be no more immune to self-examination or to external criticism than a trade union or the Stock Exchange.

There are also some limbering-up exercises in a sort of free verse: I wrote most of them while sitting paralysed at the typewriter unable to progress with my plays. And some similarly-composed anecdotal vignettes from the countryside where I live in County Galway.

Letters to newspapers: I have been writing these since 1961, and have found that this form of expression is one of the last free forms available – either the editors print them or they don't, but nobody tells you to rewrite them in the interests of public sobriety. And they *are* read, by a large audience.

I have included a dossier I was asked to prepare for the Civil Liberties campaign against the Prevention of Terrorism Act, because I am one of the few artists and women to have been arrested under the Act. Ironically, my first PTA arrest, at Stranraer, was simply because a copy of my paper *Theatre in an Age of Reform* was found in my luggage. I make no *little bridge* to apologize when I say I regard my artistic role as that of an experimenter in the breaking-down of barriers: and sometimes these barriers have been protected by the police, which accounts for my three periods inside British gaols. Each time I have come out, I have seen society from a very altered perspective, because society has clearly been telling me I am undesirable, unwanted, unfit, and a danger to all good *line-toers*. I was in Holloway this year, after my Greenham arrest, being dragged to solitary confinement for challenging their interpretation of my rights. A quiet plump young woman with dyed blonde hair whispered to me, 'Good on you, don't give in!' Later on, we chatted together. She had been sentenced to 21 days for Contempt of Court. Her crime: after the jury ignored the judge's obvious belief in her guilt, and acquitted her of Receiving Stolen Goods, she surprised herself by springing upon him: she pulled off his wig, and said, 'There you are, you silly bugger, you were wrong!' The whole court clapped and cheered her.

Women Who Have Influenced Me

published in *Spare Rib*, 1986.

A stream of childhood-remembered names comes back: Madame Curie, St Catherine of Siena, Edith Cavell, Grace Darling, St Scholastica, Pandora (science, visionary activism, moral courage, physical courage, dedicated independence, refusal to accept censorship); and the big images, Mother Nature, Mother Church: finally, Mother Cat, my personal pet, who represented love . . . Now I think about it, all these qualities were in fact combined in the two young women who brought me up.

My mother, Miriam, a Russian Jew from the East End of London: and Kitty Spain, from a small farm in Nenagh, Tipperary. Both were in flight from their family backgrounds: my mother from strict Jewish orthodoxy, Kitty from the narrow rural Catholicism of the De Valera period. We lived in Ireland, at Laragh, Glendalough, famous as the haunt of seventh-century Kevin who was sanctified for drowning naked women in the lake. There were six of us, in a small rented gatelodge, on an estate which had been turned into a hotel; my two elder sisters, Claire and Judith, my young sister Rosemary (all of us under ten), Kitty, and my mother. One of the concessions obtained by my mother when we moved in was that we could use the private lake when there were no hotel visitors around. It was my mother who gave us our faith in Mother Nature: all problems to be solved by Mother Nature,

Mother Nature knew what she was about . . . We were brought up with no fear of thunderstorms, lightning, rain, or swimming out of our depth. My two elder sisters taught me to swim: they had enormous physical courage, jumping from the highest diving board, holding their noses, down down into the deep black water, until I thought I would never see them again, until miraculously their heads would emerge and they would clamber out and jump in again.

After the cold lake water we would run naked through the woods to get warm. If we bumped into any of the hotel visitors they would smile at us and keep their distance.

We were not aware we were living through one of the most reactionary periods of Irish social history: we knew we were different, we didn't go to school, we read books instead.

We had no running water or electricity, my mother knew how to clean the well, how to stop the oil-lamp smoking, how to get the fire burning with wet sticks we had gathered: she knitted our swimming-togs, she would make a summer dress for each of us all in one night; and she also studied medicine in Trinity College, Dublin, thirty miles away. This was during the 'Emergency', known outside Ireland as World War II. There was no local transport except the bicycle. My mother did not know how to ride a bicycle when she arrived in Laragh: Kitty got one for her and taught her how to ride it. I remember the day when Kitty for the first time let go of the saddle and off my mother went, wobbling and then steadying herself, toward her classes in Dublin. We thought we'd never see her again. She returned late that night looking like a drowned cat, all covered in mud, her face shining.

I now realize, looking back, what a remarkable woman she was. And with what courage she brought us up, living alone, a Jew in Catholic anti-semitic Ireland, where many preferred to support Germany in the war rather than Britain the age-old enemy.

Kitty fed us. She introduced us to Mother Church: and also to the agony of love. Every night we would say our prayers, asking God to let Kitty marry Jimmy Timmons. She was a young woman with a great zest for life: as her appendages we went visiting and gossiping with her all day long, overhearing the cottage talk about the bad temper of the new hotel-owner and the corruptions of the black market. She never married Jimmy Timmons: and she died when she was forty.

Breaking Chains

A successful visit to the English department of Bologna University in 1985 led to an invitation to a women's seminar there in 1987: for which I prepared this paper.

I began my working life as an actress in a small alternative theatre in Dublin in the 1950s. I was attracted to this theatre after attending it as a member of the audience. The stage was so tiny we sat practically on top of it. The actors sold the tickets, showed us to our places, and then went behind a curtain to begin the play. After the show, coffee was served with the actors: it was like visiting someone's house. The theatre was run in partnership by Nora Lever and Barry Cassin. Nora was the driving spirit. That was the last time I had the experience of working in a theatre run by a woman. In fact at that time Dublin's theatres were mainly run by women. Ria Mooney was in charge of the Abbey: another small theatre was controlled by Madame Cogley and her sons. Later, when I worked in theatre in England I found that even though it was technically far superior, with a much more professional approach to the work, there was something missing: the intimacy with the audience. In a strange country with a strange culture I began to be unhappy and to feel a sense of alienation, while at the same time I was being pressured to accept, and be part of, a profession whose hierarchical structure could not be challenged. It was accepted at all levels: if you were down at the bottom, and were nice and co-operative, you would be helped to rise up in the end and take your place at the glittering first nights (even if you were not in the production itself): the intimacy of gossip and scandal was yours. But there was also the new generation of actors from the Old Vic School pressing for changes in theatre-techniques. It was out of that new generation that the Royal Court was born: George Devine had run the School, now he ran the theatre. I was part of the Royal Court as an actress, and was a member of an improvisational group there: we were in control of our own plots, characters and lines. The technique of this group was Stanislavski's, basically naturalistic, so our technique determined the form. We did not develop the technique to include the audience, but to make our own group closer and more inward-looking. We did not want to change our relationship with the audience, though we did want a different type of audience, and more social consciousness in the content of the plays themselves. I began to feel claustrophobia in this environment, and it became so bad that I decided to kill myself by jumping off the roof of the theatre. When I stood poised on the edge of the roof to jump I thought 'There is something false in the logic of my death: no-one is forcing me to stay, I do not have to be loyal to a concept that makes me unhappy. I can leave.' I could leave but where would I go? With what would I replace the theatre? How else to fulfil this need and longing for communication, this excitement of trans-cending the world we lived in, this opportunity to express feelings impossible in the normal aesthetics of our society – to laugh, dance, sing, be noisy, joyful, mysterious, silent, still, passive – and the closeness and intensity between ourselves and our audience, what would replace it?

When I met John Arden, our attraction to one another was based on our obsession with the theatre – also our dissatis-faction with it. We promised each other we would change it to accommodate what we wanted: those were the vows we made to each other. His language and sense of history excited me in his work: his provincial conservatism did not attract me.

Belonging to the theatre is more like being a member of a sect than anything else: except that when one is in trouble there is no one to go to. We are hired, and then dismissed to go out and put ourselves up for hire once again. The same applies to playwrights. At that stage, John Arden had more protection than I did. George Devine did look after his playwrights: but there was pressure on him to produce box-office hits and he had not built up an audience at the Royal Court which was loyal enough to follow him through both failure and success. So whenever the theatre was empty, there was gloom all round and the playwright in question got the blame.

So far I have given an impression of two very articulate people seriously sitting at home or in a café deep in intellectual discussion of these dilemmas. In fact, in the British theatre no one sat round tables like that: we gloried in our intuitive non-intellectual approach, and things happened spontaneously in a very haphazard way.

We moved to the countryside. This was because with small children it was impossible to get rented accommodation in cities. The move in itself brought about a change of direction in my work. We found a place to live, in a village, close beside the church. The vicar was mad about theatre, so I suggested we put on a nativity play in his church with the local people. It seems – as I write it – that it was really a very obvious thing to have occurred: but because of all the social changes since World War II the press at the time found it very strange. Class struggle was thought of as an urban activity and the countryside was only seen as an atavistic backwater, so the spectacle of one of England's leading radical playwrights involved in the writing and production of a play for a village church was news. Newspapers always prefer the simplistic, being London-orientated and run by ignorant men ignorant of the arts: so my role in the nativity play, as well as the roles of the vicar and the people, disappeared: Arden got on the telly spouting all the wonderful things he was doing, and, in fact, it was very timely. For much the same reasons as ourselves, many London-based radical artists were then moving into the countryside and regional voices were being heard. We continued working together, and at the same time Arden went on with his plays for the mainstream theatre. No one ever asked me any questions: I was just there as an appendage of Arden, but this did not worry me as I had consciously rejected London. My identity – an Irish woman working in England – was in any case a submerged one. Throughout that period (late 50s and early 60s) we worked on five 'alternative' joint plays and Arden had two 'mainstream' plays on, and everyone was happy – until the British Army overtly occupied the six counties of northern Ireland. This aroused the hidden anger in all the Irish expatriates, the ancient rallying cries rose in our throats. The eight-hundred-year-old domination of England. It all came flooding back. I could no longer live in England or work in England: I ought to be back in Ireland where my energy was needed. In fact we had been living on-and-off in Ireland – on an island, significantly, because I had not wanted to be *involved* then with my country; it had rejected me in the past, the workless early 50s, and I had rejected it – but now I determined psychologically to commit myself to the cause of a free Ireland.

By this time, in England, the alternative theatre had become 'the theatre'. The West End, the National Theatre, and the RSC were not where the excitement was. The most dynamic new work was coming from such groups as 7/84 (the first pro-fessional socialist touring company since the war), the Open Space (upmarket experimentalism) and Ed Berman's Ambience (for minorities and urban community work). Our collaborative work was now part of the mainstream. The critics suddenly heard a voice they hadn't heard before, and they didn't like it – a voice of anger and protest – my voice. The voice had to be stopped. The radical theatres became frightened: they were coerced – their grants were stopped – their venues cancelled – it was a hidden war. Our thinking began to change. We were now analysing events, no longer content with the haphazard 'in-tuitiveness' of the past. There were now problems between Arden and me: it looked as though we were now opposed to one another instead of together. Armed struggle (as in Ireland) was alien to recent English tradition, although the established British army going out and killing people was familiar enough. Arden had been in that army: but he could not adjust to a people's army, a ragged army, an illegal army. The TV images of armoured cars rumbling down the streets of northern Irish towns could not be avoided. At the start, the whole country, all 32 counties, was involved, at least emotionally; then, the English law cracked down on our work in the theatre, by means of a civil suit for libel. Mysteriously, Arden's old theatre colleagues disappeared when he looked to them for support. We were, therefore, free of them: and free of the press. In Ireland there was no one interested in the arts in the radical English manner: there was only a very small Arts Council with no influence. Irish art was still living in the past. We were free to develop our craft in our own way. In the village where we lived, the Irish traditions of rich language and music were still strong. We were able to put on a play that lasted for 24 hours. Our vows that we had made so many years before had now come to fruition. We made theatre that satisfied and excited us. We were part of it on stage: and the audience were also part of it.

In London we had one professional friend, Ed Berman, an American. He had a lunchtime-theatre and he let us use it when we wanted. The mainstream theatres could not give Arden the freedom that he now had – the freedom to experiment and to make mistakes. Financially, those days were disastrous: no one able to pay would touch us as a two-handed team. Arden by himself was still acceptable, so long as he did not handle Irish themes. He came under terrible stress. The very prohibitions prevented us abandoning that theme. Arden wanted to write about what was happening to him in the theatre. His experience was different from mine, and his rejection of the 'English' was later than mine. We decided that just because the press said he was my 'prisoner' there was no reason for us to prove them right by chaining ourselves together. We would be independent of each other. So Arden wrote on his own, and I pursued the most dynamic and explosive ideas that were then taking place – those surrounding the position of women: and I began working with women. In the 70s Arden and I worked on eight plays together, Arden by himself on one, and myself on two or three. We also worked on collective community plays.

Those years were exciting in addition to heaping a lot of troubles onto us. Now, in the 80s, I can look back and see a pattern emerging. We work together, we work separately, and our separate experiences merge into one another. We mutually recognize our different paces and our different capabilities. Through our working together, and then separating, and then working together again, I have been able to evolve and develop the original sense of loss which I always had, and I will try to develop it for you.

I will begin by questioning certain rules on how we live our life. Rules that dominate the rhythm of our life. Time: the clock, the timetable, the calendar, the working-hours; social behaviour; good manners: – all that we are told makes up 'good standards'. As we grow older and move away from ourselves, we constantly have to seek our true selves in order to be 'true to ourselves': we go in pursuit as though trying to get on a train – if only we could jump on, then we would be with others. We visit the country and 'time stands still', the clock doesn't matter, nature tells us when to do certain things – when we are cold we light a fire; when it gets dark, if there is no electric light, we don't read and therefore we don't strain our eyes. We do other things in the countryside: we ease our way into speaking with people, we wait, we exchange news, each of us is equally interested, we find a balance. We have been told that the upheavals in our natural world are set off by the earth's relationship with the sun, the moon, the tides and the fatal flaws in the earth itself. Thus the idea of perfection is itself a con-tradiction. There is no perfection just as there is no perfect circle in nature. Perfection is constantly imposed on us, quite contrary to our own experiences. We are goaded on to perfection: what it is we don't know. Someone tells what they *think* it is. I put the question: is the myth of perfection due only to a need for safety, for security? We must examine our culture, and in particular the religion based on that culture.

The predominant religion in the West is, of course, Christianity. The perfect God, controller of us all – imperfect man, fallen because of Eve, in constant pursuit of that perfection. Only through art could the male challenge the female, the source of his imperfection. An art that aspires to perfection must also aspire to permanence. Therefore all those ephemeral aspects of art – deriving from the senses of smell, touch, taste – are seen as uncontrollable, therefore not perfect, and only the static art-disciplines involving the senses of sight and hearing are recognized as constituting 'high art': literature, music, painting, sculpture. To appreciate and practise these forms strict training is regarded as necessary. To supervise the training we have to have institutions and critics who tell us whether or not perfection is near being achieved. Our appreciation of the world, therefore, instead of widening and exploring, becomes narrower and tighter.

Perfectionism in art becomes a competitive tool with which we seek to prove that our culture, our society, is nearer perfection that anyone else's. To protect that perfection we need to protect our section of society: and therefore we must develop the perfect weapon. Art has passed into the hands of the experts, to be judged by the experts, but it is executed by individuals. In the same way, nuclear weapons have now reached such a pitch of perfection that the most powerful ruler in the west, the American president, can execute the world's destruction without consulting anybody else by touching a button: because the scientific and military experts have told us all that he alone is fit to do it. We can see and hear: but we mustn't touch. Mr Reagan only is allowed to touch. Just so, Adam and Eve were allowed to see the apple but not touch it. When Eve touched it and ate it, the order was broken.

This is the point I have now reached in my development, as an artist. And this is how, through the study of the women's movement and feminism, I have changed my approach to the theatre. Before theatre and religion became functions of centralized government – which means even before the classical theatre of the Athenian city-state – they were acts of communal collective celebration or mourning. There was no dividing line between artistic activators and a passive recipient audience. To reclaim this position is the task I have set myself.

I am, of course, not alone. We live in exciting times. Many movements now are challenging the old order. And challenging the status-quo power. Marxism through class-struggle, pacifism, anarchism, liberation-theology, all searching for a way compatible with full human participation. But none of these movements seem completely to accept the excitement of imperfection, and the unlimited nature of the quest for growth.

Am I now implying that it is our turn, now, as women, to be the vanguard of the exploration? I say yes: because it is the old male-dominated culture which has said that we broke the rules, bit the apple, and so got the knowledge that caused misery to the man. So why not use the old legends to our own advantage? There is much debate in the women's movement about the role of woman as child-bearer, and thereby having a closer awareness of life and death. Each month a woman has the choice to begin life or not: and this must be considered the fundamental fulcrum of our activity. We are more sensitive and perceptive to the origins of life. And we must accept that responsibility. And be committed to the responsibility of life on earth.

Since the beginning of the 1980s I have been in an organization with other women of my profession, and I have set up – in the town where I live – a group called Galway Women's Entertainment to explore, mainly through stories and through developing the more ephemeral senses, possibilities of other artistic techniques, challenging time, challenging logical plot-structure, challenging the accepted boundaries of artistic disciplines, by means of radio, video, parties, excursions. This is now being fed back into my collaborative work with John Arden: nine plays for radio on the history of early Christianity, for the BBC. The BBC have allowed the normal conventional boundaries of drama and current-affairs programming to be dissolved, so that our plays will also be integrated with seminars and discussions, bringing our imagined ancient world into the factual modern world.

It was in this university of Bologna, two years ago, when Giovanna Morsiani, an exceptional woman, invited us here and gave us the freedom to do what we wanted, that I realized how possible it was to break down the initial dividing-line between the passive and the active. One day we had a performance where everyone expressed themselves in groups in songs, stories, or little plays. So all of us were the audience and all of us were the activators. And last year, in the streets of Dublin for two months I broke barriers down even further: I sat outside the Arts Council in protest against the rigid authoritarianism of the high art of Ireland, and calling on passers-by to support me and make their own cultural expression. Not only artists joined me, but people came to cook food for a street-party, alternative healers came with oils and massage, other people fell in love, and so it really became the art of the full five senses. This is my task now: to continue on, and I would like you to help me.

Lift The Taboo

Because I said, in the preface to Vandaleur's Folly, *that I wanted women to play men's roles, I was invited in 1981 to the first-ever Women's Festival held in Limerick. I read this paper there: and it started women questioning the entertainment value for them of orthodox theatre. As a result, I felt that I was justified in imposing the condition of 'no men' on the Galway Women's Entertainment. There was one man present at the Limerick meeting, and he thought it was his job to provoke confrontation instead of exploration: he believed that that was what theatre was all about . . .*

I am here to talk about certain directions for women in the modern theatre. Before I can go on to that specifically, let me wander a little over the general context. I want to consider the theatre as part of our entire Western mainstream culture, and within that culture, of the English-speaking areas particularly. I will not be dwelling on Irish culture as a unique phenomenon because it seems to me that there is little to my purpose today in Irish culture that is not also a part of the larger international Western influence, and that in this country our society as a whole is being influenced and organized – the more so that we are now in the EEC – by the same set of values that the West as a whole has adopted, though of course there are variations.

In the same way, there are variations between Limerick and

Galway – for instance, our political image-men, we haven't got Jim Kemmy and you haven't got Michael D. Higgins: but together in the Dail those two socialist deputies are both part of the ruling coalition, and must be considered part and parcel of the fundamentally anti-socialist government exemplified by Mr John Kelly – who has described all of us in receipt of any state subsidies as 'cannibalizing piglets': which means you, because you have paid me, in part, from public funds, to come here; and me, because I am receiving the money from you. So, despite all the difference between Galway and Limerick, I can here today be described roughly as one cannibal piglet addressing a number of others. There is of course one unique aspect of Irish culture that immediately differentiates it from most other Western societies, and which I as an artist feel very strongly about: and that is Section 31 of the Broadcasting Act, and the bizarre anomalies that it gives rise to. It is surely the worst kind of Irish joke that one half of the country can see and hear what the other half can only see but not hear. And, on the whole, we laugh about it and put up with it. Later on I will go into this kind of thing at greater length, people's casual attitude throughout many generations to equally ridiculous anomalies. Now, the exposure of anomalies that have long been accepted by society often raises hackles, and the person who brings the subject up often finds that some personal aspect of herself becomes a pretext for dismissing her inconvenient opinion without anyone having to go through the fag of actually analysing it. In this society there is one obvious way to do this, if the person does not speak with a wholesome rural accent, implying an authentic stake in the country, she can be dismissed as over-urbanized or even Anglicized. But if Ireland is, as I have suggested, now to be seen as very much a part of an international culture, it is only to be expected that speech patterns are going to become more and more cosmopolitan, and will contain thousands of variations no longer to be assigned to specific black or white areas within the local community itself.

The position of women in Western culture can be generalized

about – overall we are treated as an inferior caste, even though changes have taken place. Within this context, we can see that the variety of oppression peculiar to Ireland is one that is actually enshrined in the national constitution, and the implications of the constitution are followed through in the laws. We have the Criminal Conversation Law, for instance, and the Domiciliary Law: so, therefore, not only am I a cannibalizing piglet but I am also the goods and chattels of my husband, with no legal right to live anywhere except where he chooses to live. This legal definition of our status is reaffirmed by the general values of Western culture.

By culture, I do not mean only the arts, but every aspect of our communal life, including, most importantly, religion. Our ethical view of the world derives more than anything else, perhaps, from the prevailing religion – whether or no we are believers in it or practitioners of it – and from the arts – whether we are actually engaged in them or not. From these two sources has come the nourishment and fertilization that enables us all to develop mentally and hence indeed physically. But these two areas, the arts and religion, have not yet been challenged by the women's movement with sufficient force to make a pervading impact. What is it about them that needs to be challenged?

I am referring to the dominance of male clergy in religion and the dominance and acceptability of the male's self-image in the arts. This – the male self-image – is the main point I wish to explore today, and I hope it will be one which we can make the basis for our work this afternoon.

It is now acceptable for women novelists to write about men without inhibition: but only a century and a half ago, writers like the Brontës and George Eliot, who handled strong male characters, still found it desirable to be published under male names. Women novelists are now part of the mainstream culture in their own right but in the visual arts development has been slower: it is only a couple of years or so since the first exhibition of women artists' presentations of men was held in London – and a very mixed reception it got too. But of course novels and paintings are not essential elements of culture for the masses, who watch TV, cinema, listen to the radio, read newspapers and enjoy sport. Ethical values of mass culture and religion make their impact largely through feelings rather than intellect, and they are not today expressed by means of formal structures, that is to say the people who receive this consumerized culture do not need to subscribe to any consciously-structured doctrine, in the way for instance that the medieval public needed to accept the religious principles of orthodox christianity and the political principles of the feudal order to understand what their artists were saying to them. Interestingly enough, the very essence and strength and importance of the women's movement has been the rejection of structure, and the assertion of the ability to feel our way into a new conception of society. So our culture is the very thing that we are most receptive to, and therefore the very weapon that we are using to change society's attitudes and values is being used against us, subliminally, and with far greater force than we are often aware of.

This is reinforced by the daily spectacle we see around us at street level, army, police, the law courts, political assemblies, church processions. How is it, then, that we are able to see men all around us in public, in fancy dress, showing off? Very simple, they don't allow women to join.

In the very early days of christianity, before the new religion became the structured dogmatic church we now know, it seems to have consisted of a large number of local communities, with many variant practices: particularly in the eastern regions of the Roman Empire where these practices included a far greater degree of sexual equality than is now recognized. For instance, according to Elaine Pagels in her studies of the gnostic gospels, god was symbolized sometimes as both male and female: the holy spirit constituted the maternal element of the Trinity: or, as another gnostic text suggests, the spirit was both Mother and Virgin, the counterpart and consort of the heavenly Father. One text gives a poem spoken in the voice of a feminine divine power:

For I am the first and the last.
I am the honoured one and the scorned one.
I am the whore and the holy one.
I am the wife and the virgin . . .
I am the barren one, and many are her sons . . .
I am the silence that is incomprehensible . . .
I am the utterance of my name.

Women as well as men were often appointed to such religious offices as existed in those days – they were called priests, evangelists, bishops and so forth – and this reflected the status of women that already obtained in non-christian society in certain areas of Greece, Asia Minor, and particularly Egypt where they were prominent in education, the arts, and professions such as medicine. In the second century AD women were everywhere involved in business, social life, such as theatres, sports events, concerts, parties, travelling with or without their husbands. According to the satirists, they took part in a whole range of athletics and even bore arms and went into battle. But in the Jewish culture they had no such equality, and the Jewish element in christianity was strongly opposed to cultural manifestations from the pagan world. So, by the end of the second century, all this female participation in the religion was condemned as heretical: and groups that continued the practice were hunted out of the church.

One further possible explanation is that christianity by this time had improved its class position from the lower orders to the middle class, and in the middle class the free and easy attitude held in the upper class towards women's activities was frowned upon. This would imply that in the early period those christian communities that sponsored women's leadership were largely lower-class; where women had always taken an equal part in labouring work (in India I myself have seen men and women working on equal terms upon the building sites). In the fourth century, christianity became the official state religion: and with its male-dominated values caused the disappearance by degrees of women from the mainstream of public social life, particularly the performing arts. Creative women soon were only able to find an outlet in the cultural activities of nunneries, where they did put on plays, paint pictures and so on, within an exclusively female environment. As christianity flourished, the medieval church took over the theatre more and more, with its formal church plays, and its associated sponsorship of the lay guild-drama, which excluded female performers. Of course, throughout this period there was always a disreputable and often persecuted element of unofficial entertainers, men and women, who carried on the pre-christian traditions of Roman times. From this artistic underworld emerged the Italian *commedia dell'arte* theatre, which brought first into France and then into England the professional actresses of the seventeenth century.

This century marked the final collapse of medieval culture based on the total authority of God and the secular authority of the church. Humanism and enlightenment became the prevailing cultural norm, and this led to the growth of naturalism in the theatre, and naturalism carried with it at one and the same time the employment of women to play female roles and the use of realistic painted scenery. The plays, however, remained reflections of a male-dominated society, even though female playwrights emerged in some numbers. Sheridan's *School for Scandal* is a typical play of this 'enlightenment', where the wife is her husband's chattel and her reputation must be preserved for the better preservation of her husband's social image.

By the nineteenth century women had obtained more control and were themselves running theatres: dramatists were writing major roles for women. Some women even played male roles: this was a development from the all-male casting of the Elizabethan theatre where boys playing women often extended themselves to women disguised as men – for example in *As You Like It* or *Twelfth Night*. When the actresses appeared they, too, were given such roles, known as *breeches parts* – the Irish Peg Woffington specialized in them. This degenerated into the

Principal Boy of our modern pantomimes: but such 'high-art' performers as Sarah Bernhardt did perform regular male roles, Hamlet or the son of Napoleon. By the end of the nineteenth century, the Ibsen period, there was serious exploration, in the drama, of women's psychology vis-à-vis the male-dominated society, which coincided with the political movement for female emancipation. At the same time, serious plays were being written about the working classes. Today these themes have been extensively developed, and a whole range of hitherto stereotyped roles has been brought forward for serious and sympathetic examination on the stage – e.g. 'funny' Irishmen, 'funny' black men, 'sinister' handicapped people, 'posturing' homosexuals, and so on: while these social minorities have also demanded that their members in the acting profession should not be cast only according to colour, ethnic origin, or physical characteristic. This is a development of the humanism that began in the late renaissance, in which the wholeness of the human being rather than his or her superficial marks of identification becomes the substance of the actor's role.

Of course, this is by no means uniform, but it has achieved general acceptance as a theoretical position, most obviously in the US where the ethnic lobbies have been strongest. For example, a TV series like *Mannix* can now include a straight character, Peggy, the hero's assistant, who is black: and the colour of her skin is hardly ever mentioned in the scripts. The contradiction, however, is that theatre and TV – taken as cultural industries – are more dominated by men than ever. To look for an example in our own country – Lady Gregory was one of the original controllers of the Abbey Theatre, Ria Mooney both managed and directed but the last woman in a post of authority at the Abbey was Lelia Doolan, and that was ten years ago! Similarly with the Irish Touring Company (ITC) and Radio Telefis Éireann (RTE). It would seem that as the state subsidizes, and, therefore, takes over the culture, more and more, so men become entrenched in its power structure.

The recent advent of the 'women's theatre movement' has

opened doors for women, primarily in England. But, as it stands at this particular moment, it is still only peripheral. Take the National Theatre in London, the imperialist culture house: for the first time this season a couple of women dramatists have had plays on there directed by women – but in the smallest of the three auditoria, which only holds 240 seats. While in the big auditorium, about 2000 seats, Sir Peter Hall is to present a great ballyhoo production of the *Oresteia* of Aeschylus with an all-male cast, thus going back to the most anti-feminist days of ancient Athens where women were excluded altogether from participation in the drama. As far as I can see, this is a throwing down of the gauntlet against the emerging women's theatre: war has been declared. In New York, Joseph Papp, more subtle than Sir Peter, put on another ballyhoo production of a play about gangsters and their molls, with an all-male cast, but with a female director and an all-female technical crew whose work was done in full view of the audience. An Irish feminist who saw it said that the result was very curious: it was publicized as a gesture to women's skill in technical theatre work but, in the event, the men actors dominated the proceedings with their machismo vitality while the women appeared to be little dolly-girls assiduously serving them in the exercise of their fantasy.

This type of production is in fact a sophisticated side-effect of the backlash against the advances made by the women's movement in all aspects of life: there is a clear attempt to establish a new ghetto-ization of the sexes – all right, they say, let the women set up their exclusive women's theatre groups, we'll show them that we men can fight back from our own trenches. It runs parallel with complaints among certain trade unionists that equal job-opportunities for women are unfair to men in a time of high unemployment. And it has a far more sinister side in the less rarified areas of mass culture, I mean the alarming increase of films dealing with the rape and murder of helpless women, which we must all have observed lately obtaining enormous publicity in the press and even on the, supposedly, harmless advertisement interludes of RTE. I don't need to remind you of the type of journalism the Yorkshire Ripper case gave rise to earlier in the year. The deliberate cultural separation of men and women under conditions of growing equality and hence increased rivalry can produce a highly-aggressive pornography which is of course used by the advocates of male supremacy as a means of discrediting the gains of the women's movement.

And it is significant that in this war between the rival sexual ghettos in the arts, the male side has the permanent advantage of the taxpayers' money – Peter Hall, for instance, can operate with the full resources of the National Theatre behind him while women's theatre groups in England often work without any subsidy. Likewise in the trade unions, the reaction against women's improved job-opportunities is a reaction against a victory that has not yet been won, indeed, you might say that the situation for women is, in fact, getting worse. In this country our culture is affected by some very heavy male battalions indeed, the Pope's visit, for example, when his main message seemed to be for women to get back to the home and carry on with their breeding. The Church, both Catholic and Anglican, has firmly rejected any present notion of women becoming priests: which is why the EEC legislation on job-equality specifically excludes the church (which means that the Judaeo-Christian male ideology is still alive and well in spite of Karl Marx . . .). Now there is another specific exclusion from this legislation: and that is the entertainment industry. It is assumed by the EEC that women in drama will be employed to play women and men to play men and that the number of either sex in the cast of a play will depend on the proportions between the sexes laid down by the author of the play. In other words, if one writes a play about three men and one woman, then three men and one woman are employed by the theatre to act in it. It may seem to you, as it has obviously seemed to the EEC legislators, that this is perfectly natural and logical and what is all the fuss about? Equal job-opportunity applied to the theatre would mean that such a cast would consist of two males and two females, and therefore one male role would have to be played by a woman? Which would, you might think, be absurd. But would it really?

I now suggest that it would only be absurd if we seriously believe that the sexual difference between men and women is the most important and overriding characteristic of them as human beings, and the most significant aspect of their personalities to the author writing about them or the actor portraying them on the stage. If we do believe that then we are surely guilty of sexism in its clearest most elementary form. Acting is not a process of exact imitation, and it has never been necessary for an actor to represent every exact detail of the person he or she is portraying. We are perfectly accustomed to a youngish man playing the aged King Lear, to an Irish actor playing a German, to a twentieth-century actor playing a sixteenth-century character, to the mother of children playing the virginal Juliet, and as we watch their performances we are well aware of the discrepancies: but if the actors know their business we very soon forget to notice them. We are in the theatre to be persuaded by the exercise of artistic skill, which is in turn dependent upon the actor's training and many years of theatrical tradition. I see no reason why the principle of playing members of the opposite sex should not become as accepted a regular part of actors' professional education as all the other examples I have listed. The revision of the EEC legislation to include equal employment in the theatre would necessarily bring this about. Now let me explain what I believe would be the long-term cultural advantages of such a system.

1. Sexual stereotyping and hence sexual exploitation in the drama would become impossible: so, therefore, soft porn would disappear and genuine imaginative eroticism would emerge to take its place. Censorship has never solved the problem of the exploitation of women's sexuality, it has only driven such activities underground. I do not think that the women's movement (which has

always itself been subjected to censorship) should use censorship as a means of changing social attitudes. Rather should we seek for positive action that would render censorship obsolete.

2. There would be an immediate deflation of the glamourization of power, political power in particular. Anyone who watched the recent *Disraeli* series on RTE will understand what I mean – it dealt with a period when women had no votes, so therefore all the parliamentary scenes were filled with male actors. This programme came next door to the evening news programmes filled with real-life male politicians – if the men in *Disraeli* had been interpreted by women, how effective a contrast between the pretence and the reality?

3. Similarly with the glamour of war and violence in general.

4. The understanding of one sex by the other would be enormously encouraged and developed.

How can all this come about? Am I not suggesting that I can change society simply by getting a woman to stick on a moustache and become a man? That is exactly what I do not want. The art form itself will have to change to adapt itself into a new technique for the imaginative understanding of the physical differences between men and women. It will be through this understanding that we can remove the concept of macho supremacy, which is what attracts men into the army and into any similar aspect of the power-structure. Of course, it cannot happen at once, but we can begin working towards its eventual achievement – as professional cultural workers through our trade unions, as members of other sorts of trade union, and indeed just as citizens able to lobby and agitate for the EEC legislation to be extended.

Cultural change by itself cannot change society at large: but if the images of that culture can be consciously developed, a shift in perception will inevitably take place which will reflect the progressive directions of change that already are indicated. If the images are allowed to remain static, then progressive change, as I believe is now the case, will be immeasurably slowed down. The representational arts are mainly concerned with the human being and the human form. In the beginning the human image in art was diagrammatic and symbolic. As human beings took on more and more control over themselves and their lives, the image became all the more *humanized*. This process has been regularly accompanied by a series of reactionary backlashes against artists who have dared to tamper with the image accepted as the norm in any given period. (Veronese got into serious trouble with the Inquisition because he showed servants doing the washing-up in his picture of *The Marriage at Cana*: Picasso got into serious trouble with the critics because he apparently distorted the human image by his analytical cubist dissection of it, and so on).

Now, in 1981, for the removal of the most immediate existing barrier to the complete comprehension of the totality of the human being, embracing both male and female, I am simply asking for the taboo to be lifted: and for women to be allowed to play men.

Forward To Ontophany

(published in *Theatre Ireland* 1984)

Nina Simone, an aging squat black woman, comes onto the stage of Ronnie Scott's Club, London: this is her second performance of the evening, she is not unduly late for it. We have been charged a higher entrance-fee than usual, we are a predominantly white middle-class audience and we must pay for the privilege of hearing an artist who has wholeheartedly given her services to the cause of black liberation.

She comes on, does not bow, just sits at the piano, and in a business-like fashion starts to play. She is indifferent to us: she is paid to sing, we have paid to hear, there is no expression on her face as we applaud each number. I have not heard her before, not even been to Ronnie Scott's before, but some of the audience obviously have and they understand their role. I observe them and begin to understand mine. If we are passive she will be passive, we must show her we want her – but we have to want her very much, working hard, putting our heart and soul into that wanting until it turns to love for her, until from loving her we come to understand her, understand what it is for a black woman to have to perform, pour out her heart to expose her emotions, pain, struggle – and then and only then she in turn, reassured, begins to trust us: first a little smile (in spite of herself): and still we must work. Victory! we have passed the test, come out with flying colours – what singing she gives us now, and also dancing – she is transported, all mistrust broken down, she enjoys her skill, abandons herself in that enjoyment, she is high: and so are we.

She goes on long past her scheduled time to end, we won't let her go, her brother who is her personal manager comes on to beg us to let her go as her voice is cracking – so it is and she is aware of it, she laughs as she fails to reach her top notes. In the end the club-management (all male) begins dismantling the equipment. It is over: it was magic: a reaffirmation of humanity at its potential height.

Cynics may shake their heads, what a naïve person the writer of this article must be – wasn't it all stage-managed? Isn't that what's called show-business? Haven't we seen it all a dozen times – the false modesty, the disingenuous but rehearsed reluctance, wooing the public by apparently scorning them . . .? Yes, that was what *I* thought too: until I asked some people present, was it always like that? and their answer was – no: on the previous night, for instance, she had ended as she started, that audience hadn't sweated at all, they got no more than what was advertised.

> 'The communal vocational self-awareness of women is a *creative political ontophany*. It is a manifestation of the sacred (*hierophany*) precisely because it is an experience of participation in being, and therefore a manifestation of being (*ontophany*).' *Mary Daly*

Nina Simone gave what was very nearly an exact example of this: she knew who she was, politically and personally: but she also knew – and demonstrated her scorn for – her exact place in capitalist society when the management terminated her performance. They were making money out of her work; they were indeed committed to her work, but not to an experience that would have prevented her performance the next night.

Women can in fact provide no complete 'communal self-awareness' within the existing capitalist imperialist patriarchal culture – 'management' must always step in – only when women are politically and creatively in control of themselves and of their environment can a genuine fulfilled expression of feminist culture emerge, or for that matter of any culture from any oppressed class or group exploited by and suffering under the same unholy trinity.

I have worked in live theatre for 35 years: and I have now come to the point where I realize I might just as well be working in an asbestos factory or a leaky nuclear plant. In the theatre, not alone must we combat sexism, racism, political censorship, but as a craft we have the highest rate of illness (mental and physical), the highest unemployment, lowest wages, highest death-rate – check it out with any insurance company, compare premiums demanded from actors with those of other trades – and yet we still have this myth that out of these terrible conditions a terrible beauty is born. Collectively, we have to rethink our profession. But, as a woman, even if general conditions change, where would I fit in? In this ancient art-form which began its recorded history (male-story) in sixth-century Athens with the deliberate exclusion of women? And here I must intuitively invent: there was an earlier beginning to the theatre, a culture of total participation and being, which derived from the creativity of women. In some way we cannot yet reconstruct, this was utterly rooted out and replaced with what we know, the obsessive telling and re-telling by male dramatists and male actors of the same basic theme – the conquest by the male of the female; with no opportunity for dissenting members of the audience to participate or con-tradict: the male actors on stage were the active controllers of the art and the audience remained passive and controlled. In essence, our culture today is the same as it was then and our society is the same – the passive public in the twentieth-century war-theatre allows the controlling actor to push the button of nuclear holocaust for all of us.

True participation by all of the people is still considered to be the most dangerous of all revolutionary weapons, whether in Central America, the Churches, the North of Ireland, or even just at ordinary street-level when, as in Dublin, people organize themselves to expel the drug-pushers.

Viola Spolin ('Games and Improvisation') set up the Chicago City Theatre over 50 years ago on anarchist/pacifist (though *not* feminist) lines, and she did to an extent open our art to participation. But the money-men have stolen her generous theories.

In the post-referendum 26 Counties, my civil rights are no greater than those of a stray sperm: in spite of all the 'cultural renaissance' north and south and its plethora of community-theatre, performance-art, white-faces, tumbling out onto the pavements under the ever-increasing hysteria of competitive festivals for which the businessmen and multi-nationals scatter their loose change like Nero at the Circus while pocketing the paper they have gained at the expense of their own un-employed. In our rethink (our return to the 'manifestation of being') let us determine that this cannot happen again.

County Galway Vignettes

B's mother had a tightening in her chest, could not breathe. At about one in the morning they took her to the doctor. She was sitting beside him in the car, he glanced at her and thought she was in a coma: his wife said she thought she was dead. The doctor confirmed this. They were not able to arouse the undertaker, so B. had to drive his mother to the Regional Hospital. In hindsight he thought the doctor had said a strange thing to him: he asked where the mother would be buried. 'In K—, of course.' 'I wouldn't be too sure of that . . .'

When B. went to the catholic parish priest of K—, there were problems. The mother was a protestant and wished to be buried as one. The parish priest said she couldn't be buried there, and he wouldn't let the protestant minister take the service in the chapel. In the end a compromise was worked out, with B. having to buy two plots in the K— burial ground; one for his own family who are catholic, and one for his mother. They were put beside a path in the graveyard where no one goes.

On the day of the funeral B. had hoped that the priest would say a few words, or at least read them. The priest said he hadn't got the book. B. and his family were very upset. The catholic neighbours were shocked. They came to the funeral service in St Nicholas (the protestant church in Galway City) and thought that the ceremony was fine.

A friend of D.'s fell in love with a woman, not his wife. His wife and mother-in-law got him admitted to the Psychiatric Wing of the Regional Hospital. He escaped in his pyjamas and went to D.'s office looking for help. D. got him de-certified: and he then went voluntarily back to the hospital. They drugged him. Later, he visited D. with the wife and her mother, saying he was returning to the family home, thank you very much but he could manage his own affairs from now on.

D. was upset. He wrote an obituary in the local paper for Liam O'Flaherty – it had been stated in the press that O'Flaherty had been reconciled to the Church before he died. The gist of D.'s article was that the wild men of our society are tamed by mental hospitals and death-bed conversions, so the myth is engendered and goes into the annals: there are no Irish rebels.

H. was in great form, playing cards. He gave young P. 50 pence to place a bet on the horses. He was over 80, suffered from angina, his wife was in a worse state than him. That day as he sat at the cards she was walking with his stick in the kitchen, saying, 'If I had your stick I would get rid of my hump.' He said, 'Take the stick, I'll never use it again.' At that moment his head fell forward and he was dead at the table.

Her house is finished now. She said she will live for at least another two coats of paint. I said that meant she would live till she was 120: she said she wouldn't like that, then she cheered up when I said time passed so quickly. 'All right, I'll live for two coats of paint – or maybe even three.'

Met Mrs E. in the Post Office. Tells me Marianne R— is dead, from cancer. The mill stands there, Marianne's flowers and roses in the front of the house. Her large studio windows are broken, the wind and rain creep in, the back doors are boarded up now with card: hay scattered from her stable. The river still runs, but F. is dead too, found in the river where he went for death: no one had sent him a card for his birthday. The R—s had gone down the river in their shallow boat to find his body and now Marianne is dead. Her flower-designs are lying in the mud. She thought she was a survivor, hoarding seeds in case of famine, a child who escaped the Nazis in Holland, not knowing that in County Galway the Nazis have another name, *banks*. They lent money to set up a business, a design centre, and then foreclosed before the business could get off the ground. Marianne poured her heart and soul to make a presence, hoping that a group of unemployed young people would find fulfilment in design: there is nothing left now. O death where is your sting, O banks where is your conscience, O government where lies your responsibility. Another woman, too, died of cancer. I can no longer walk at night through the country roads but in the gaps left by my dead neighbours their ghosts intrude and voices call me. It is not good enough: we must change.

M. was working in the Post Office. His son was in the IRA, was imprisoned: when he came out he was offered a job in the Post Office, and was asked to sign a form renouncing his belief in a United Ireland. M. was so shocked he resigned *his* position and became a self-employed man doing odd jobs. The wife couldn't understand it. Later, M. became a priest, in Rome.

Censorship In Ireland

1978

It is a great honour for me as an Irish writer to be invited by the Norwegian writers' union to read a paper at this conference. Our Irish contemporary culture owes a considerable debt to the writers of your country – at the end of the nineteenth century, when Irish writers, particularly in the theatre, were seeking a literary means to express their sense of an individual national culture distinct from that of the imperial power Great Britain which politically controlled the country, they looked to the newly-emergent Norwegian literature as a model. It is possible, for instance, that but for the work of Ibsen and his colleagues in establishing the new Norwegian theatre, the famous Abbey Theatre in Dublin would not have existed, at least in the form that it eventually adopted. At the same time the influence of Ibsen upon the young James Joyce is well-known and his play *Exiles* is an admirable transposition of the Ibsenite style and character to the subject matter of bourgeois Dublin – which, as the capital of a small dependent nation had a great deal more in common with Oslo than with London or Paris. However, the parallel between the rise of Norwegian national identity and that of Ireland has not continued. There is still a portion of Ireland under direct foreign domination, and this partition of our country naturally affects the political, economic, and therefore the cultural development of the re-mainder. There is still a national liberation struggle, under arms, in process in Northern Ireland: and any attempt to examine the phenomenon of censorship in the Irish Republic must take this into consideration. I will now give a brief breakdown of the official censorship structure presently obtaining in the Irish Republic.

Cinema is censored by the Official Censor of Films, a person appointed to this function by the Minister for Home Affairs. He or she is paid a salary by the Government. There is also an appeal board of nine members appointed by the Minister. The Censor has the responsibility under an Act of Parliament for ensuring that films presented to the public are not 'indecent, obscene, or blasphemous' or tending to 'inculcate principles contrary to public morality' or 'otherwise subversive of morality'. The Censor may refuse to allow a complete film to be shown, or he may demand that certain portions of the film be removed before it is shown. Exhibitors of films who show them to the public after the censor has prohibited them, are liable to fines not exceeding £50, and additionally £5 for every day during which the offence continues. The Act of Parliament laying down these regulations was passed in 1923, one year after the country obtained independence from Great Britain.

Books and other publications are subject to the Censorship of Publications Act, which was passed in the Dublin Parliament in 1929. A board of censors is established under the terms of this act consisting of five members. They are appointed by the Minister for Justice, and their function is to examine all books and periodicals that are brought to their notice as worthy of such examination upon the following grounds:

1. that they are indecent or obsence.
2. that they advocate prevention of conception or the procurement of abortion or miscarriage, or the use of any method treatment or appliance for the purpose of such prevention or procurement.
3. Periodicals that have devoted an unduly large proportion of space to the publication of matter related to crime are also brought under the censors' examination.

The censors have the power to ban, from entry into the country and sale and distribution within the country, all literature they regard as coming under the above categories. The police have the right to enter any premises, under warrant, by force if necessary, to search for prohibited books, if they believe that these are for sale or distribution. The Minister may grant permits for the importation of specific banned books, for the personal use of individuals. Offenders against the decision of the censorship board may be subject to fines or imprisonment. In 1967 the act was amended, allowing the ban on any book to last no longer than twelve years. Periodicals are now only banned for six months at a time, except for those on contraception which are banned permanently. There is an appeals board established by the government: an author, publisher, editor, or a group of five elected politicians, may appeal to have a prohibition-order annulled.

The criteria that the board of censors must take into consideration when examining a book are

1. its artistic merit, importance, etc.
2. the language in which it is written.
3. the nature and extent of the circulation.
4. the class of reader expected to read it.
5. any other relevant matter relating to it.

Unlike the Censor of Films, the members of the Censorship of Publications Board do not get paid, and they only meet four times a year. The present membership of the board consists of

a lawyer (there always is at least one lawyer on the board)
a professor of English
a wife of a senator
a librarian
there is a judge regularly as chairperson of the board.
Before 1946 there was always a clergyman member.

The membership of the appeals board:

the chairperson is a judge.

there are also

  a teacher
  a business man
  a theatrical director and actor
  a professor of English

In the present day Ireland the complaints to the board, about particular books or periodicals, are generally from the Customs Officers at ports of entry. Ordinary members of the public contribute only 10% or less of the complaints received. One reason for this is perhaps that in order to register a complaint about a book, three copies of the offending book have to be sent in to the board and the number of people who are prepared to buy three books merely to secure a prohibition is limited. But these figures do suggest that Irish people on the whole are sufficiently broadminded to get along most of the time without censorship, if it were not for the officers of the Customs Service doing their vigilance for them.

The Censorship of Broadcasting. The national radio and TV stations are controlled by certain powers of the Minister of Posts and Telegraphs. Generally broadcasts are affected by the Offences against the State Legislation and the Laws of Libel. But the Minister has the power to ban specific material from the air if he considers it against the interests of the state – though he has to have such decisions ratified by the Parliament. The Government may at any time remove from office a member of the Broadcasting authority, and the Government appoints the chairman of the national broadcasting authority.

Censorship of Theatre. There is no censorship of theatre in Ireland.

The Offences against the state Act (1939) is directed against political subversion and as amended in 1972 it prescribes heavy penalties of fines and or imprisonment for statements and documents upholding unlawful organizations that are deemed to pose a threat to the security of the state or statements or documents that are deemed to constitute an interference with the course of justice. The definition of document in this act includes maps, plans, drawings, photographs, discs, tapes, etc., films etc, as well as written texts.

It will be seen from these arrangements that the state is concerned to control the freedom of the writer and consequently of the reader in two main areas: sexual expression (in particular in regard to the freedom of women to plan their own sexual activities); and secondly, political expression where this calls into question the legitimacy of the present Irish constitution. This could be interpreted in two ways – either the Irish Republic is an archetypal Catholic fascist state, or it is an extremely insecure society dominated by an inferiority complex, petrified lest the lower orders are about to arise and kick out their masters. If it is the latter, it would seem that the ruling class have an unexpected understanding of the theories of Reich and that they recognize only too well the relationship between the orgasm and liberationist politics . . . I do not believe that Ireland is a Catholic fascist state; my reason is the existence of our national constitution, by which democratic liberties are guaranteed, minority rights and freedom of religion or no religion are guaranteed, and the rights of the family are guaranteed. This constitution can be invoked through the Supreme Court and no change can take place without a national referendum. Nevertheless, it will be asked how can a country with a comparatively liberal constitution contain within its legislation such draconian political censorship as the Offences against the State Act – does not this appear to indicate that the state is arrogating to itself exactly that dogmatic supremacy over the lives and opinions of its citizens that is characteristic of fascism all over the world?

Explanation in one word: 'Partition'.

The subversive organizations feared by the Dublin government are the militant underground groups that have consistently, since the foundation of the state 1922, regarded themselves as legitimately at war against the British control of Northern Ireland, and regard any government in Dublin that is *not* so at war as at best illegitimate and at worst actively traitorous. And yet here is the extraordinary contradiction in the whole affair – one might expect the Dublin government to totally renounce these organizations, to offer complete recognition to British-ruled Northern Ireland, and to impose fascistic regulations to repress all opposition to such a policy. This does not happen – the constitution of the Irish Republic itself declares that all thirty-two counties of Ireland belong *de jure* to the Republic, and that therefore the Northern Six Counties have no legitimate right to membership of the United Kingdom. The recognition by Dublin of British rule over the Six Counties is therefore only *de facto* – and therefore the repressive legislation to safeguard this recognition – the Offences against the State Act, the Broadcasting Act, etc – is equally *de facto*, and thus liable at any time to modification or abolition entirely in response to developments between Dublin and London and the growth or diminution of violent rebellion in the North.

So, to clarify – we have a divided country, but one in which three-quarters of the total population believe in an *eventual* united Ireland, the three main political parties in the south are formally committed to a united Ireland, and the constitution lays claim to the whole of Ireland under the name of the Republic of Ireland. All this, however, remains theoretical and the present governing party finds that its practical day-to-day political problems impose practical day-to-day solutions that are by no means consistent with the theory. The political censorship is one such solution, and it has serious repercussions upon the overall cultural life of Ireland.

To properly discuss the nature of this cultural life we must first understand that the political censorship in Ireland is a long-standing institution, which may be traced as far back as the middle ages. From that time until 1922 it was imposed by the British Government upon the whole of Ireland in order to prevent rebellion against colonial rule. The Catholic sexual puritanical censorship is a phenomenon of post-1922 independent Ireland and derives from the political history as follows: in 1798 a rebellion against Great Britain took place, both of Catholics (the peasants, and the new petty-bourgeoisie) and of Protestants (also including peasants, as well as the supposedly loyal ruling-class that had been imposed upon the country by British military conquest in the seventeenth century). This rebellion demanded an independent Ireland to be governed according to the principles of the French Revolution and posed a very serious problem to the general security of the whole of the ruling class of the United Kingdom. The rebellion was defeated: and future ruling-class policy was to be directed to ensuring that no such combination of classes and sects would ever again be possible in alliance against the power of the British Crown. It was therefore necessary to isolate the Catholic bourgeoisie – not only from the Protestants but also from the Catholic peasantry and urban proletariat, although the latter was at this stage neither large nor very influential. One of the techniques employed to achieve this isolation was to encourage the church hierarchy in Ireland, through British diplomatic influence at the Vatican, to impose a strict control over the social behaviour of their flocks. As one Irish Catholic bourgeois politician said – during the middle of the nineteenth century – 'why need the British Government spend so much money upon police in Ireland when our Catholic clergy can act of their own free will as a moral police force upon the disaffected people, a beloved and acceptable force, who will not be liable to assassination and outrage . . . ?' The church was strongly opposed to the political legacy of the French revolution, and this opposition was combined with the puritanical suppression of sexual freedom so characteristic of both Catholic and Protestant churchmen all over Europe at this period. Sexual licence was equated with political radicalism: and the peculiar situation of Ireland ensured that in that country legislation for sexual behaviour became an integral part of the general political doctrine of the Catholic bourgeoisie. Now, as the nineteenth century progressed, this Catholic

bourgeoisie became more and more disaffected with the con-
tinuation of British rule: but did not modify its horror of
proletarian revolutionism or of moral liberalism. So the revived
movement for Irish independence became closely identified
with the most restrictive aspects of contemporary Catholic
thought: and the independent Ireland of 1922 was in reality a
country in which the Catholic bourgeoisie alone became
liberated – at the expense of the working-class and the
'freethinking' elements of the educated class.

Since 1922, of course, there has been a great deal of
opposition to this state of affairs, but so firmly entrenched has
been the prevailing opinion that every opponent of the Catholic
political-social morality has to overcome enormous prejudice
even today to present his or her ideas to even a highly-educated
public. I will quote at this juncture some remarks made only a
week or two ago by a distinguished intellectual at a learned
colloquium. The occasion was the annual summer school of the
Social Study Conference, and the speaker was Senator John A.
Murphy, Professor of History at University College, Cork. He
said, – 'It is astonishing to hear some leaders of public opinion,
including bishops, still use the divisive concept of faith-and-
fatherland, developed in the late nineteenth century and per-
sonified by the then Archbishop of Cashel. I am referring to
recent statements made this year [1978] by the present Bishop
of Cork and the Bishop of Kerry . . .' Senator Murphy answered charges that the secular state, of which he is one of the
most prominent advocates, was a godless concept leading to a
wholesale permissiveness and a collapse of morals. 'The only
way forward is a secular state and a pluralist society.' The
Senator said that he is not a 'mere Bishop-basher': but bishops
should be prepared for criticism when they made pronouncements outside the area of spiritual guidance, and which
impinged on legislators and the civic powers.

'They must be prepared to accept the same criticism as any
other citizen, particularly so when their pronouncements

endanger a real spirit of reconciliation in Ireland.' In the past
10–15 years – he added – the age of paternalism and moral
childhood, including passiveness, had gone. 'The new
criticism is a sign of maturity and no more than the new
image of the Church presented by Vatican II.' He pointed
out that he not only criticized the Catholic tradition but also
the other traditions – 'We should not pull punches when we
come to criticize the entrenched attitude of Protestant and
Presbyterian . . .'

But the big question was whether the common values,
common to Protestant and Catholic, could be reconciled in
civil rights before the law. You will notice that Senator Murphy
assumes automatically that Irish people will expect the values of
one or other aspect of the Christian faith – either Protestant or
Catholic – to be taken into consideration when the laws of the
land are being framed. The point he is making, and for the
making of which he has, even in 1978, risked considerable
unpopularity in influential circles, is that the laws of the Irish
Republic reflect far too closely the doctrines of only the
Catholic church – and the strong emphasis laid by the
censorship regulations upon the theme of contraception will
well illustrate this point.

It may be thought that the absence of censorship in the
theatre is odd, given this overall picture of a nation where free
thought has for so long been held to be dangerous both morally
and politically. This seems to be a historical accident, and may
have something to do with the fact that at the time of independence (1922) the only theatres operating in Ireland were the
Abbey, which was a national theatre and under direct influence
from politicians; and the rather low-quality commercial
theatres in one or two towns, which did not boast permanent
companies, and only presented a fairly light sort of entertainment – it was probably felt that these theatres could
easily enough be controlled by the ordinary police regulations
regarding obscene public behaviour, etc., and that

pre-censorship of plays would not be needed as so few plays were presented. The Abbey, on the whole, could be trusted to censor itself. And, indeed, it has generally so proved. Another quotation, this time from a newspaper interview, again only a week or two ago, with Mr Cyril Cusack, the most celebrated of our contemporary Irish actors. Mr Cusack's remarks may be taken as representing a strongly-felt body of opinion in the Irish theatre at the present time. He says, first, on the subject of politics, that he is very much a traditionalist and loathes modern staging, such as pushing the acting-area out into the audience. He dislikes message-plays, and modern politically-orientated theatre leaves him cold.

> 'I've turned down many parts for aesthetic reasons: and on points of principle. The actor, I feel, carries a major res-ponsibility, because in a play, what is presented as a particu-lar is often interpreted as a general: and an assault upon any kind of morality, publicly presented, gives an unfair advantage to the assailant . . . What I would like to see is a rejection of vulgarity, and that can apply to the moral climate as well as to the aesthetic . . . Licence in the media can forward the destruction of society . . .'

Over the past fifteen years, however, there has been radical change in Ireland – industrialization, discovery of minerals, free education, membership of the EEC, and the troubles in the north have all affected hitherto stagnant attitudes towards social development. The search for a solution to the northern violence has led to increased understanding of the concept of civil liberties in all walks of life, the women's movement, the gay movement, as well as purely political affairs; this has gone hand-in-hand with a movement by the middle classes towards the secular pluralist society I have already mentioned to you in my quote from Senator Murphy. The most important develop-ment as far as censorship is concerned took place this summer – when the whole concept of the censorship board was challenged before the Supreme Court in an unprecedented legal action. A book describing techniques of family planning had been banned by the censors. Two individuals, Mr and Mrs Crummey, together with the Family Planning Services Ltd (a voluntary body), took the board of censors to court on the grounds that the decision to ban the book infringed their constitutional rights as citizens who desired to read the book in question. Mr Crummey claimed that as he was a mature student and unemployed, he needed his wife's income to enable his family of five children to live, and that it was therefore essential that they had access to essential information about family planning. (Contraceptive devices may not be purchased* in the Irish Republic, but they can be supplied free of charge by voluntary bodies – this is in itself a permission achieved only because of another court case in 1974, when a successful challenge was made, again by private citizens, to the right of the Customs Authorities to seize their contraceptives on arrival in the country.) The verdict of the Supreme Court on the Crummey case was that the family planning book should not have been banned because the publishers had not been consulted first and allowed to prepare a defence against the board's decision. Unfortunately the hoped-for court verdict that the censorship board was in itself an offence to constitutional rights did not take place: but the significance of the case has been well described in a newspaper as follows: 'The censorship of Publications Act *allows* the board to consult authors, editors or publishers before reaching a decision. In practice it has never done so. The effect of the court's decision is now to *force* the censors to consult with authors or publishers of serious works before making a decision. Effectively, anyone who has had books banned can now apply to the high court to have the ban lifted . . .' This in fact presents the censorship board with a serious problem. As it is a voluntary organization that only meets four times a year, it is simply not geared to the possibility

* No longer the case: 1987.

of having formally to justify every one of its decisions: but of course this will depend upon the vigour with which writers and publishers take advantage of the court's judgement. It is really quite extraordinary that no publisher should have hitherto challenged the censorship board, but that two working-class individuals have had to open the way for them. I regard this as a very hopeful sign for cultural freedom in Ireland. Nevertheless, the hitherto apathetic attitude of publishers – not so much in Ireland, where publishing is still very much an underdeveloped industry, but in England, where most important Irish writers have had their work printed – has led in the past to untold witchhunting and persecution of Irish writers. Many have had to leave the country, simply because they had their work banned, and thus were unable to obtain employment – in such areas as teaching, librarian-jobs etc – because they were thought to be morally depraved as a result of the censors' stigma.

Now, the censorship of films. Here I will quote from a paper recently written by a well-known cinema critic, Mr Ciaran Carty of the Irish *Sunday Independent*:

One of the worst obscenities of censorship is the hypocritical assumption that there are two classes of people – those who can be allowed to view whatever movies they choose, and those who cannot. Such arrogance revolts me. By what right can any person presume moral superiority over his neighbour? This insulting dual standard, which is rooted in class-distinction, is not unique to movie censorship. In Ireland, if a person is affluent enough, and comes from the right social background, he or she has always been allowed to circumvent the legislative restrictions upon contraception, abortion, and divorce intended to keep the general body of society in order. Censorship laws, like other laws, are primarily designed to restrict the rights of the poor, the dangerous masses, rather than of the well-to-do. That was the whole point of the famous *Lady Chatterly's Lover* trial in England some years ago. The whole prosecution in the trial hinged on the outrage that Lawrence's novel had been made available in a cheap edition which 'even the servant girl' could read! I go along with Sartre, who says that freedom is indivisible: to limit that of others is ultimately to destroy one's own. But don't let any of us be smug. None of us is blameless in this hypocrisy. It is now possible for members of film clubs and societies to see uncut whatever movies we choose. But in doing so we are letting the censorship authorities off the hook. They can now cut and ban with an easy conscience, using the justification that – well – it's okay, all those intellectual types won't cause any more bother, they're taken care of, they can see what they want. People who care most about cinema have in effect been bought off at the expense of the vast bulk of cinemagoers who don't want to – or are not in a position to – become members of a film society. An example of what can happen has been the shameful treatment of Fellini's *Casanova* – in my opinion one of the great movies of recent years: but instead of finding the large audience it has been restricted to a few showings at a film society, the censor having refused to pass it for public release unless damaging cuts were made.

If, like me, you attempt to break through the official secrecy and demand information from the Dept of Justice, you will be informed that 'the Minister for Justice has always felt precluded – on the ground that it would involve a breach of confidence – from disclosing information about films submitted for censorship.' The censor has told me that he personally would have no objection to divulging the information. The renters have told me the same: but the Department of Justice stands firm. And this secrecy applies to every movie going back to 1923. The Cabinet papers dealing with the deliberations of Mr De Valera's government during World War II are now available for scrutiny in the public record office. But by a bizarre circumstance of bureaucratic arrogance, information about the antics of Laurel and Hardy in the 1920s is still too dangerous to divulge. 'You can't see these records because the Official Secrets Act still applies,' a Dept of Justice spokesman solemnly informed me. But information that I have gathered from unofficial sources reveals, that particularly in the period immediately before our present censor took over, appalling acts against cinema were committed by censorship authorities. In 1971, for instance, ferocious cuts were made in Visconti's *The Damned*, Bergman's *A Passion*, Antonioni's *Zabriskie Point*, Nichols' *Catch 22*, Widerberg's *Adalan 31*, Schlesinger's *Midnight Cowboy*, Fellini's *Satyricon*, Altman's *MASH*, Ashby's *The Landlord*, Roeg's *Performance*, Petri's *Investigation of a Citizen above Suspicion*, Peckinpah's *The Wild Bunch*, Lean's *Ryan's Daughter*, Rafelson's *Five Easy Pieces*, Penn's *Little Big Man*, Cate's *I Never Sang for my Father*, Kershner's *Loving*, Wexler's *Medium Cool*, Van Peebles' *The Watermelon Man*. That's to say nothing of the banning of Pasolini's *Theorem*, Black's *Cover Me Babe*, Friedkin's *The Boys of the Band*, Yates' *John and Mary*. Why are the censorship authorities so obsessed with cutting and banning? I think it goes deeper than individual prejudices. It is a manifestation of fear – fear of the unknown. Many people are genuinely uneasy about cinema because of its very nature it is ambiguous. And in being so it becomes an implicit challenge to the fundamental order of society. It is in nature of movies to exult in the sensual, to appeal to intuition more than reason, to annihilate logical concepts of time and space, and create instead ribbons of dreams. Cinema is inherently a re-volutionary medium, a threat to the status quo, for it challenges people's habitual ways of looking at the world and experiencing life. By its ambiguity and inde-terminateness it questions the order and certainty of every-day social conventions and norms. Cinema doesn't corrupt, it liberates. That's what censors are afraid of. Puritans are hostile to cinema because they sense that it undermines the framework not of their own lives – because puritans only speak for people they claim to be less mature than themselves – but of ordinary mortals' lives, by exposing them to different worlds and alternative modes of behaviour.

I will conclude by summing up the general effect of the political censorship imposed by the Offences against the State Act, the Official Secrets Act and the Broadcasting Act upon the radio, TV and newspapers in Ireland. The most important of these is the Offences against the State Act, the other two merely reinforce its effect. This act was made much more severe in 1972 – its amendment in parliament at that time had been strongly opposed by the civil liberties lobby, and it even seemed as though this opposition could cause the government to fall. At the same time there was a strike of national TV reporters because one of their number had refused to divulge his sources of information about an interview with a member of the IRA. A few hours before the act was due to be voted on in the Dublin Parliament, a number of bombs went off in the streets of Dublin – killing several people. This was the first serious bombing outrage south of the border in the current troubles. It is widely believed that it was the work of the British Army SAS – for the purpose of influencing the opposition in the Irish Parliament. If so, it was successful – the Act was passed more or less unopposed: and the government clamp-down upon any public manifestation of hostility to Britain's presence in Northern Ireland became complete. In 1973, there was a change of government. Dr Conor Cruise O'Brien, internationally-known playwright, critic, political analyst, etc., became Minister of Posts and Telegraphs which gave him control over the news media. The press was not strictly under his authority, but his censorship as applied to TV and radio had a definitely intimidatory effect upon the newspapers as well. During his period of office there were two important law-cases concerning newspapers which had commented unfavourably upon the standards of justice obtaining for political offences in the Irish courts – the *Special* Courts, where such offences are judged without the normal use of a jury. The newspapers were fined, and threatened with closure if they continued with their criticism, indeed the editors could eventually have ended up in gaol. The offices of another paper, the organ of the Provisional Sinn Fein party, were closed down, and the editor served a term in prison for allegedly being a member of the IRA. Many people have been sent to gaol for alleged membership of the IRA, and the crucial evidence against them has been their possession of certain proscribed political books which are prohibited under the Offences against the State Act. A number of TV producers and writers have been shifted from employment in current-affairs programmes and put into work where it has become impossible for them to give the free expression of their views on public matters. The result of all this intimidation has been to make journalists extremely conservative and nervous of sticking their necks out. Unfortunately, because the country is so small, and because of the overall insecurity of the Catholic nationalist in the face of constant British-inspired world-wide hostile propaganda, the Irish press has tended to become very uncritical of public men in general and the policies of authority. There is not much money behind the Irish papers and editors are unwilling to expand too far in the region of investigative journalism. They have to rely a great deal on the work of the British press for their foreign reports. There are about ten little left-wing papers in the country: but once again, because there is no education in investigative journalism, their efforts to uncover the truth of what is going on in the country are comparatively weak. There is one exception – *The Irish People*, which has an excellent record of exposing monopoly-capitalist and government malpractice.

When I was doing research for this paper I had an interview with the deputy editor of one of the leading Irish newspapers – I asked him how much pressure were the papers subjected to? The feeling I got from him was 'quite a lot'. There is a move in Washington by congressman Biaggio, who with 100 other congressmen belongs to an 'Irish lobby' – he is anxious to get congress to debate the Amnesty Report on police torture in Northern Ireland. If their findings agree with those of Amnesty the result could be the cutting-off of aid to Britain. There was sympathetic coverage of this congressman's activities in the Dublin paper. A Minister immediately rang up and told them to leave it alone. Our Prime Minister, he said, had been assured by the British Prime Minister that if the British Labour Party obtained a good majority in the forthcoming election, the British would consider withdrawal from Ireland: so, therefore, the Irish papers must not complicate the negotiations going on between the Irish, British and US Governments. Also, through conversation, I became aware of insecurity among journalists stemming from British propaganda about the likelihood of a 'bloodbath' if Britain were to withdraw – also the Irish Government's own fear that southern Ireland could be 'swamped by refugees from the North'. On the whole, Irish journalists did not seem to consider the Irish situation in a general world or even European context, but held a very insular view. The other very embarassing thing for the Irish government recently has been the Amnesty report on their own treatment of political prisoners in Portlaoise Prison, and on their own police 'Heavy Gang' who have been beating up suspects to obtain confessions. The government were able to silence journalists' comment on this issue by a promise of investigations, so that a deep-reaching inquiry by an Irish Times investigatory team was, as it were, halted in mid-stream. The most recent glaring example of the timidity of Irish press has been the case of a judge who was constantly falling asleep during a political trial. A defence lawyer tried to have the case stopped because of the incompetence of the judge and wanted the journalists present in court to act as witnesses to the behaviour of the judge – the journalists refused. With one exception – the man from a weekly news magazine. Fortunately, the judge suddenly died – proving that his sleepiness had in fact existed and had been pathological – and the case therefore had to be postponed for a re-trial. The journalists themselves are very open in private: but there is a general feeling amongst them of cynicism and apathy towards any public demonstration of their complaints. This feeling permeates the country and is a direct consequence of the repressive attitude of the authorities in Ireland towards open reporting. In other words all the years of official censorship have succeeded in rotting the spirit of inquiry among the very persons who should most fervently maintain it.

It may seem that I tend to lay the blame for the ills of Ireland almost entirely upon Great Britain – in fact I do so lay the blame. Much of the censorship situation in Ireland is the work of the Catholic bourgeoisie, who have as a class paid lip-service to revolutionary concepts of independence and national liberty, but who, because of their economic relationships with Great Britain, have proved unable to divorce themselves from the control of their larger neighbour. Why will Britain not leave, when it is so obvious that she has impeded the industrial, economic, and cultural fulfilment of the small country? The main reason, I would think, is strategic – the Six Counties are part of NATO, whereas the Irish Republic is not.

There have always been the two strains throughout modern Irish history – revolutionary socialism and bourgeois nationalism. Which of these forces will finally win through? I leave that perhaps for general discussion: but I will finish by stating that in my opinion the tension between these two is the basic reason for the heavy amount of censorship in the country and the repressive attitude taken for generations by our political and ecclesiastical authorities, both colonial and post-colonial.

At the present time the whole Western world is troubled by a series of movements demanding independence for national minorities, independence from monopoly capitalism, independence from big-power military alliance, etc. The censorship in all these countries is being used to reinforce the status quo of each country. We, as writers, must be very clear which side we are on. We must all fight for the freedom to express it, and this – I hope – will be the way in which your discussions here will develop.

Theatre In An Age Of Reform

1978

In an interview with the *Guardian* in 1975, Hugh Jenkins, Minister for Arts in the British Government, stated: now that Britain no longer had a use for an imperial Army, her culture should become that Army's replacement. Last Sunday, in the *Sunday Times* colour supplement, the following appeared: 'The British theatre is one of the few areas at which this country still excels, and one earning dollars as well as prestige: a cultural asset also combining glamour and big business.' Some time ago another *Sunday Times* article, by an American writer, said that Britain should be envied because of the grace with which she was able to cope with her leisure. J. W. Lambert, the drama critic, has pointed out that the percentage of public money expended on the Arts has risen over the past few years much more than the percentage allotted to the National Health – in other words the authorities would appear to regard the sponsorship of the Arts as being more important than the physical health of the community. That portion of the world influenced by anglo-saxon culture is loud in its admiration of what is going on in the British Arts, the National Theatre in London and the community arts projects all over the UK are visited and studied by experts from every country.

This festival in Belfast, the presence at it of *Vandaleur's Folly*, my presence as one of the authors of the play, are all part of this boom in the theatre. As Northern Ireland is officially part of

Great Britain naturally enough these activities would be expected to be observed here too. A quotation from the London *Times* – 'after surviving a decade of violence, the Arts in Northern Ireland are undergoing general expansion, thanks particularly to generous government subsidies ... Government expenditure aimed at revitalizing the province has helped to treble support for the Arts in the past three years.'

A flourishing cultural programme would appear to suggest a fairly stable society – or at least a fairly stable and united *section* of society for whom and amongst whom the Arts can be developed. Mary Kenny, in the latest *Sunday Telegraph*, says: 'Ulster revisited felt to me like an Ulster waking up to the calm after the storm.' And in the same article she describes the section of society from which this calm is apparently proceeding: 'What has happened in Ulster, ironically, is the opposite of the Marxist prophecy: it is not the workers who are uniting but the bourgeoisie. It is the workers who are most bitterly divided and most constantly hurt. But I had the impression that both Catholics and Protestants are beginning to think of themselves more as Ulstermen than as Republicans or Loyalists: that a new sense of national identity is emerging from the heap of suffering.' This analysis, I suggest, can be summed up as a fairly precise definition of a society entering what I have called in my title 'an age of reform'.

My presence here would therefore logically imply that I had a role to play in what Mary Kenny considers to be the calm after the storm. And yet, *Vandaleur's Folly* is a play which we have deliberately written in order to demonstrate the impossibility of reformist policies succeeding so long as the basic reason for the reforms is to keep the ruling classes in possession of their wealth and political power. This was what was happening in the 1830s. The French Revolution, and its Irish development, the Republican revolution of 1798, the aims of which were summarized by Wolfe Tone in these terms: 'To subvert the tyranny of our execrable government – to break the connection with England, the never-failing source of all our political evils –

and to assert the independence of my country, these were my objects. To unite the whole people of Ireland, to abolish the memory of past dissensions, and to substitute the common name of Irishmen in place of the denominations of Protestant, Catholic and Dissenter – these were my means' – this broad revolutionary movement had been apparently defeated through the long process of the Napoleonic Wars and the repressive activities of the British Government: and yet the dragon of resistance in Ireland had refused to lie down. John Vandaleur's dream of communal harmony imposed from above, by the very ruling class against which the violence of the underprivileged was directed, could not and did not succeed. I believe that this is exactly the situation we are faced with today.

My own political views are effectively those of Tone (Revolutionist, Republican). And yet here I am, as a playwright, a member of a profession officially characterized as one of the strongest bastions of the new reformism. My play has been shown in Queen's University – which should be a haven for the bourgeoisie who are, as Mary Kenny says, uniting in harmony in spite of Karl Marx, as a beautiful object-lesson to the surrounding proletariat, who obviously have not yet discovered what is good for them. But how far in fact does Queen's University really and deeply concern itself with the imposition of communal calm? I read recently about the sums of money granted from various sources for research projects here. £3,500 for research on 'Neuro-transmitter Imbalance in Psychoses and Animal Behaviour', £100 from the Bayer Drug Company for research into drugs of a general nature, £500 into research into the causes of the present conflict in Ireland, £10,000 from NATO to investigate 'rock-weathering' in the Six Counties, £180,000 from De Beers Industrial Diamond Division Ltd to research the properties of tungsten carbide under complex stress. This is a very varied and at first sight not very significant list of funds: but break it down and you discover that scientific research here is being backed by (and is therefore presumably very useful to) the military power of the Western alliance, the industrial power of racialist South Africa, the multi-national drug monopolies. Psychoses and Animal Behaviour is not such an innocent object of research in an age which has institutionalized systematic torture – and you don't need me to tell you in which particular local context this has had most effect. Set all this against the parallel expenditure upon the Arts, and what do we see – an image, I suggest, of sensitive and beautiful people playing elegant chamber music in an upstairs drawing-room while downstairs in the cellar human bodies are chopped and hacked upon tables and red blood trickles slowly out through a blocked-up gutter in the corner.

In other words, the Arts are being used as another department of the British psychological war machine in its programme of 'normalization' or, as the Americans put it in Vietnam, pacification. With these terms we also associate Vietnamization and Ulsterization. Ulsterization involves 'criminalization', whereby the ongoing war in the province is refused recognition as such. It is therefore very difficult for people not immediately involved to identify with it. Unfortunately the position amongst artists and theatre-people is one of severe unemployment, poor wages, and very heavy work. This makes it very difficult for them to analyse the effect of their activities as a whole. They are, one might say, in much the same position as private soldiers in the British Army. And with much the same mentality – 'We don't ask any questions: but from a sense of duty we know that the show must go on.'

This does not only affect the UK and Northern Ireland. The piece in the London *Times* about the Belfast festival also included this sentence:

'In the recent past the border has proved a greater barrier than the Irish Sea; however, as the atmosphere in the north becomes rather more relaxed (despite the bombings last Tuesday) the political sensitivity of artistic links with the south is being overcome.'

And, indeed, the important press coverage of the recent meeting between the Northern Irish Arts Council and its Dublin counterpart indicates the truth of this. A couple of years ago Colm O'Briain from the Dublin Arts Council was able to obtain money from the Gulbenkian Fund to pay for a consultant visit from the British Arts Council to the Republic: a report was made out as a result of this visit saying that there was a fantastic amount of lively artistic activity going on all over the 26 Counties, which deserved official support and encouragement. Since that time Arts centres and community theatres are concepts on everyone's lips. To take an example, in Galway they are trying to get an Arts Centre established, also in Athlone, and in the small town of Oughterard, Co Galway, there is a most beautiful community centre built very recently, opened by Bobby Molloy the Minister of Defence. All this, we ought to applaud and encourage. But if we look at the other side of the picture: when the Coalition was in power prior to 1977, Dr Conor Cruise O'Brien was continually harping on the theme that the support given to revolutionary movements was largely emanating from frustrated idealism which could and should be channelled into artistic activity of a harmless nature. This attitude was confirmed by the furore that took place in Dublin a couple of years ago when Gay Sweatshop came to perform at the Project Theatre. An enormous amount of idealistic energy was expended upon defending the right of the Project to present this group's work in the face of puritanical objections from City Councillors and religious pressure groups. The effect of this controversy was more support for homosexuals and enhanced understanding of their problems within society. Again, a very progressive circumstance. But at the same time, the Project would not allow the English 7/84 Company, playing there on tour, to publicize opposition to the death-penalty imposed upon two people – the Murrays, who had been convicted of shooting a policeman. Normally speaking, a campaign for homosexual liberation would contain much the same crowd of people as would take part in a campaign against hanging. But in Dublin, among the artistic liberals, a split took place between these two issues. Why? Because the death sentence imposed on the Murrays was part and parcel of the Government's anti-subversion law-and-order policy, to which Dr Cruise O'Brien himself was heavily committed. Hence opposition to hanging was to be equated with support for armed insurrection: and was exactly the sort of thing that the new emphasis on community arts etc was supposed to be rendering redundant among all right-thinking people. I do not believe that opposition to hanging the Murrays could by any stretch of the imagination be called a revolutionary activity. It was no more than an ordinary liberal twentieth-century point-of-view: but the Dublin Government was determined that it should be seen as revolutionary. As far as the then administrators of the leading Dublin avant-garde cultural showplace were concerned, this is the view that was allowed to prevail.

Another case from the 26 counties that illustrates my point here. The Galway Theatre Workshop: a small community-theatre group which consisted of a number of people drawn from no particular political ideology, and, (except for two members) with no real experience in theatre at all, but we were all interested in making plays to demonstrate the implications of various social and political events in Galway in particular and Ireland in general. We did a play about the problems of university lecturers as members of a trade union, we did a play about a factory strike in Galway, another one about the death-penalty, another one about the housing of itinerants in Galway, and one about the status of women in the 26 counties. We did have a small grant from the Arts Council in Dublin. But at the time of the general election in 1977, when Liam Cosgrave came to hold a Fine Gael rally in Galway, we felt it necessary to present some sort of comment on his policies. This took the form of a theatrical happening in the square during the meeting. We had placards demanding the release of political prisoners etc. attached to our clown costumes and we sang a little song.

We were dragged away by the police through the thick of what they hoped would be a hostile crowd, so that the supporters of Cosgrave could beat us up and no doubt get rid of us altogether if they could make it look sufficiently like an accident. We were held for two hours in the police station and then released without any charges being laid. The police said we had been 'taken in for our own protection'. Afterwards when questions were put to them by the press they denied that we had been arrested or detained. They very nearly denied that we existed at all. The result was that it proved impossible for us to get any support from the type of people who had all flocked to support the Gay Sweatshop even though the Galway Theatre Workshop had written strong letters in support of the Project Theatre during that controversy. The Dublin liberals took the view that either nothing had happened to us at all, or that if it had happened, it had happened because we were engaging not in regular theatrical activity but in political heckling etc., and anyway if you opposed Cosgrave you must surely be in favour of all manner of subversive violence.

There was also a rather crafty pseudo-Marxist point of view put forward in this connection, that we had had no business doing this kind of thing in the west of Ireland anyway: that if the state machine was to be confronted by the artists then it should only be confronted in Dublin where the power-centre was, and all the best artists were, and that any sort of provincial theatrical agitation was only repeating the idealistic errors of Synge and Lady Gregory with their romanticism of the peasant culture . . . But what followed was significant. Because there was no support from Dublin the members of the Theatre Workshop were very vulnerable to local political pressures, upon their families and employers. Some of them had to leave town altogether and go to England to get work. And when an advertisement was put out the following season to re-establish the Workshop, no one wanted to take part in it. A lot of people expressed interest, but only as spectators. The whole thing in fact had become muddled by a sustained campaign against us in the conservative local press, which deliberately confused the issues of artistic expression and terrorism: so local people supported us from the outside but did not feel sufficient commitment to Art (in these confused circumstances) to put themselves in danger of the same harassment that we had suffered. But, on the other hand, when *Vandaleur's Folly* travelled to Galway last month, five-hundred people came to the play and another two hundred were turned away at the door: so we cannot say that there is no desire for political theatre in the town.

There is another significant contradiction involved in the whole question of the Art for Society exhibition and its treatment at the Ulster Museum during this festival. Again I quote from the *Times*: 'The trustees of the museum decided that some of the exhibits were unsuitable for display. They apparently included pictures showing police interrogation in Ulster and two pieces of feminist art.' Here sexual politics is linked with anti-subversion politics – just the opposite of what happened at the Project in Dublin. But that is by the way. To continue with the quote: 'The trustees denied making their decision because museum attendants threatened to walk out if some of the pictures went on show. Nevertheless the trustees' action led to the cancellation of the exhibition.' Now, earlier press reports had laid the whole responsibility for the cancellation on the shoulders of the ordinary people – i.e. the museum attendants. There is a certain similarity here with the way the police in Galway made out that the Theatre Workshop had not been arrested but had been taken in for protection against grass-roots popular feeling. But one thing is clear about the Art for Society censorship, it has not gone without protest, and the protest has been widely reported in both Britain and Irish newspapers. And no doubt American and European papers as well. Which is splendid. There is a liberal consensus apparent on the ground which is justly outraged by such occurrences. So long as they take place within the framework provided for them by the officially-sponsored museums and theatre-establishments.

But I would like you to ask yourselves what would be the attitudes of the liberal consensus if people who wished to express their views on feminist questions (by means of what their opponents might smear as 'obscene pornography') or on police interrogation, or on the atrocious conditions caused by the criminalization of political prisoners in Long Kesh, were to do so by painting pictures and graffiti on the walls of the streets near the Ulster Museum? I am sure the police would have a very clearly defined attitude. If the artists were caught arrests would no doubt take place. Who would defend them? Because they would not be working within the art-gallery cocoon, does that mean that their artistic credentials would automatically be rejected? And if so, why?

This seems to me to be the crux we must face up to in a reformist climate. All manner of expression is tolerated, provided it takes place in the *correct places*, where it can be insulated from the mass of the people. If it proves not to be tolerated in such places, then there will arise a host of defenders. But once let the artists remove themselves from inside the safety barriers: then they are literally Outside The Pale: and are deemed unworthy of serious public endorsement. Which means that if they adopt a certain political stand they can be denounced as giving aid and succour to terrorist organizations, which means, in the Northern Irish context, that they render themselves liable to be put into Long Kesh. Thus, they themselves would have to take up the posture that they are political prisoners: and Mr Mason would then have to go off to New York to reassure American artistic people that these terrorists are not of course artists but criminals. But this in turn would raise the spectre of the Russian dissident artists who have been put into labour camps and lunatic asylums on the grounds that they are anti-social psychopaths and hooligans. Now, all good liberals in the West have invested a lot of denunciation-power in attacking the Soviet authorities for their disregard of human rights . . . This may be thought to be something of a fantastical scenario: I do not know how many people would have sufficient sense of experimentation in the cause of 'Art for Society' to try it out in practice: but it is not altogether a fantasy. A recent outburst in the London *Times* has so far led to no observable protest from the poets in Britain or from those in Ireland who would not object to being seen reading the London *Times*. This quote is from an article by Christopher Walker about the H-block prisoners' protest. He says: 'The prose in the republican newspapers is often accompanied by poetry written by protestors anxious to boost up their role as patriots. One recent composition by an anonymous versifier described only as 'H5 Blanket-man' ended "For it is criminals they call us, and criminals *we are not*".' One is reminded here of an Elizabethan description from 1562 of the Irish bards active against the English domination of those days – 'the poets who by their ditties and rhymes in commendation of extortions, rebellion, rape and ravin, do encourage lords and gentlemen against the Queen' – and therefore had to be exterminated . . .

On the other hand, I don't know why Mr Mason would not be clever enough to use the fact of the Provos in Long Kesh writing poetry as a propaganda point to prove that as there is so much cultural activity in the prison, there cannot of course be any inhuman or degrading treatment taking place, and so therefore philanthropic American businessmen can safely invest their money in the Arts in Northern Ireland.

Within our own work we have become very conscious of these contradictions imposed by the reformist preconceptions of our present society. Vandaleur's Folly, although the plot contains a good deal of complex detail, is nevertheless a simple enough play and its basic message can be summarized in two sentences, thus: Where the reform of injustice is prevented by political manoeuvring, the people themselves must take measures to protect themselves against their exploiters. If they cannot do this democratically, then they must do it through force of arms.

We have shown in the play how this has happened in Ireland. Now, even within an overtly political theatre company such as

7/84, the presentation of this statement caused extraordinary problems. Some members of the company, believing in the reformers' need to make clear at all times their good intentions, began to boggle at lines in the text where they thought the play seemed to support and advocate violence. They seemed to think that the softening or removal of such lines was more important than the overall struggle within the production to analyse *why* there is *already* violence. If we had not resisted their resistance to the statements of the text, the meaning of the play could not have been presented to the public. Such a situation, of course, can make it impossible for individual playwrights to put forward their own analysis of their subject matter undiluted by the ifs and buts of collective insecurity – and I see this insecurity as part of the cultural climate imposed on us today from the controllers of the state – it is all of a piece with the official attitudes that identify opposition to capital punishment with a desire to carry out assassinations and robberies. There is another problem about producing plays which seek to make clear the contradictions of our society. Actors need to entertain and to be liked by their audiences. If they are not liked, and if this is reported in the press by the reviewers, the performers will suffer in their professional reputations and will find it harder to get work at a time when work for actors is very hard to come by. But society is divided: divided in Ireland to the extent of actual armed conflict. How can an audience drawn from a divided society be expected to unite in liking any one play – if that play in any way explores the roots of the society and the passions and interests that are instrumental in dividing it? And yet such plays, which are known as 'serious drama' are the very plays which the Arts Councils are supposed to be encouraging, and which cultural export agencies such as the British Council are so proud to send overseas as examples of the liberal reformist enlightenment of the modern age.

Mention of the British Council and the export of culture inevitably leads us to examine the other main invisible export of the modern age from the United Kingdom. This is the new expertise in what are known as 'counter-terrorist' techniques. Police and military experts from the UK have already deployed themselves alongside the security forces of the Irish Republic, at the time of the Herrema kidnap, the West German security forces in the Mogadishu hi-jacking, the Italian security forces when Signor Moro was kidnapped. There is a constant expansion throughout the Western world of the lessons learnt by ten years of this counter-terrorism in Northern Ireland. You might think that the present state of Northern Ireland is not all that good an advertisement for successful *counter*-terrorism: but the very existence of the Belfast Festival is significant to frightened foreigners. There is no comparable Arts Festival in Salisbury, Rhodesia, for example: nor did they manage to hold such an event in Saigon during the Vietnam War. Cultural exports and repressive policing techniques are not in opposition to one another: they are the left hand and the right hand of the modern propagandist state, and all artists and audiences who are the subject of the one activity cannot afford to forget about the other.

The role of the Arts Councils is crucial in this arrangement. Not only the British Arts Council and the Northern Irish Arts Council, but also the Arts Council of the 26 Counties. There is an obvious overt political and cultural linkage between London, Belfast, Dublin and Washington which is paralleled by the undercover activities of the CIA. We all know about the way in which Western capitalist interests are upheld by infiltrated assassins, subsidized mobs, labour agitation directed against the working class on behalf of the bosses and the encouragement of reformist peace movements which only demand peace from one side of the social struggle. But there is also the infiltration of cultural and artistic movements – ironically, in 1966, Conor Cruise O'Brien himself did much to expose this when it was going on in connection with the *Encounter* magazine. This cultural infiltration and manipulation began nearly twenty years ago, when a new concept of the 'alternative society' was starting up amongst the artists and students of America. This was seen by the authorities as a threat to the integrity of capitalism and imperialism, and measures were therefore put in hand to take it over without anyone noticing. The principal method of doing this was by means of subsidy. If people are determined to *do their own thing*, but are dependent upon payment for it from somewhere else, it was clear that it would not really be their *own* thing for very much longer. After the defeat of the American War in Vietnam the administration of that country became less and less willing to engage in further overt military adventure: so accordingly the cultural manipulation on a global scale has been stepped up.

Now, in Northern Ireland you have a state that can only survive by keeping a certain level of the heaviest repression continually on the go. And yet the state must appear stable enough to encourage business investment, particularly from America. With the emphasis these days so strong upon 'human rights' this stability must be seen to have a liberal reformist image. What better method therefore than to bring in a new subsidized cultural task-force drawn from a generation too young to have actually experienced the spontaneous, unsubsidized, untheoretical naïve beginnings of the concept of the *alternative society*? They will be well enough able to talk the right language of community arts, social involvement, non-violent participatory celebration and all the rest of it: but in practice they will be completely missing the original totally revolutionary innocence of the whole thing.

Let us consider wall slogans. In America, these have become a seriously regarded form of artistic expression and are of course disapproved of by authority. Most of them are the product of Black, Puerto Rican, Mexican minority ghettos. Reformist community groups are funding projects of mural painting to channel, as it were, the talent for wall-decoration away from dangerous political dissent towards a more general and non-controversial improvement of the environment. Is not the same thing now happening here in Belfast? But does it not totally miss the point? Political slogans on walls are not intended to improve the environment. Generally speaking they are in fact a fierce protest against the environment or at any rate some marked aspect of it. If the ferocity of the slogans is replaced by pretty pictures of nothing in particular, where does the ferocity go? It surely hasn't disappeared. It has merely been deprived of one particular means of expression so, inevitably, it will find another one. The artists who contribute to the mural-painting programmes do so in the belief that they can improve the environment without first totally destroying it. The original slogans themselves suggest that the people who put them up would not share this point of view. A society that can be improved is a society that can be made stable. Artists involved in making our present society stable are playing the game of government, however much they will insist that they are doing their own thing and are completely non-political. Their reformism in fact has become overtly counter-revolutionary, and thus is an active part of the military techniques for forcible control of the population. To shift people's indigenous forms of political expression – by means of government money – into bland hand-me-down all-purpose decorative nothingness is in itself to play a highly political role and the a-political people who are persuaded to play it must not be surprised if they are eventually treated as the cultural wing of the British Army. A genuinely non-political artist who is working in a sectarian ghetto will inevitably become political either by identifying with, or by being repelled by, the politics of the community there.

In other words, under these conditions of subsidized arts programmes at a time of severe civil disaffection, armed rebellion, armed repression etc., there are only two possible ways for reformers to operate. They can either become political and commit themselves to one side in the struggle: or they can keep on proclaiming their non-political stance and unwittingly support repressive Western state power in defence of the three hundred or so multi-nationalist monopoly-capitalist companies who in effect control our world, and control it at the expense of the liberties and democratic aspirations of the mass of the population. Those portions of the masses who resist such control are systematically isolated by their very acts of resistance. In Northern Ireland the Republican minority has been put into this position. The required stability of the province cannot be secured until the Republicans are crushed. Even if this means the establishment of a small allegedly-independent six-county overtly Fascist statelet. A letter in the London *Times* from one of the painters principally involved in the Art for Society row is very much to the point here. He is Conrad Atkinson from the Slade School, London, and he says: 'Northern Ireland has added another new and depressing anti-democratic group to its list – the cultural paramilitaries.' He is referring to the Trustees of the Ulster Museum: the people who would be the Arts establishment of an independent Ulster, and who have, as Mr Atkinson also says – 'Confirmed the message of my painting, which generally speaking is that once you erode freedom of speech, all kinds of unsavoury mechanisms emerge. The sleep of reason produces monsters.' As I have already indicated, that is more or less the message of *Vandaleur's Folly* as well.

But do not misunderstand me – as a citizen of the 26 Counties I am not in Belfast to abuse the Northern Irish and let my own society off the hook. The Gombeen Government of the Greengrocers' Republic (where incidentally you cannot get a fresh vegetable west of the Shannon), is part and parcel of the whole sordid set-up. If beautiful Arts festivals and jolly clowns running all about the poverty-stricken streets are to be used to disguise Fascism north of the border, so, too, in the south. The press will fill up with images of Arts Councillors and equivocating politicians congratulating themselves upon their cultural exchanges, and fostering the agreeable picture of jolly rivalry between Ulster and the rest – when on all grounds, cultural, social, economic, the two halves of the divided island are crying out to be treated as a whole, whatever political arrangements can be finally arrived at. The natural mineral resources of the 26-counties are pouring out of the country into the pockets of the multi-nationals, and any attempt by the people to resist this can lead to little else than a replay of the Chilean situation. The land is undeveloped, the gaols filled with political prisoners, the dole queues get longer every week our so-called economic miracle progresses, . . . But so long as there is a Wexford Opera Festival, a Dublin Theatre Festival, vigorous arts centres improving environments all over the country, who will point the finger? The people who will suffer most from the economic and political manipulations are the ones who will not be receiving these cultural goodies: so it will not be necessary for the theatres to direct attention to their plight. In any case such attention will be in bad taste and will only serve to reduce the chances of social stability: who knows, it might even instigate violence? And violence, we all know, never comes because there is a need for it: it is always brought in by self-seeking criminal agitators.

Theatre In Ireland

1981

This is the last piece I wrote for Dialog, *an annual Polish theatre magazine with international coverage. When the Solidarity movement was supressed many cultural journals and theatres were temporarily closed,* Dialog *among them. I had been invited in 1976 by the editor (an ex-prince of great sensitivity) to contribute a yearly article after I pointed out to him that by always including Ireland in the 'British' entry he was unwittingly perpetuating cultural imperialism, despite his sympathetic identificaton with the Irish struggle.*

'And now for next year' – a headline on an Arts page in a leading Irish Sunday newspaper, referring to the optimism that is in the air for the Dublin Theatre Festival of 1982. The Dublin Theatre Festival is Ireland's main theatre showcase: the policy of the new programme director, Michael Colgan, is to influence through the festival the development of theatre in Ireland in general. So, with that in mind, he had no major Irish plays this year: instead he invited a medley of foreign companies to show off their wares. 'Next year it will be the festival for the Irish playwrights': so this year we had, for example, from Poland, the Wroclaw Contemporary Theatre. In the words of Kazimierz Braun, their director: 'For us, *Birthrate* is an invitation for spectators to create with us. It is a journey to Rosewicz's "internal theatre" . . . to the mystery of the art of the theatre.' In the text of *Birthrate* there are no dialogues, no lines for actors. The majority of the audience at the Gate Theatre, where the production was shown, were bewildered and some felt insulted, as they were led into the dark cellars below the theatre to be locked up and churned about – what did it mean?

For too many of them it was an experience they could well do without, in view of the paranoiac political climate that obtained in the country during the aftermath of the ten hunger-strike deaths in Northern Ireland's H-Blocks earlier in the year. These deaths (which included one MP of the British parliament and one elected deputy to the Irish parliament) carried a significance which effectively destabilized the political balance of the entire country, thereby causing the British government's intelligence services to become extremely worried about the future development of British interests in Ireland. On April 6th, 1981, one month after the late Bobby Sands MP and his comrades recommenced the hunger strike to the death, for humane treatment in the North of Ireland concentration camps, a writer in the Dublin *Sunday Tribune* recorded that 'British Intelligence has more than 600 operators working north and south of the border', in Ireland. 'Fifty operate regularly in the south.' One secret document obtained by the *Sunday Tribune* is described as 'graded *Secret – UK Eyes "B" Only*'. The classification is a hangover from colonial days when "UK Eyes" meant "To be viewed by white British only". In Ireland it means that the paper can be seen only by people with a "mainland" background.' There are eleven separate agencies – apart from MI5 and MI6 – involved in military intelligence in Ireland. In addition to these, the Special Air Service, the Royal Air Force, the Royal Ulster Constabulary's Special Branch all have independent intelligence organizations. There are also GS (Int) units attached to fourteen security and intelligence companies – whatever all that might mean. 'Men with field intelligence links usually pose as businessmen, journalists, and tourists' – social classifications which make up the greater part of the Dublin theatre audience! It is no wonder therefore that Michael Colgan – in this particular year – seems to have felt reluctant to expose Irish playwrights to a public largely consisting of foreign spies. He did say proudly that he had managed to get 300 American tourists over for the Festival – could they, one wonders, have been a block-booking from the CIA? And if they were, what agencies in what nations were employing the remaining sprinkling of non-Irish and non-English visitors to the festival?

Along with the Polish company we had such groups as The National Theatre Company of Bath (England), Zippo the Clown, the Danish Street Theatre, the *Optical Figurenbühne* (West Germany), the Repertory Theatre of St Louis (USA), and the *Commedia dell'Arte a l'Avogaria* (Italy). Many of the visitors were street-theatre companies, and paraded the pavements to seduce and usher in the lone tourists who either had nerves of steel or else were quite ignorant of what was going on in our unhappy country at the time. Buntings and street banners were out advertising the festival, mingling with the black flags which had been put out in hundreds to mourn the dead hunger strikers (the last of whom was Mickey Devine, died in August: although during September and October, there were still eleven on the hunger strike who eventually were forced to abandon their protest).

As a playwright I have no choice but to be subjective when I write this article. The shock and revulsion at the stench and carnage of what was happening in the H Blocks has prevented me from taking other than a jaundiced view of this year's theatre in Ireland and, in particular, of the Dublin Festival. Readers should understand that all over the country, when hunger strikers died, there were in some areas total general strikes, in other areas token strikes, businesses were closed, hundreds and thousands of people marched through the streets: and not one professional theatre so much as hung up a black flag, or even announced a token closure. There were no major Irish plays: indeed, how could any serious writer produce a work this year that did not in some way reflect the horrendous nightmare of 1981 that gripped our country? One of Ireland's best known dramatists, Eugene McCabe (whose reputation has not been based upon political polemic) had intimated to the Abbey Theatre that he wished to write a play about the H Blocks: but his idea was incontinently rejected by the authorities of our national theatre.

How many of the visiting companies realized that shortly before their arrival in Dublin there had been a change of government, and that the first directive of the new administration to the radio and TV networks was that day-by-day bulletins were no longer to be issued on the condition of each hunger striker: that the funerals of the dead men were not to be covered in any meaningful detail? So, month after month, there continued this macabre and spectacular theatre – of prisoners tortured and murdered by British imperialism (and even, when their naked and wasted bodies were given to the relatives for burial, the remains had been dragged out of the coffins by police and desecrated) – in full view of the whole world – except in Ireland where our censors would not permit us to share a complete knowledge of the endurance and suffering of these young men, who were giving up their lives in the cause of Irish liberation. This censorship of news naturally had its effect in the theatre, which relies on government funds to keep going. The official policy meant, in effect, that all national sympathy had to be switched (in the interest of good relationships with Great Britain, and her 600 spies) from the nationalist resistance in the North to the unionist element of the northern population who insist on continuing the political link with Britain. This unionist element was, incidentally, providing a macabre theatre-spectacle of its own – and one which was disagreeably reminiscent of Nazi spectaculars in Germany in the 1930s – the Rev Ian Paisley, Westminster MP and protestant bigot (whose ideology derives in part from the Ku-Klux-Klan-ridden areas of the southern-USA 'Bible Belt', where he obtained his doctorate of divinity) proclaimed, to a gathering of journalists and a rally of para-military hoodlums on a moonless night on top of a mountain in the wilds of County Antrim, that he was forming a 'Third Force' (i.e., a private army) to wipe out republicans in Northern Ireland.

It was clearly not easy for playwrights in the south to feel or express much sympathy with such a repulsive figure as Paisley (and indeed any attempt to treat him on the stage would make theatre-people terrified that they would be a target for his vengeance – loyalist bombs in the centre of Dublin in the early seventies killed 33 people in one blast): but there are aspects of the unionist social classes which do lend themselves to a certain sentimental and nostalgic artistic benevolence. And this has been very acceptable to the Dublin government in its attempt to defuse national tension and anti-British emotion. I am referring to the protestant-ascendancy landowning gentry class, put into the country in the seventeenth century by the British Crown in gratitude for military and financial services rendered, and to oust the native Irish from their confiscated lands. Like the white colonies in Algeria, 'Rhodesia' (Zimbabwe), or South Africa, they have been determined to hold on at all costs: but because of their allegedly gracious ruling-class life-style it is assumed that their hearts can be wooed into acceptances of a united Ireland where they may still have some civilized part to play and their values may be appreciated.

So our national theatre, the Abbey, in tune with British and Irish government thinking about this class, commissioned a play from William Trevor (better known as a novelist and short-story writer) concerning an English family which received grants of land in Ulster three centuries ago and, ever since, 'fair-minded and generous in different ways and in different generations, they find themselves repeatedly caught between Ulster extremes and never more so than in the present.' Decadent and all as our Irish bourgeoisie is, when confronted with a play sympathetic to the landlords, the gall rose in their throats and they would not be seduced into the theatre. As one professional Dublin man put it to a journalist (who had liked the play and wanted to know why the theatre had been only half full with so large a proportion of foreign tourists): 'Oh, you know, asking for sympathy for the poor old Prods, and making out how noble they are compared to the rest of us . . .' (*Scenes From An Album* by William Trevor. Director, Joe Dowling; Designer, Bronwen Casson; cast included: Ingrid Craigie, Fedelma Cullen, John Kavanagh. Abbey Theatre, Dublin.)

The other two major Irish theatrical events of 1981, also part of the Dublin Festival, were two new Irish versions of Chekhov.

Field Day Theatre Company presented *Three Sisters*, translated by Brian Friel. (Director, Stephen Rea; cast included: Sorcha Cusack, Eileen Pollock, Olwen Fouere. Gaiety Theatre, Dublin, and on tour). The Irish Theatre Company presented *The Seagull*, adapted by Thomas Kilroy. (Director, Patrick Mason; designer, Frank Conway; cast included: Rosaleen Linehan, Alan Stanford, Kevin Flood. Olympia Theatre, Dublin, and on tour). The spectacle of Ireland's two major modern dramatists both at work on Chekhov at the same festival provided great knockabout entertainment for the theatrical salons (i.e. the Dublin pubs) Mr Kilroy was at an initial disadvantage in the rivalry. His *Seagull* had been made as a very free adaptation for the 25th anniversary of the Royal Court Theatre in London, and he therefore inclined his text towards the *mores* of a British audience: although he removed the action of the play from Tsarist Russia and set it in the west of Ireland at the same period. The young playwright in the story was converted into a figure of the Celtic Revival literary school of W. B. Yeats, and similar local adjustments were made throughout the text. The first performance in Dublin was heckled by an element in the audience who complained of inaudibility and actors not knowing their lines. It has however been said that this complaint perhaps concealed a strong hostility felt towards the play by a section of the public who were suspicious of the adaptor's motives in mocking Irish cultural and social institutions for a British audience.

Brian Friel, however, was much craftier. After all, he had been the public's darling the previous year with his immensely successful *Translations*, and it was perhaps not to be expected that the critics would acclaim a Chekhov adaptation so highly this year. But audiences throughout the country seem to have thoroughly enjoyed *Three Sisters* (except in the north, where business was very bad, not surprisingly in view of the H Block deaths and aftermath). Friel's approach differed from Kilroy's in that he retained the original Russian settings and names: but he used a very vigorous colloquial Irish dialogue which had nonetheless the effect of *placing* the play into an Irish garrison town with all its local class bickerings. It should be mentioned in passing that productions of Chekhov in Ireland in 1981 do inevitably carry a certain subliminal sympathy with present government thinking about Anglo-Irish relations and the necessity for looking with comparative favour upon the land-owning gentry class: and that both the Friel and Kilroy versions fell comfortably into the same cultural ambience as William Trevor's play.

Theatrical treatment of the landowning ascendancy class may not, therefore, yet, be entirely acceptable to an emerging country still in the throes of its national liberation struggle: but on the other hand, neither does the bourgeoisie accommodate itself happily to the element of marxist ideology in that same struggle. Ireland's only independent producer, Noel Pearson, mounted a spectacular production of *The Informer*, adapted by Tom Murphy from Liam O'Flaherty's famous Conrad-like novel about revolutionary organizations in the Dublin of the 1920s – to quote the programme note: 'symbols and de-clarations of political freedom change: the life of the poor in the slums goes on unchanged.' The play was not a success: critics disliked the overall style and technique of both adaptation and production. This, however, would not normally deter a Dublin audience if the content of the show had been to their taste. In

October, the British intelligence in the North had coerced under torture a couple of middle-grade IRA volunteers into turning informer: the O'Flaherty story, therefore, was a little too near the bone to be comfortable . . . And presumably the same discomfort would affect the British 'tourists' . . . *The Informer* was presented at the Olympia Theatre, Dublin.

The smaller theatres during 1981 had a motley bill of fare, plays ranging from studies of mental illness to divorce.

Back among the natives, however, interesting and potentially exciting developments have been taking place. Why are the playwrights silent? If they are given better conditions and status, perhaps they will produce? Anthony Cronin, an intellectual liberal-minded republican, put forward a plan to the last government for forming a body known (in Irish) as the *Aosdána* – a partly-independent institution to represent artists in Ireland. This is based on the old Celtic idea of artists as the guardians and inspirers of cultural values in the society. (The ancient Celts were noted for their love of 'truth, arts, and science'.) Membership of this modern-day *Aosdána* is a recognition of achievement and distinction in a 'creative discipline'. Eighty-nine practitioners have now been selected, painters, composers, poets, writers, and playwrights. The playwrights include Samuel Beckett, Tom Murphy, James Plunkett, Michael Molloy, Brian Friel – and myself. We are now entitled to various moneys from the state if our circumstances require it. The other development in the professional circumstances of artists is the amalgamation of all the artists' organizations (i.e., Musicians' Union, Painters' Union, Society of Irish Playwrights) under the umbrella of the Irish Transport and General Workers' Union, the largest union for workers in the country, founded by James Connolly, himself poet and playwright as well as workers' leader, who was executed by the British for his part in the Easter Rising of 1916. The union HQ in Liberty Dublin (where the Rising was planned) now contains an office for all the artists' organizations with a full-time paid secretary.

So: in one stroke, from being nothing, we now seem to be

everything – we are recognized by the state: and on equal terms with the industrial proletariat, and form, in effect, its 'cultural wing' . . . For our physical needs, as nothing is too good for the workers(!), the famous theatre-director, the late Tyrone Guthrie (who, ironically enough was himself part of the land-owning ascendancy class) has left his ancestral country house to be made into a retreat for writers. This house is very close to the border with the north, it is the last stop in the 26 counties before entering into the part of Ireland controlled and occupied by British forces, the very area where the most intense fighting is at the moment taking place. The writers' retreat is to be administered by both northern and southern Irish arts councils in tandem. As a journalist put it in the Dublin *Irish Times*, on the occasion of the auspicious opening: 'Nobody was tactless enough to mention political martyrs or constitutional prob-lems. It was left to writer Niall Quinn, a merchant seaman who lived in a lightless caravan until arriving at Annaghmakerrig, to explain the experience of working here. "Every day I wake up here and think to myself, if this is heaven, why aren't I dead?"'

So, for the vast improvement of our individual and collective status in society, we can thank a living writer, a dead theatre-director, and the working classes: but what do we owe our government, or what are they going to do to encourage the words of the writer actually to be heard? They have curtailed the money to the Arts Council, who have removed altogether their grant to the Irish Touring Company, the only pro-fessional company to tour plays through the provinces: the Abbey Theatre is only getting a six per cent increase of grant: and the Dublin Theatre Festival looks as though it will be able to run only for two weeks in future instead of three. A tightening of belts all round means that no theatre will be able to take the risk of putting on any playwright's work that contains controversial matter – as for example, spies in Ireland, or the national question – lest it jeopardizes the image of the country to tourists in search of 'smiling Irish eyes' and the famous Irish blarney. The Arts Council's justification for these cuts is the need to build up arts centres throughout the country, at the same time as the Tourist Board hopes to build up the major industry of tourism.

But if the future is to contain well-fed playwrights, working away in splendid isolation, but with little hope of having their work heard by the people at large, their imagination may turn from the theatre to the wider arena of republican revolutionary traditions, such as brought so many dramatists into the 1916 Rising . . . 'And now for next year' – what kind of surprises will the Irish playwrights have in store? Because in spite of the repression inflicted on the Irish people during the past year, and in spite of the Dublin government's subservience to its British perpetrators, the spirit of resistance continues unabated: and is surely bound in the long run to give courage and inspiration to the Irish playwrights.

Letter To The Press (1)

Galway,
3 Oct 1983.

To the Editor
The Irish Times

Sir,

The official opening of the 25th Dublin Theatre Festival at the Mansion House last week looked as though it was going to be an event worthy of the occasion – red carpets, a gracious building, musicians, street-theatre groups in exotic costume, representatives of equally exotic foreign theatre-companies, and all that. Press reports suggested that this promise was in fact fulfilled: but my own dire experience of the speeches after the preliminary drinks-and-chat makes me wonder if the reporters and myself had really been present in the same room at the same time.

Although President Hilary gave formal welcomes (100,000 of them) to the visitors from abroad, none of the speakers even thought fit to specify who they were – from China, India, Japan, Poland, Italy, Britain, the USA (to say nothing of Cork, Belfast, Galway . . .) – why, Dublin was host to artistic representatives of something like three-quarters of the world, surely in itself a remarkable circumstance? Ironically, the only country to be mentioned by name in this context was Britain.

We were, however, treated to a lengthy series of mean little self-congratulatory remarks about money (and that silver cup), combined with some poor-mouthed crypto-political parochial requests for more money and complaints that it was not forthcoming, all too reminiscent of the worst and narrowest type of bardic verse from the depressed fag-end of the Middle Ages.

The speakers were all greyish, male, and admirably in tune with the non-aesthetic nature of the tired State which they have helped to make. The Lord Mayor did say that street-theatre was near his heart and that he hoped there would be more of it: may I recommend that a change of cast in the 'state-theatre' of the Mansion House at the Festival opening might be a good idea?

Dr Tim O'Driscoll referred to the 'hidden women' behind the Festival: again an anonymous tribute. Women in Ireland in some ways resemble the major visiting companies of this year's programme: not *really* part of the First World, with all its wonderful values. If some of these hidden women (e.g. Grace Parrott, Helene Montague, and many more whom I did not meet personally), who in fact *created* the Festival with their intelligence, vitality and goodwill, were to be on the platform, there might be less bureaucratic gobbledegook and more sense that a Theatre Festival could be in reality an artistic free zone where international practitioners can meet as individuals unimpeded by the crude power-politics of their respective governments.

Also, the sterility of the Mansion House had in its turn a detrimental effect upon the body-language of some of the women artists who spoke at the press conference the following day. They tended to cling to the wall, or sit coyly, deferring to their male colleagues, as if subconsciously responding to their diminished status in this republic (on a level with the unborn).

Yours, etc.,
Margaretta D'Arcy

Statement For The National Council of Civil Liberties Concerning the Prevention of Terrorism Act

1985

To begin with, I should explain that what follows is not alone the work of the Prevention of Terrorism Act or PTA (which I see as just one arm of a state determined to prevent objections to the eradication of those civil liberties normally considered part and parcel of a western democracy): the specific effect on my life of the PTA is combined with the effects of my arrest for protest over artistic freedom (see details on your proforma) and with a second arrest (1979) and 3-month imprisonment in Armagh. This latter sentence was for joining a street protest in that town against the conditions I had already observed in the women's gaol: and I was charged with breach of the peace and with disorder. Together with a second detention at Stranraer under the PTA while I was awaiting trial, I accumulated so many paper charges as to make me appear a thoroughly undesirable person. The total dossier thereafter had a strong effect on my life.

My four sons, at that time attending school in north London, became marks for local police harassment. One of them (second eldest) was stopped and searched by the Special Patrol Group or SPG outside his school 15 times in three months. The eldest, picked up by police outside a disco when there was some small disorder found himself singled out for a charge, unjustly: and was found guilty of disorderly behaviour. The third was twice arrested on similar grounds: on one of these occasions he was roughed up by the police to get him to admit a robbery of which he knew absolutely nothing – they took off his shoes, stamped on his feet and told him 'Your mother is in the IRA'. The fourth was beaten up by the police, using a truncheon – he was in fact not charged with anything. Several years later, when he wanted to join the Territorial Army, he was, first, accepted, then suspended for a 'background security check', then told he could not be a member of the TA, and was not to go near any military base. The second eldest son, who had no court record, applied to join the police and was never even asked to an interview. I must emphasize that none of these four boys were in any sense 'criminal' types. They had no interest in politics, either: and they certainly considered themselves as loyal Britishers. All this has made them feel bitter towards me, for my involvement in civil liberties issues: they feel I have stymied their free choice in life.

As a theatre worker, my career has been strongly affected. When I was first stopped under the PTA (as described on proforma) I was carrying a letter from the Nottingham Play-house inviting me to discuss with them a major production of one of my plays. Subsequently this project was never mentioned: and I have had no further communication with that director. I can only assume the police got in touch with him . . .

In 1980, I was invited by a theatre group in New York to go over there, stay on their premises, and work on a production of my plays about Ireland. After some time the people who had invited me cancelled all their part in the work and ordered me off their premises without explanation. This left me in a highly vulnerable situation. The critic from the *Village Voice*, at about the same time, invited me to meet her to discuss a big publicity spread on my work: but when I went to her she suddenly became highly abusive, saying that I was not going to seduce her into supporting terrorism etc . . . I believe that these reversals had nothing to do with my plays themselves, but everything to do with the British Embassy in the US. I had been talking freely in NY (on radio as well as face to face) about the state of the gaols and the Irish prisoners, in what one might call a traditional 'civil liberties' manner: and thus was subject to a *destabilizing operation*. The '*Voice*' had just been taken over by Murdoch: the theatre group was dependent on miscellaneous fundings which could be politically affected . . . I have frequently found that when I talk to people who have some inside knowledge of the media, they hint that my work is refused production, or I am refused publicity, because I am thought to be a terrorist.

In the Irish 26-county republic, of which I am a citizen, and where I live, I have found this boycotting much more overt than in Britain. I think the effect of the British PTA and its spin-offs is taken strong note of here and the hostility towards presumed 'terrorists' is manifest in left-wing, liberal, and literary circles as well as managerial areas. When my book *Tell Them Everything*, about my experiences in Armagh Gaol, came out in Ireland, a radio interview and general publicity appearances *etc.* were set up for me, and then mysteriously cancelled. Only last month a friend asked a TV producer why I had not been invited to a conference of socio-political history, where she thought I would have been able to make a specialized contribution: she was told that I was 'mixed up with the provos', with all that may be understood to imply . . . I have never met the producer in question, or had any dealings with him of any sort whatever, so what I am talking about here is a noxious climate of unattributed rumour.

People have come to my house for quite casual reasons: and then have displayed nervousness and asked 'will their names get on to a list?' Reviewers of work I have done in collaboration with John Arden – or, gratuitously enough, of John Arden's own sole work – have implied that I am the terrorist in the partnership, and the work of either or both of us must be judged from that standpoint.

This last June Michael Billington in the *Guardian* wrote an extraordinary attack on my statements at a theatre conference in London, which bore no relation to what I had actually said, but could only be understood on the assumption that he thought I was presenting some sort of 'terrorist strategy' there. My image in the theatre and literary world is thus constantly tarnished with a smear.

Not long ago, in Dublin, I asked a well-known painter to paint a portrait of John Arden. He declined, in an oddly unexplained manner. Sometime later, at a meeting, he implied that I was a 'provo'.

I have often proposed resolutions (in Ireland) at union meetings and the like on civil liberties issues. There is always someone there to oppose them on the unjustifiable ground that my motives are not what I say they are: i.e., I am an undercover Provo. I have found Northern Irish poets to be regular pursuers of this tactic.

No established person in cultural life has ever come directly out stating these subterranean charges, or even asking me about them: and yet I feel constantly that I have been for a considerable time the subject of hints and allusions – sometimes when I meet people I have never met before they show surprise that I seem an ordinary human being. In general the climate produced by anti-terrorism legislation is extremely unhealthy and disturbed. Rumour becomes fact: fear is induced in persons who have nothing to be afraid of: public affairs cannot be openly discussed without preliminary 'dissociations from terrorism' by the participants. This would not be surprising in a country where there are no claims for public liberties and democracy: but when it happens in democratic states which still parade their virtues of freedom and open government etc., it becomes alarming in the extreme.

The combination of the legislation and the British military intelligence blackening-operations spread all over the world wherever there is any sort of British link. I have been invited to speak at cultural conferences in Norway, Greece, Italy, West Germany, France: it is normal to find at least one British person in the room who gets up and denies that there is any such thing as harassment and intimidation of the sort I have described above. Often these individuals turn out to have some local connection with the British Council. The implication of the remarks is, once again, that I am an agent of Irish terrorists: and that no one should take any notice of my cultural credentials. People in foreign universities, I may say, have recently been telling me that the absence of my name from books and articles on aspects of the modern theatre has become quite blatant, and they wonder why it should be so? I have to tell them all the details I have written above.

Lately, there has been some easing off, as far as I personally am concerned, in that the BBC has put on radio plays with my name as an author. But nevertheless irreparable damage has been done to my general reputation.

To have been the victim of the PTA is like being a carrier of a plague-germ. You can never tell who will have heard about it, or what attitude they will take to you. This produces in one a fear of mixing in social circles where there is no experience of the PTA: and thus one slowly becomes ghettoized. When one meets people who *have* had direct experience of the PTA it is possible, and only possible *there*, to talk frankly about the situation produced by its operation. One finds, for example, those who have had their houses searched in an overt fashion in order to frighten them off from political activity and also to notify their neighbours that they are plague-carriers. In my particular way of life the threat is more subtle and less crude: the effects of it are exactly the same.

In 1983, I was commissioned with John Arden to write a text about Irish history for the Kurt Weill/Bertolt Brecht cantata *The Mother*, to be performed at the Queen Elizabeth Hall. Shortly before the performance, the Arts Council cancelled its financial guarantee for this avant-garde musical event. When they were asked why, they said they did not provide funds for art that supported terrorism – even though they had already agreed the money, a quite unprecedented decision, and one taken without their having read the script. Luke Rittner of the Arts Council appeared just at this time on Channel 4 TV, talking about music, and how it must not be subverted by politics. People who heard it told me they recognized it as a veiled attack on my working on *The Mother* project . . . This had major repercussions because, after it, no group which relied on major Arts Council subsidy would ever employ me. I also noticed my unions far less inclined to make a fuss about it, than would have been the case a few years ago.

Organizations to which I belong (or have belonged), and where the PTA has become an issue:

The Theatre Writers' Union (UK): When I was arrested, they supported a resolution condemning the PTA.
Haringey Irish Association: also condemned the PTA.
Women in Entertainment (UK): at their first meeting in, I think, 1980 – condemned the PTA.

I do not belong to any political party. Prior to 1972 I was, for one year, a member of the Official Sinn Féin, in Ireland, which subsequently became the Workers' Party. While I was in it I did not suffer harassment in Britain or in Ireland. I do belong to the Irish Council for Civil Liberties and the Irish Anti-Apartheid Movement: and also the Irish Nicaragua Solidarity Campaign. I am a member of the Society of Irish Playwrights (part of the cultural wing of the ITGWU). Also the Writers' Guild of Great Britain.

Verses

I want to probe and swim in the sea
But not so deep as to get my foot caught
Tangled in the weeds
Get sucked down to drown.

*

My pen in here is my lifesaver
No I will not give it up
For who else can I talk to
Except this prison paper?

*

Whichever way it could go
There would have to be
An end
From me to you
Or
You to me.
I do not agree with you
And you do not agree with me.
So therefore
A collision

Would take place
Which would hurt
Both of us.
So why not now
Rather than later?
It will take the same time
To heal.
Each of us can feel
That the other does not
Understand
And so can not
Truly feel.

*

The letter came today
I was not expecting it.
Only, on Sunday
I had a
Flash in the
Sunday Press,
When I opened it
And saw a name
I did not want to see.

So I pulled
Myself together
And said, 'This is
Nonsense,
A woman of your
Years
Should not be
Living in
A Mills-and
-Boons
Novel . . .'

It worked.
I read Foucault
About the origins
And meaning
Of sexual power.

Today
Reason leaves
Me
And I open
Mills-and
-Boons.

*

Instructions how to talk:
A leisurely game of tennis in the afternoon
One two three over we go
Are you there? Well caught. I'll send it back to you.
Not so hard. A gentle flick of the wrist and over it goes
I'll gently run to send it back
O how we skim and spin
One sentence at a time, two
At most three: no more
Or else it's rude.

*

In the beginning was the word.
Just one.
A torrent of words drowns and sweeps all before,
Gives some women headaches, drives others to the pub,
Engulfs envelopes and destroys all before:
In the avalanche the word gets lost
And then we are free to use
Any damn words we want. Sisters.

*

I sit in the kitchen
And type
Words
To help myself
More than anyone else
At the moment.

Piscator
Says you cannot
Have Revolutionary
Theatre without
A Revolutionary
Audience.

I agree.
But you cannot
Have
A Revolutionary
Audience
Until they
Understand
And feel the need
For a Revolution.

Today the *Guardian*
Exclaims Never, never, never
Has there been such
Militant Nationalism
In the republic as the result of
Maggie on TV pouting and uttering
The famous or infamous words
Out Out.
The people however are not saying
Out Out to Garret
Nor will they say
In In In to C. J. Haughey.

*

The aged rams,
Their twined horns now
Barely noble:
A blast of wind or thunderous shower
Would reveal the transparency
Of their matter,
Ravenna Cathedral would not
Praise God through these ragged age-bespattered artefacts.
They stand herded together against the lean-to on the hill.
No plant lives: trodden-down
By sharp hooves never still
As they repossess their territory,
Leaving their black pellets hardening in the sun
And snow.

Spring never comes: or if it does
It cannot capture the eager stirrings
Of New Season.
For no space is left
By these ancient animals
Too stagnant to give room to
Something other than themselves.

The maggots creep out and fall unmolested on the
Earth, they nest and creep back in to sanctuary.

O ragged rams roughened by eternity.

No ewes go near because they would
Sap the energy and so threaten that which rules.
Sky encircles these constant shapes, guardians
Of our culture and our aspirations.

Fall fall into the crevice of the dry ruts left by the
Forgotten rains
And move no more.
A monument to ramness.

*

I am allowed to write a poem now.
Mr Arden, a very educated gentleman,
And quiet too,
Says so.
My poem is:
Who controls the army
Controls the culture.
Very nicely put:
But is it true?
It is very easy
To set down slogans –
Why should we accept
Her doggerel?
Strident too,
Not written by
Any sort of
Educated lady
But by a bloody
Cow
Who for all we
Know is
Herself
Paid by the very
Army that she
Wants us to den-
ounce.

                    *

When I want a clear story
Arden always complicates it
By putting in too much.
Like yesterday –
A simple joke in a short scene:
One philosopher has taken five years to
Develop an argument,

The other has
Five hours
Before they are both eaten by lions.
But Arden
Has to put in how
Long they've lived,
Who they are,
I say I say
Old boy,
A shouting match –
All to show that
Arden can write.

*

Is there a more secure sight
Than to see a man
Kneeling on the floor
With a hammer in his hand
Head bent in concentration
As he prepares to
Put a nail in wood:
A shelf for books?
The house must be quiet
And no one is allowed to move
Near this one
While he completes his task:
All-important as a testimony
To him as a caring
Husband and
Provider for his
Mate.
He made the rules: let him
Keep them.

*

To John Who Complains I Never Write Nice Poems to Him.

If you died
I
Would have
No
Past
Or
Future
Only
Now:
No dreams
No time.
Conscious for only each second that passes
As the earth spins
With
Me
On it
With out
You.

*

If I were to write a poem what would I say
About the Condition of the Human Race?
John Berger says that only the poem now
Can speak the truth.
Poetry speaks the immediate wound.
The future cannot be trusted.
The moment of truth is now.

So I am told.

A young Garda beats a wino
Outside the Garda Station
And the other Guards laugh.
Is that the truth?

One thousand nine hundred and thirty-two questions
Were asked of Joanna Hayes
At the state's Kerry Baby Tribunal:
By men.
Men alone
Speak.

*

I heard the Irish windbag crane-bag field-day national poetry
– oh really? – on the telly,
A plethora of words
That turned into turds
One evening on the telly:
In the presence
Of the Attorney General
Who, having finished his fun
Of putting his fingers
Up a prisoner's bum,
Turned to smile to us at home:
Goodnight
Sleep tight
We have ended the fight
And Maggie is here to stay.

*

The poor are being screwed
To pay for the art
The rich can pay for.

The poor are being screwed
To pay for the heart
That screws the poor.

Doublethink In Aosdána.

These two statements in support of resolutions are the consequence of an ever-present schizophrenia among our leading artists. The first one was passed: with some dissent, which was censored from the (edited) minutes of the Aosdána assembly. This editing of minutes made me look far more closely into the workings of Aosdána's Committee (the Toscairí). Hence my second resolution, two years later, which called for unedited minutes, the suspension of the highly-restrictive Standing Orders, and the open conduct of all business in full assembly. My speech was heckled and booed all the way through, by a prearranged claque led by male visual artists, the group wanting to be closest to the gravy-flow of the international art hypermarket. My socialist-feminist political ideas had angered them, they felt threatened by them at feeding-time, and they determined I should never speak publicly in Aosdána again. Since then, however, and following my two months' sit-in, radical changes have taken place. Minutes are now fully recorded, members of the public may attend meetings, and it is now possible to make informal speeches. The Toscairí still sit on their mystery-box of votes, but I am confident it will not be long before it is opened.

On Censorship: 23 January 1984.

I am aware that my sending you this document instead of appearing in person to explain my resolution on censorship is an unsatisfactory expedient. Unfortunately I do have to be in Germany on January 23rd for a professional engagement: and I therefore hope either that a summary of my remarks can be read out or that the paper can be duplicated and distributed to members so that they can read it for themselves.

I have put forward again my resolution against all forms of state censorship, even though – at the April meeting – it was presented by the chair and passed unanimously. However, at the same time as it was being put to the meeting, the newly-elected Toscairí were engaged in the new committee arrangements, and I do not know whether they were aware, or were later made aware, of the nature of the resolution. In the report that was sent to me by the Toscairí there was no mention of any discussion upon my resolution.

Censorship has existed since the foundation of the State: although at all periods enlightened voices have been raised against it. The introduction of TV, (and in recent years, the extension of RTE in two channels both TV and radio), has however meant that many more people are now directly affected by official censorship. The opposition to the latest developments of censorship comes chiefly from journalists whose profession is threatened by Section 31 of the Broadcasting Act. It has been argued that this is because journalists are embarrassed by their colleagues outside the 26 counties being able to broadcast material denied to the home team: but nonetheless it is a welcome development.

The nature of censorship in this country reminds me of a Hindu, Buddhist or Taoist sage saying 'Those who desire the information can seek and find it: but those who do not desire it shall be denied it'. It in fact splits our society in an intellectually-damaging way. The more so as we have a whole new generation grown up since the Broadcasting Act was passed, who may not even be aware how much censorship there is.

If Aosdána is to be an intellectual and cultural 'beacon of light' for our young people, the whole question of censorship and its implications needs urgent debate. I am not expecting an immediate call for the end of state-censorship, and I am not expecting that even if there were such a unanimous call from Aosdána, the Government would at once repeal the legislation. But I do believe that by bringing it in to the arena of our debate we will find our members forced to take up a position one way or the other: and those, like myself, who oppose it entirely will therefore be given confidence to bring the issue more and more into the full open forum of our society. Ideally speaking, Aosdána should issue statements to the press to say that we are at least debating it.

To those who may think that I am wasting my time and that no one listens to us – may I remind them of the remark attributed to the gentle pacifist Sheehy-Skeffington to the effect that 'a crank is but a small arm which produces revolutions'?

On The Spirit Of Aosdána Broken: 21 March 1986.

My purpose in putting forward my resolutions: the fundamental element of Aosdána was the honouring of artists for their originality and creativity. But I now feel that its present direction cannot fulfil this aim. It is going the way of a conservative and traditional bureaucracy, upholding values which in the past have destroyed original and creative artists or forced them to leave the country. I do not use these words lightly. So alarmed have I been at the direction Aosdána is going that I decided I should test my judgement by referring, privately, to the opinions of a civil rights lawyer who works in an eminently respectable firm of solicitors; of a progressive sociologist at one of the national universities; of two women, a social worker and a psychologist, employed by the Health Board: and also of a trade unionist who negotiates on behalf of her branch. I did this to find out whether or not I was over-reacting because of my inexperience of state-funded organ-izations.

The opinions they gave were all roughly in agreement and may be summed up as follows. There is no doubt at all that the spirit of Aosdána as declared by the Taoiseach and James White, and published in the press at the time of our inau-guration, has been breached, in that the Standing Orders are unreasonable, demonstrating an extreme insensitivity to indi-viduals' rights, a total lack of imagination, and determination to quell all spontaneity and creativity, as from men reacting in extreme fear to bodies of people whom they do not know and are afraid they cannot control – they read like an attempt to perpetuate the rigid class-structure already inherent in our national education system. The idea that a resolution cannot even be considered for the agenda without first finding a seconder clearly indicates all these repressive symptoms: and it may be that Article 40: 1/3 of the national Constitution is being contravened, at least in spirit. Any body set up by the state does have to abide by the Constitution. And what about the UN Human Rights Charter, UNESCO, and the principle of Equal Employment? Also, it may be that the Toscairí, in relation to company law, are acting *ultra vires*. It is no coincidence that among the Toscairí we have a professor of music, the head of a college of art, a lecturer, an ex-RTE producer, a teacher, and various administrators.

It might interest Mr Munnelly to know that the personal cost to me of having to find a seconder by circularizing the membership was £229, instead of the £22 which I understand he so airily estimated. I would like to thank the thirteen members who took the trouble to reply to me personally. Their letters showed an openness and generosity towards debate, even from those strongly opposed to me: and this, to my mind, is the springboard for creative vitality. In contrast, I received no personal replies, either for or against, from anyone under fifty. And a reason why I think the under-fifties did not respond, given to me by a member in private conversation: he said, 'If I rock the boat I might lose my Cnuas*.' I see this as the most terrible indictment of the present state of Aosdána. It has become an organization held together by fear, not only of losing money and being kicked out of Aosdána, but also of social blacklisting in the world of the arts. This shows a complete lack of confidence in ourselves. The Toscairí have done nothing to reassure us; there is no 'Bill of Rights', no one has ever said, 'You are free to say what you like here!' The Toscairí have shown no understanding of the fact that we live in a highly secretive class-ridden suspicious society where there is very little in common between people who do not mix economically and socially with each other, and where information is constantly denied to those who have no 'pull'. Suspicion and mistrust is bred by us never having full information on such simple things as –

who has applied to be a member of Aosdána?
how many people take part in elections for the Toscairí: [and who votes for whom?]
which Toscairí turn up for their meetings?
by whom and how were the Standing Orders drafted?

We need a 'Bill of Rights' to protect individuals within Aosdána: we also need a 'Freedom of Information Act' so we can find out what Aosdána is doing and how and why it is doing it. And we need a recognition from every member that we will not be fulfilling our function as described in the inaugural statements unless we all accept that a vibrant culture cannot exist without the full diversity of cultural threads in our society. That means recognition of working-class culture, feminist

*Financial grant.

culture, community culture, popular culture, and recognition of unlabelled individuals who do not easily fit into any particular cultural clan. I wonder why such artists as Pat Murphy, Alice Hanratty, Desmond Egan and Jer O'Leary, for example, are not in Aosdána?

I am coming straight out and saying that the Toscairí have exercised their power to create cliques and factions and have rejected applicants with whose ideology they do not agree. This, to my mind, is the abuse of power: it is no good to attack, for instance, the treatment of dissident artists in the USSR, when we are going so far to reproduce the worst features of their system without copying any of its real benefits. There is no social responsibility shown here at all for the overall development of the arts in this country. Instead there is a petty-minded envy and a determination to crush any artist who threatens the social positions of those who hold the power. Our purpose should be to defend the right of artists to express themselves in any form they want, even if it appears to subvert the status quo and to tarnish the docile image of artists for the snobbish culture-vulture clientèle of the multi-national market.

How can we expect the people of Ireland to support us with their money and how can we expect support from those artists who are not members, when they all see that we do not even respect each other, and that our organization not only mirrors the worst aspects of the state but does things that would not even be tolerated in the Dail? On the question of the Saoi:* I would personally prefer not to have them at all, they seem to me to be in breach of the Constitution's prohibition of titles conferred by the State – but I do think that we should create, as I stated in my paper, a celebration for everyone, where we could all remember past artists as well as present ones.

We must have generosity to one another, and then we will have generosity to other artists who are not in Aosdána. It is Aosdána that can create – and create in public – a climate of

---

* 'wise ones': a title of honour accorded certain eminent members of Aosdána.

excitement and debate about the importance of the arts. Of course we need more money for the arts, but we are better able to negotiate if we show that we are concerned about ourselves as artists, our working conditions, the difference between us, our mental and physical infirmities, the stresses and strains – the late Brendan Behan said he regarded an artist as a healer, and I will add: 'Physician, first heal yourself!' The resolutions on the agenda about race and anti-apartheid are excellent: but unless we apply them to our own society, and indeed, with all their implications, to our own organization, it could appear that we are only using these resolutions to gain ourselves a good public reputation while in our hearts we remain the same.

The greatest crime that can be done to the human being is the killing of the spirit of that person. If we do not change our modes of procedure we are well on the way to killing our own spirits. I am finishing now. And if you do not understand what I am trying to say – that it is not just a question of passing resolutions – it is something of a much more profound and fundamental nature, to do with our relations as human beings and artists – then I must take the debate outside Aosdána.

Dr Margaret MacCurtin, the historian, has said, 'For some reason we on this island and particularly our menfolk, are prone to that mysterious mentality which has been described in Europe as Fascism. What it is in Ireland, I'm not quite sure, but it's the authoritarian mind.' Can an organization with this authoritarian mind be an inspiration to liberate and fulfil the creative instincts in our society? I will carry on this debate in public outside the Arts Council offices, where I will be asking for public participation and support.

Letter To The Press (2)*

Galway,
3 April 87

To the Editor,
The Irish Times:

Sir,
   'Human rights' now seems to be an obsessive priority with the leaders of the Western World. Let me recount my recent experience in the magistrates' court at Newbury, Berkshire, and the denial of human rights to the hundreds of women charged with civil disobedience at the Greenham Common peace camp.
   On 13 December 1986 I was arrested with nearly 100 other women for entering the Cruise-Missile base at Greenham. I attended my trial at Newbury court on 19 March 1987. I observed (and indeed suffered) the following anomalies in the procedure of justice.

---

* This was published in Irish papers, and in The Irish Post in England. It was not published in other English papers to which I sent it. I received a lot of support: but John Arden had one anonymous letter (British stamp) asking him if his wife was a 'Lesbian Pervert like . . . (a list of well-known contemporary women, concluding with the name of the late Countess Markievicz).'

Defendants were not allowed to question the Ministry of Defence Police as to where exactly they were in 'the prohibited area' when they were arrested. The magistrates ruled such questions 'irrelevant'. When defendants asked if this was because of the Official Secrets Act, that question too was ruled 'irrelevant'.

Defendants wished their cases adjourned so that they could seek legal advice as to the legal status of the byelaws under which they were arrested – these byelaws having been specially brought in to deal with the Greenham Peace Camp. This was refused.

Women who insisted on making statements from the dock questioning the morality of the laws protecting nuclear weapons were threatened with contempt of court. But when they ignored this threat they were not charged with contempt but forcibly removed from the dock and thrown out of the courtroom by the police, and the court was cleared.

Dates on which arrests were made did not tally with the prosecution evidence. This should have resulted in the dropping of charges: but the court ignored it. Women in court who drew attention to this were brutally evicted from the premises.

When women are convicted and fined, no effort is made by the authorities to collect the fines on the dates given: months, even years, can go past, and then the women are suddenly arrested and imprisoned for non-payment. The length of such imprisonment seems to bear no relation to the amount of the fine. In addition to gaol sentences, women who refuse to pay their fines are pro-hibited from entering certain counties of the UK for specified periods – a device amounting to internal exile, and regarded with horror when it takes place in the Soviet Union.

In my own case I was subjected to the following phenomena:

On the charge sheet there were no specific charges and the date of arrest did not tally with that given by the chief witness for the prosecution.

In my defence, I began by saying that the laws under which I was charged had been 'abused for the political and military interests of government' and that as an Irish citizen I was aware of a long history of such abuse of the British law . . . As soon as I came to that point my statement was torn out of my hands by the police. When women demanded that I be allowed to continue, I was forcibly removed from the dock and sentenced to seven days imprisonment. I did not hear the court find me *guilty of trespass* (with which I was charged), nor did I hear them give me time to pay a fine – which is normal, 28 days being the regular condition. I was told that I would serve my time in Newbury Police Station which is quite unsuitable for convicted prisoners – no sheets on the uncovered foam-mattress, no light except artificial light, no exercise facilities, and no copies of prison-rules available. I had not expected prison and had no change of clothes or toilet articles, and none were given me.

Imprisonment in a Police Station seems to be a legal grey-area: relatives and friends cannot find out from the authorities where you are serving your sentence, and there seems to be no machinery for providing this information.

When I constantly questioned my legal situation in the Police Station, I was moved – after two nights – to Holloway Gaol. In Holloway, I was knocked down and dragged off to solitary confinement because I said I wished to attend Sunday worship at both the Catholic and Anglican services. I had been told that other prisoners were allowed to do this: but, in my case, it appeared I had to declare myself as belonging to a specific religious sect.

These abuses against the Greenham Common women have been going on with increasing intensity over the past three-and-a-half years. Because they are now considered 'normal practice', they are no longer considered newsworthy by the British media. Greenham Common women, because of our constancy and non-violent determination to get rid of weapons of mass destruction, are dangerous to the governments of Thatcher and Reagan: our human rights, therefore, are irrelevant.

Yours, etc.,
Margaretta D'Arcy

P.S. During the 48 hours I was in Holloway I was strip-searched twice.

Power to the Sisters!

Two weeks at Greenham, July/August, 1987

'I want the names of those women who blockaded the *Morning Star*, I want Sarah Hipperson – who I know took part in the blockade – to expel herself from Greenham, I'm going to publicly publish Sarah's home address. If Wilmette Brown had been a white woman, she would not have made such a fuss when I publicly insulted her at the Moscow Workshop on Greenham. I am not a racialist. There is reason to believe that the King's Cross Women are infiltrated by the CIA. We have access to computer files: so we can investigate everyone at Greenham.'*

It was on Thursday morning, 6 August 1987, I was in the Friends' Meeting House at Newbury where Greenham Women gather to use the washing facilities, when this phone-message was delivered. It was for Sarah Hipperson, to be passed on to her 'by any of the women at "Yellow Gate"' where she lives. My blood ran cold: *I* was one of the women who had *picketed* the *Morning Star* – now it was being referred to as a 'blockade', a CIA-led operation, our backgrounds were being 'investigated' from computer-files – what computer-files? where? who had fed what into them?

---

* Ironically, Sarah Hipperson *was* banished from Greenham – in October: but by the State, as part of a bail-condition.

One might think we were in the middle of a reversed McCarthy witch-hunt, or an all-women gangster-film – 'Get outa my territory or you'll be liquidated!'

What *was* going on?

The background

Moscow, 23–27 June 1987, World Congress of Women 'Towards 2000 – without Nuclear Weapons! For Peace, Equality, Development.' Ten British women, from Greenham, and from Greenham Support-groups, attended this congress. Breakdown of the ten: three from Yellow Gate (the main gate); one from Violet Gate: permanent residents of the Greenham Women's Peace Camp outside the RAF/USAF cruise-missile Base. Two from the local Newbury Cruise-watch. Four from the Camden Greenham Support-group (London).

Tensions and Splits in Moscow

The Yellow Gate women made three public interventions in three separate sessions of the Congress:

1. They challenged Gorbachev's right to speak at a Women's Congress when his wife seated beside him was silent.
2. They denounced the cheap exploitative emotionalism of an American woman millionaire who presented a childrens' ballet resembling a Coca-Cola ad: her message, 'If every child throughout the world had a computer, it would save the world.'
3. They questioned Soviet women, asking them to justify their government's deployment of nuclear weapons.

The Camden women called a meeting in an attempt to bring the Yellow Gate women to heel, saying they were disruptive and were giving the Greenham-image a bad name: they should have been satisfied with the standing ovation that Gorbachev had procured for them.

The Non-Aligned Third World Intervenes

The Moscow Greenham Workshop: this was held during the Congress as one of the public subsidiary activities. It was attended by about 30 women, from all over the world. Who was to define what was to go on in it? There had already been discussions in London. The women from Greenham had stated that only those who lived permanently at the peace camp itself could give an accurate picture of the daily life there. The support-group women agreed.

But in Moscow the support-group women said that no one was really interested in the anatomy of Greenham, that they wanted the slogan 'Greenham Women Are Everywhere', with everyone singing Greenham songs, a much more generalized and sentimental approach.

Sarah Hipperson said, no: and insisted on the original agreed format, with women from Greenham talking about their specific work (the monthly stopping of the cruise convoys, the daily evictions, the arrests, the court-appearances, the imprisonments, and their involvement with the support-groups); the support-groups would then have an opportunity to make their own statements of their involvement.

This went very satisfactorily, until Wilmette Brown (from the King's Cross Women's Centre in London, representing 'Black Women for Wages for House work' and 'Housewives in Dialogue') got up to speak of her groups' involvement and support at Greenham Common. The King's Cross delegates – Wilmette and Selma James – were at the Congress as part of a world-wide movement, with a petition which called for implementation of a 1985 UN decision to count women's unwaged work in the GNP of every country: and also they welcomed the new Soviet *Glasnost* policy reforming women's workload in the USSR. Wilmette's main contribution was to analyse why black women should support Greenham, and why they felt alienated by the present white predominance in the women's peace movement. She had laid this out very clearly in her book *Black Women and the Peace Movement*, published a few years back, and now she recapitulated the same argument: that it is third-world women 'who have paid the highest price in hard unwaged and low-waged labour for the enormous world military budget', and that the black women's struggle for peace (i.e., Vietnam agitation in the USA) has virtually vanished from official peace-movement history.

No sooner had she begun, when the six women from the support-groups ostentatiously left the workshop. As she concluded her speech, they returned. Katrina Howse (from Yellow Gate, Greenham) was later to claim that one of them made 'a blatantly racist verbal and physical attack on Wilmette Brown'. A Native-American at the workshop got up and said this was a classic example of why black women do not feel they are part of white women's struggles – as soon as a black woman speaks, white women refuse to listen.

The crisis was not resolved in Moscow.

Continued Crisis at Greenham

Two long and painful meetings were called at Greenham, after the Moscow Congress, to try and find out what had happened, from the parties involved, and to heal the split. Demands were made by the Yellow Gate women (including myself, who had not been to Moscow: but I was that week at Yellow Gate) that underlying racism in the Greenham movement and the British peace movement generally, must be recognized and eradicated. I had always felt that the general silence of the peace movement towards England's-Vietnam-in-Ireland was in part racist. But Wilmette was present at both.

I was at the second one: I witnessed racist behaviour. Some women tried to prevent Wilmette from speaking, and both she and the only other black woman present were heckled, sneered-at, jeered-at and laughed-at. Wilmette said it was a 'lynch-mob', reminding her of what she experienced in early days of Black Civil Rights in the USA. Nothing was resolved.

The Falling Star

On 14 July, an article had appeared in the *Morning Star*, largely consisting of the impressions of the support-group women; it was headlined, 'GREENHAM GOES TO MOSCOW' and reported: 'British peace women have returned from the recent world congress in Moscow with some positive images of the Soviet Union. It didn't take them long to see through the anti-Socialist propaganda rampant in Britain and they found the only barrier was language.'

The three women from Yellow Gate who had been to Moscow – Sarah Hipperson, Katrina Howse, and Beth Junor – objected strongly to the article.

Sarah demanded a right-of-reply. When it was refused, she wrote a letter in which she said:

For nearly 6 years we have consistently taken a firm non-aligned position on Nuclear Weapons and Nuclear Power. Rejecting them all. Resisting justification and deterrence. Defending peoples and the planet earth against all of the Nuclear States. We have taken our position not as a tactic but as an 'absolute' – a commitment to a non-violent non-nuclear world. This article deliberately sets out to undermine this long-held position – it suggests a pro-Soviet stance. What a gift to President Reagan, Mrs Thatcher, and all those who brand us as puppets of the Soviet State, from the *Morning Star* and all those who participated in this article. There is more to be said about this article and all that happened in Moscow at the Congress but since you have refused us space it will be said somewhere else . . .

Our position is clearly shared by President Mugabe of Zimbabwe. At the closing of the congress he said: the Nuclear threat was too serious to leave to the Super-powers – an élite club of privileged – to solve. He spoke out with confidence for the non-aligned.

This letter was refused publication in the paper. Greenham

women then decided to put a picket on the *Morning Star* until the editor came to speak with us.

The *Morning Star* was at a historical crux. The building had just been sold over the heads of the workers without their being told, the workers themselves had been given two-weeks notice. On the day we arrived there, a big meeting was to be held to discuss the future of the paper. I don't apologize for the cliché: men, whether MOD police or workers on a communist paper, always seem to behave in the same way in a crisis – no matter how sympathetic they are as individuals and supportive of your cause; when the boss calls they run behind his locked doors and shout sexist abuse at any body of women that appears to be threatening them. In this case, pseudo-political abuse too: we were a bunch of CIA agents and we deserved to be beaten-up (fortunately the presence of some women with cameras prevented this).

Finally the *Morning Star* went to higher authority and brought in the Metropolitan Police to clear up their self-inflicted mess: we were as astonished as the police when we faced each other on the communist steps. A sergeant stepped forward and said he'd been called in 'by the firm, to negotiate,' and that the chief executive of the *Morning Star* (who was a woman, Mary Rosser) was prepared to talk to us in her office. We said, 'Are you aware that the "firm" is the *Morning Star*? whose stated policy is to overthrow the state and your role in helping to maintain it?' He said he was not aware: he was just doing his job.

So Wilmette Brown and Sarah Hipperson went in to speak with Ms Rosser; who told them that *she* had not been aware, of Sarah's letter. On her desk, however, was lying another letter, or card from the two Newbury Cruisewatch women who had been at Moscow, thanking the *Morning Star* for its funding* of

---

* The four women from the Greenham peace-camp had not been able to get sufficient tickets for the Congress from the British National Assembly of Women who were organizing their distribution: but they wrote to Mrs Raisa Gorbachev, who sent them four free tickets. The *Morning Star* funding was in fact a 'whip-round' among the *MS* staff, about £10 odd; according to Lynette Edwell.

their trip . . . The message included thanks from one of the Camden support-group, to the *Morning Star* for its excellent article. It seems likely that Ms Rosser had not intended the picket's delegation to see this letter.

But she was very polite: she said that as Greenham women had put in a complaint to the Press Council she would have to wait for the result before taking further action. The editor of the *Morning Star*, meanwhile, was in the corridor downstairs, 'holding the barricades': we saw his frightened eyes behind spectacles in a puffy white face.

Our picket commenced at one o'clock and at 5.30 we left.

1 We had had support on the doorstep from the King's Cross Women's Centre, women representing 'Wages for House Work Campaign', 'Black Women for Wages for House work', 'English Collective of Prostitutes', 'Legal Action for Women', 'Wages Due Lesbians', 'Win Visible', 'Women against Rape'.

Savage Aftermath

The MOD police had obviously read the *Morning Star* piece: and were now confirmed in their opinion that Greenham women are all KGB agents. A day or two later, when the cruise went out, for the first-time ever four arrested women were handcuffed, on the ground, their faces pressed into the road, and then dragged face-down to the police vehicles. They were dragged face-down out of the vehicles and thrust into the cells at Newbury Police Station. One of the women thus mistreated lost consciousness. The four were later released without being charged.

I was thrown down by PC4781, in what I can only describe as a foul-tackle from the Rugby field. I sustained badly-bruised ribs and a lacerated arm which then went septic, one of my legs was also heavily bruised. The CID came to the peace-camp with warrants to search campers' belongings at all the gates. This was the first time such a search had happened there for years. They took away numerous articles such as paint and bolt-cutters, Sarah Hipperson's bicarb-of-soda, a woman's family notebook, and a manuscript of mine containing the text of an opera I have been working on for the past year. They refused to give us receipts. Mr Bull, the chief of these detectives, uttered an unfortunate joke, which I took seriously: I understood him to say that receipts were 'irrelevant as documents can always disappear'. I have since made a formal complaint about this remark.

Conclusions

What can we make of all this strange story, and what was the reason for the extraordinary phone-call to the Meeting House?

Because I am a dramatist, and because I have been writing at length about sectarianism among the early Christians, I will quite brazenly put forward some possible scenarios.

1. On Thursday, 23 July, Gorbachev announced that he would remove the last obstacle to the withdrawal of cruise from NATO countries. Had we won? Would we soon be leaving Greenham in a great victory parade? The press came down to ask us. We said, no: the camp would continue until all nuclear weapons were withdrawn and the resources given back to the people. Our principled decision was a grave embarrassment to the British Communist Party, which was anyway in internal disarray. They had already bragged to Gorbachev that Greenham was *their* operation, as implied in the *Morning Star* article. So they had to destabilize the inconveniently independent Greenham women by means of internal faction led by their subsidized excursionists from the Support-groups. They hoped, in their muddle, that if they could thus *deliver* Greenham successfully into the Soviet bloc, Gorbachev would quid-pro-quo save their collapsing newspaper.

2. Why did Greenham support-groups so viciously attack the involvement of the King's Cross Women's Centre at Greenham, and accuse *them* of being the destabilizing influence? When some middle-class Englishwomen play at politics – one foot into feminist revolution and the other still clinging on to the mediocre career-values of a patriarchal

imperialist Britain – they are thrown off-balance by the sophistication, knowledge, and experience of two such internationally-minded women as Selma James and Wilmette Brown. The idea that the wage-value of house work, and of ostensibly non-productive low-waged women's labour, should be included in a nation's GNP, is one that would turn on its head the whole in-stitutionalized vulgar-marxist concept of the industrial proletariat in developed countries being the vanguard of the revolution: and by implication it diminishes the role of the Communist Party. It also threatens the *détente* between East and West by bringing in the *South* – the non-aligned countries of the third world – to determine its *own* future. For Wilmette, a black woman, to propound all this with so much certainty, in the demoralized *un*-certainty of the left under Mrs Thatcher's third successive government, was too much to take: and the white middle-class women unconsciously retreated into a traditional 'memsahib' *whites-only* enclosure.

I could throw in other convoluted scenarios: that it was all to do with the rapes at Molesworth peace camp by male peace-activists, which the peace movement in general, and some women at Greenham, had attempted to deny – that it was all to do with the piece of Greenham Common land acquired for Greenham Women with the help of Yoko Ono's money – that it somehow related to a current court case challenging the legality of Newbury Council's bye-laws – or that it arose from the classic contradictions of the gospel parable, where those that had worked the vineyard all day in the heat of the sun got no more money than those who turned up in the last hour (i.e., how to evaluate the labour of women who had given up everything over the last five years to live permanently at Greenham, in contrast to those who claimed to be Greenham Women but still lived in their own homes?).

It is probably a mixture of all these complexities.

But the slogan 'Greenham Women Are Everywhere' most reminds me of the struggle in early Christianity when St Paul effectively bypassed Jesus' message of the immediate Kingdom of Heaven on earth, in favour of the Hereafter, mythologizing, institutionalizing, nullifying.

However, unlike St Paul, I feel confident that the confusion and faction-fighting, which has always been part of Greenham, is only an indication of the continuing revolutionary development and dynamic of the camp: it *strengthens* commitment, in fact; commitment to a women-only movement without the 'orthodox' old-guard structures. As a result of all these experiences, we made a new slogan: 'Up-front, In Public, At The Time!': which completely, I hope, throws out-of-the-window for ever the memsahib mentality of covert character-assassination behind the filofax combined with overt white gloves and a visiting-card.

Epilogue

An experience with the Thames Valley police (who are also the police used to protect the Greenham-Common cruise): it took place the day after I left Greenham to return to Ireland.

Galway,
20 August 1987:

To the Editor, *The Irish Times*:

THREATS AND THE LAW

Sir,

I wish to protest at the treatment accorded passengers on Slattery's coach from London to Tralee on August 7th.

The coach stopped at a service station near Chippenham, on its way to the Irish ferry at Fishguard. The driver locked the door so that we could not get out, and then said there had been a complaint, one of the passengers claimed to have been robbed en route of £150. The police had been called and we were all to wait for them.

When they arrived (uniformed police and CID plain-clothes) they entered the coach and announced that unless the money was recovered – and they didn't mind how! – we would *all* be arrested, strip-searched, and collectively charged with the theft in Chippenham Police Station, thereby missing our boat to Ireland.

During all this, a five-year-old child wanted to go to the toilet: her father was not allowed to accompany her, and she had to go with a total stranger from the service station.

No £150 was forthcoming as a result of these threats, and in the end – after threequarters of an hour – the coach was allowed to proceed without further action from the police.

As far as I understand the British law, the police were acting outside their proper powers. They have no right to make a collective arrest and strip-search, I believe they only threatened it because we were an *Irish* coach-load; they were calculating that knowledge of the Prevention of Terrorism Act and its ramifications would prevent us standing up for proper treatment.

What tourists will want to travel through England to Ireland if this is the treatment they can look for as they travel? I hope and expect that our Government will take some action to prevent a repetition.

Yours, etc.,
Margaretta D'Arcy

Letter To The Press (3)

This letter was published in the Irish national press and the local County Galway press. It gave me my first experience of the professional anonymous 'pro-life' letter-writing lobby. One reply (British stamp) was addressed from 'Bethlehem': 'Madam Herod – will you tell the press why you had us murdered? Hoping you will not die roaring.' Another said, 'If you show your face in Dublin, you will be burnt to death . . .'

Galway,
18 Jan 1987

To the Editor:

Sir,

The logical conclusion of the High Court order (preventing women's centres from counselling and assisting pregnant women to travel abroad for abortions) is that any individual citizen giving such advice to individuals can be criminalized. I have helped women in this way in the past and will do so again. As an Irishwoman under Irish law I will thus be a criminal? But I will also be upholding the UN Declaration of Human Rights – Article 19: the right to give, receive, and impart information – which, upon this issue, I would put above any Irish law that attempts to deny it.

Yours, etc.,
Margaretta D'Arcy

PART THREE

Arden & D'Arcy

Whose Is The Kingdom?

Two essays on the background to nine radio-plays for the BBC, which took us six years to research and complete. They were written in 1987.

Pious Founders by John Arden

'You shall pray,' the headmaster used to pronounce in our school chapel twice a Sunday during the 1940s, 'for the memory of our pious founders . . .' and then followed a long list of English gentlemen from the sixteenth century onward who had given portions of their incomes (however earned, and *that* was not gone into) toward building, equipping, and staffing the establishment in which we were fostered. The same headmaster had a nice line in indoctrinating school-leavers: 'Always remember, you have been trained here, not to lead but to *serve*.' And then he would hand out booklets giving details of possible careers in the Palestine Police, the Indian Civil Service, or the East African Rifles. When, in his classrooms, I learned Roman History, it fell easily into this pattern. We understood that the 'good emperors' ran an empire very much on the model of the one that Queen Victoria's great men had left to us, and the 'bad emperors' did their best to sabotage it by wanton self-indulgence (although the *tradition of service* in the Roman army and civil administration was usually strong enough to prevent too much damage being done).

Constantine, for example, was obviously a 'good emperor'. He had to be: he was a sort of 'pious founder' himself, being the first one to adopt Christianity, whereas the persecution of Christians had been a notorious feature of the reign of the most notorious of the 'bad emperors', Nero. Roman History, however, was not a very important subject in my particular course of study, and my lessons in it terminated just at the point where a few contradictions and ambiguities were becoming apparent. Politically-speaking, it seemed that Diocletian, who was emperor at the end of the 3rd century just before Constantine, had been 'good'. He was not personally debauched, he put his army and civil servants under very proper control (tradition of service or not, they *had* been getting debauched), and his reforms in general made it possible for Constantine to exert a 'moderate and humane' rule. But Diocletian had also been the most deadly determined persecutor of Christianity. This particular period of the Roman Empire was therefore rather difficult, and indeed the school curriculum tended to shy away from it. Everything after the end of the first century AD was treated in a perfunctory fashion, and the emperors who followed Constantine were briefly summarized as symptomatic of 'Decline and Fall', which we were not encouraged to worry about – 1946 and 1947 were not good years for either the Palestine Police or the Indian Service, even though East Africa was still going strong: and morale had to be kept up.

Later on, I discovered that Constantine was held responsible (by such as Dante) for all manner of things that went wrong with the Church in the Middle Ages, and also that during the English Reformation there were calls upon Henry VIII and his son Edward VI to become 'new Constantines' and place England, under their leadership, in the forefront of revived European Christendom. Some of my old school's 'pious founders' might probably have contributed to these calls.

So a series of plays for the BBC on the rise of the religion from a persecuted underground cult to the official faith of a great empire seemed, at first glance, to be inevitably a series of plays about Constantine. If credit was to be taken, he had already grabbed it all: if blame was to be allotted (and by 1981 I had read Gibbon who thought that the main cause of 'Decline and Fall' was in fact Christianity), then he would be taking the lion's share. Most modern historians seemed to agree. The character of the emperor, they said, was murkily enigmatic, superstitious, power-hungry, often cruel, always efficiently pragmatic: his personality was crucial to the events of his reign. He had seen a vision, or had thought he had seen a vision, or let it be put about that he saw a vision: a cross in the sky with an order-of-the-day in letters of fire, 'Win with this battle-flag!' And from then on he did it more or less all by himself, just as Diocletian, all by himself, had tried to annihilate the Christians. On his arch in Rome, Constantine's inscription still stands to inform us of his personal responsibility: 'with the guidance of divinity and the loftiness of his own mind, he freed . . . the republic . . .' *etc.* Of course, at other times, he also let it be inferred that he was a *servant* rather than a *leader*, although such protestations are not necessarily worth any more than those of British headmasters laying their charge upon cadets of the old imperial officer-caste.

We read in the *Concise Oxford Dictionary of the Christian Church* that '*Constantine's* policy was to unite the Church to the secular State by the closest possible ties.' Paul Johnson in his *History of Christianity* asks, 'How could the Christian Church, apparently quite willingly, accommodate *this weird megalomaniac* in its theocratic system?' Fr. Ricciotti, author of *The Age of the Martyrs*, describes the enormous changes that took place under Constantine's rule, states that no one at the time could know how they would finish or when equilibrium could be expected to be restored, and then adds: 'No one was able to answer such questions, perhaps not even the *main cause of the changes, Constantine himself*.' (My emphases in these quotations.)

So it looked, when Margaretta D'Arcy and I began to read all the books we could get together on this period, that as we would be dealing with one main historical character – a Napoleon or a Queen Elizabeth I (whose lives we had already seen serialized on TV), or a James Connolly (about whose involvements in revolutionary struggles we had already written a series of six stage-plays), our dramatic form would be quite a simple one: Youth, Maturity, Old Age, with a crowd of subordinate personages floating in and out of the events as they went along. Our commissioned theme – the development of a religion rather than of a man – would be automatically reflected in his words, actions, and internal meditations. He would, of course, be partnered, and at times opposed, by a 'second lead', a figure – or figures – representing 'the Church', just as he represented 'the State'. The assumption was that Christianity had at that time a fundamentally unified voice, with certain disruptions from 'heretics', and that when Church and State entered into debate they would do so in scenes like that in Shaw's *Saint Joan* between the Earl of Warwick and Bishop Cauchon. We started our preliminary reading at least three years before we were sufficiently on top of the material to begin writing. By the time our first words were on paper, all the preconceptions had completely changed.

It had, for instance, become apparent that Constantine was by no means the great decision-maker: nearly everything he did came upon him out of the blue, he spent his whole life trying desperately to keep up with the forces that were swaying his empire, and he died without having anywhere secured any form of equilibrium. When he tried to handle this strange phenomenon called Christianity he was even more at a loss than are modern Western governments trying to 'stop communism': and just as the word 'communism' can be used to cover all varieties of dissidence from liberal American film-scriptwriters to black nationalists in South Africa, to Trotskyite red-brigades in Europe, to British coal-miners on strike, to the IRA, to post-Maoist China, Sandinist Nicaragua, or post-Stalinist

Russia, including by the way, the Women's Movement, CND, Greenpeace, and Polish Solidarity, so the Christian community at the beginning of the fourth century contained so many different schools of thought that to talk of 'the Church' and 'the heresies' totally begs the question. Moreover, all these variations claimed to derive directly from Jesus of Nazareth, and most of them had books to prove it. Even so apparently simple a statement as 'toleration and imperial favour were given (by Constantine) to the Church' – from the *Oxford Dictionary of the Christian Church* again – became almost meaningless. What Church? And what was to be tolerated? And how did he – or anyone else in the empire – understand any of these terms?

By the time Constantine made his bid for empire, his world had filled up, without his being aware of it, with an enormous number of drifting individuals and groups, all of them believing themselves to be Christians, and very few of them in any unity with each other. They all represented what Diocletian's government had termed 'subversion', and had frantically, unwillingly, attempted to suppress. Constantine made one big decision: not to suppress but to encourage. And then, after that, he was as it were at their mercy. The very nature of his decision is historically in doubt. A vision? Perhaps. Or perhaps such a description was no more than a convenient shorthand for a state-of-affairs to which he had come without really understanding how. At all events, his centrality in any dramatic setting-out of the events began to be less and less important. Our plays took on an entirely different shape. A number of stories about the interweaving lives and ideas of these individual 'Christians' took over the narrative structure, and the figure of the emperor was almost lost in their ebbing and flowing. One central point in the overall story remained: the Council of Nicaea, a formal meeting-place between the old State and the new Church, a little over half-way between Constantine's vision and his baptism and death. In our episode dealing with the Council there are two long conversations, duologues of the Emperor and the Bishop of Cordova, which approach nearest to the Shavian model. The second of these, although at first sight it seems to promise a regular debate between Church and State, turned out to be more of an exposition of how decisions of great weight are often made almost by accident before they are actually decided upon. The first conversation also emerged on the page as rather an odd one: it ought to have been an explication by Bishop Hosius of the basic difference between Christianity and Judaism, but it ended up as a confrontation between two different ideas of history.

The more our work on the plays progressed, the more I became aware that these two ideas of history were the very root of the problem of this period. The history of Rome, by which Romans understood 'the history of civilization', commenced with myth and legend – Aeneas on his travels, Romulus and Remus fed by the wolf, gods and goddesses overseeing the foundation of the City which was to master the world. Livy, who wrote the 'definitive' account of all this, was not unduly credulous: he told the old stories in the full knowledge that they were a kind of fairy tale, and he introduced a commonsense political and sociological comment into them from his earliest chapters. In this, he followed the Greek tradition of Herodotus. Later writers, such as Tacitus, were sceptical critical observers of the political facts of life: when we read them today we are aware that they lived in a society run on much the same principles as our own – power of money and armed force, party-intrigue, class-rivalries, concretely determining the people's destinies. Again, the Greek tradition: Thucydides, Xenophon. The nearer to their own day they approach in their narrative, the less reliance they place on paranormal phenomena. Of course, they describe portents: Romans believed in the scientific validity of extra-terrestial signs and did not see how government could be carried on without taking them into account. But there is a great deal of difference between, say, ghosts walking in the streets just before the Ides of March (which notably did *not* deter Julius Caesar from going to meet the Senate), and the miraculous ascension-into-heaven of Romulus (even though Livy does hint that he may actually have been secretly murdered). 'The Gods', in short, issued warnings and encouragements: but in general they did not physically intervene. Humanity was responsible for its own successes and failures, and rational history is the reporting of them.

But according to Christianity (of whatever sect or tendency) a vital and unprecedented divine intervention *had* taken place, only three hundred years before Constantine became emperor. Which meant, of course, between seven and eight hundred years *after* the divinely-blessed Foundation of the City. If the Nazareth Carpenter was what the Christians said he was, instead of being merely an obscure rural philosopher who fell foul of the colonial police, then mythological magic was much more up-to-date and decisive in its operations than any educated Roman of the early Empire would have cared to acknowledge. And moreover the Christians were able to produce an entire corpus of hitherto unknown history-books to show this to have been the case.

Once you accepted the divinity of Jesus Christ, then you had to accept the truth of the Jewish scriptures (and their sequels – not only our 'New Testament', but a bewildering array of other gospels, epistles, apocalypses, and apocryphas, not at all reduced to a canon) wherein God's intervention had been constant in human affairs since the creation of the world. To read Livy alongside the *Book of Judges*, or Tacitus alongside the *Acts of the Apostles*, must have been a disturbing experience. To start with, the authors of Holy Writ were not really its 'authors': they took dictation, as it were, from the Almighty; and such a source could not be doubted. If it said in the *Book of Kings* that Elijah was caught up into heaven in a fiery chariot, there was absolutely no room for any cynical alternative version (such as Elisha privately knifing him and disposing of the corpse in order to obtain leadership of the prophetic cabal). And yet it

was clear that these books did contain real history, not necessarily more erroneous than Herodotus (and everyone knew
Herodotus had made certain mistakes). And if Elijah and Ahab
were basically 'true', as they certainly seemed to be, then what
of Herod, and Caiaphas; what of Jesus himself, whose
miraculous resurrection and ascension had somehow slipped
out of the regular imperial records? The arguments fed each
other, both forward and back . . . It was as though modern
history had been retouched by Homer, with Jerusalem and
Galilee as his narrative centres instead of Troy and Ithaca.
Pontius Pilate was a real Roman who could be looked up in the
archives: and he had signed the death-warrant for the Immeasurable Infinite . . .?

Did this therefore invalidate the whole of Livy and his
colleagues? How could it? Rome existed, still in charge, still
civilizing the world.

Two possible explanations. One: that God's Adversary
rather than the old gods had made Rome great, reaching its
height of power just in time to damn itself by presiding over the
Crucifixion. And, two: that the Christians' One True God had
been disguisedly fostering the greatness of Rome throughout
those previous seven-and-a-half centuries, expressly for the
purpose of providing an imperial system that could most
adequately receive the New Gospel (after, of course, a certain
time-lag of hostility and misunderstanding).

The first explanation was obviously impossible, except to
thoroughly subversive elements who would have opposed
imperial power in any case. The second one was in fact adopted
almost as soon as Constantine's government began to accept
rather than repel Christianity. Eusebius, Bishop of Caesarea,
wrote his *History of the Church* as an immediate ideological
justification of the new policy and a guide to its fulfilment. He
made it clear that he was compiling the definitive sequel to
Holy Writ, taking up the story from the end of the *Acts of the
Apostles*, and fitting it carefully into both traditions of history,
Greco-Roman rationality and Hebraic credulity. His book

was taken by Constantine's government as an official expression of its historical philosophy: and it led to certain consequences.

1. Faith rather than reason became essential to political technique.
2. Eusebius's view of the Church (i.e., that St Paul had been correct, with his acceptance of the right of Empire to rule the material world while the Church disposed of humanity's eternal destinies) prevailed over all alternative schools of thought (e.g., that the Kingdom of God meant social revolution here-and-now, casting the mighty from their seats, exalting the humble and meek). From which followed, that the Pauline strand of Christianity was correct in other ways too: the hierarchy of bishops and clergy, the subordination of women, the deprecation of individual prophetic voices, and so forth.
3. All those who did not agree with the Pauline view could officially be described as 'heretics', a word which previously had been meaningless to those, outside the Christian community, who saw all sorts of Christians denouncing each other but had no standard by which to assess the merits of the disputes.
4. Hostility to Jews by Christians was assured for ages to come. If the Roman Empire had been pre-ordained as the worldly receptacle for Christ's Spiritual Kingdom, then the guilt of the Crucifixion could hardly be Roman, and those parts of Holy Writ putting all the blame on the Jews must be absolutely true.

But Eusebius's book alone could not have supported these huge alterations in the imperial way of looking upon the world. The theory it put forward had to be confirmed by administrative action. So Constantine and the Pauline bishops found themselves arranging the Council of Nicaea in what appears to be the very year Eusebius finished writing. The

Council was intended to clear the decks of all ideological and legal and historical confusion by establishing the main aspects of Eusebius's argument as an official part of Empire: and it did this, finally, through repression and censorship. Dissident Christians were banished by government edict, and their books were burnt. Constantine himself was accorded the title of 'Thirteenth Apostle' and his 'vision' became part of history. Within little more than half a century, indeed, the Emperor Theodosius was to take Nicaea to its logical conclusion: and *all* canonically-authorized Holy Writ became a mandatory part of history, all imperial servants were compelled to be 'correct' Christians.

Myth and legend had been brought in to surround the person of a living emperor, and to shore up his groping policies. Constantine's invocation of the miraculous was not at all comparable to the formalistic deification of dead emperors that had been happening for generations: it was much more akin to the hysterical assertions of Caligula or Elagabalus, who identified their own persons with various pagan gods and so incurred the scorn and hatred of their better-informed subjects. The only difference was: those 'bad emperors' failed, while Constantine – at least partly – succeeded. Nearly everything else decided at Nicaea was very soon evaded: heresies did not disappear, bishops did not remain invariably closely associated with, and approving of, secular state policies, and the authority of the 'Thirteenth Apostle' gave way (in the West) to the authority of the Bishop of Rome as Pope. But even today the idea of immediate divine intervention is still surprisingly strong in Christian parts of the world. Only recently, for example, I read that the President of the United States is impressed by prophecies of 'Armageddon', and may well be conducting his Middle-East affairs on that basis. If he doesn't really believe this himself, at least he finds it useful to have many of his voters believe that he believes it . . .

If heretics were censored and repressed, so, too, was official history. It is remarkable how hard it is to discover what really went on in the years covered by *Whose Is The Kingdom*? When Acts of State are presented as a religious revelation to be accepted by an act of faith, the world is given one big lie and must learn to make the best of it. For dramatists living and working some 1,650 years later, there is only one course: to invent. By and large, we have invented the areas of dissidence which church-and-state 'magic' endeavoured to 'wish away'.

The Moon of The Dispossessed
by Margaretta D'Arcy

I came to explore the wreck.
The words are purposes.
The words are maps.
I came to see the damage that was done
and the treasures that prevail.

Adrienne Rich

Patriarchy is a religion of the entire planet and whether it takes
the form of Hinduism or Buddhism or Christianity or Judaism
or Freudianism or Marxism or Maoism, it is a religion of male
worship . . . (women should therefore leave patriarchal religion entirely, not just because its laws and rules are unfair but
because) its whole symbol system and mythic system is utterly
gynocidal.

Mary Daly

I put these and other cuttings (from daily papers) on the wall of
my workroom to prepare me for *Whose Is The Kingdom?*

Scholars Defend Liberation Theology.
A group of leading Catholic theologians sharply criticized
Vatican officials yesterday for attacks on liberation theologians
whose followers are linked to Third World political struggles
(and) on feminists. 'Within the Church we have also seen
people defamed, forbidden to teach theology, rendered suspect
of infidelity to the Christian message . . .'

Irish Times

If a man murders his wife, it is only natural to ask why? My starting-point for these plays was to find out why Fausta, wife of Constantine, was murdered by her husband. I could not find an answer in any of the history books written by men shaped within the Judaeo-Christian culture. They skipped rapidly over the murder, implying a kind of regrettable accident . . . 'This dark and unaccountable occurrence would seem to detract from the greatness of Constantine's blah blah blah . . .' It had never been fully documented in the minutes of the efficient Roman administration, so, therefore, it could not have been 'important', so, therefore, it is not necessary for us to know . . .

Unexplained gaps in history cause historians to pass them by and carry on: if they were to stop and really explore they would discover that most of history in fact consists of gaps. To fill them in would be to divert the flow of interpretation from a comfortable 'mainstream' into a series of eddies representing the so-called 'losing' side in one historical conflict after another. 'Mainstream' is winners' history: eddies and backwaters are where the losers still survive, refusing to be entirely written-out. I have never accepted that ideological conquests have ever been complete, or indeed that it is possible for them to be complete until the root cause of the conflicts are understood and dealt with.

I believe that all conflicts are at root one conflict: the rivalry between *we* and *I*, between co-operation and domination; and the constant refusal of the human race to recognize this. A little story: recently, at the Celtic Film Festival in Inverness, where I was showing my polemical video *Circus Exposé of the New Cultural Church*, I was engaged in an ancient argy-bargy – 'why were there no women on any of the public discussion-platforms?' – with a very 'important' media-executive, a sort of ITV Constantine. I asked him did he resent having been born from his mother's womb? His reply was: 'When I was in the womb, we were *we*, I was a dependant. When I was born, I became *I*, an independent.' *I* am the Lord thy God. Thou shalt have no other gods before *me* . . .

In 1981, John Arden and I accepted the task proposed by Richard Imison of the BBC radio-drama department, to write a series of plays about the beginnings of Christianity. We decided that we should focus our story upon the consolidation of Christianity in Constantine's reign at the Council of Nicaea. Richard's own interest in Constantine was that he, like the emperor, had had a vision, at the age of nine . . . The last big series of broadcast plays on the Christian theme was Dorothy L. Sayers' *The Man Born To Be King*. She was a committed anglican Christian: in the middle of World War II the plays were her statement against Nazism and neo-paganism. She also wrote a stage-play in 1951, *The Emperor Constantine*: this coincided with the onset of the Cold War and the beginnings of the McCarthyite persecution in the USA, circumstances reflected in her evident approval of the orthodoxy of Nicaea. To me, Nicaea represented a triumphalism of conformity which has led directly to the triumphalism of those who would sacrifice the whole world to nuclear destruction for the sake of Christianity. And it was a male triumphalism: in the early church women had often held positions of high authority – even bishoprics, we now discover from certain feminist historians. But after the Council, never again . . . and also, never again, the free circulation of the 'gnostic' gospels alongside the four 'canonical' ones. In some of these works there are texts stating outright that the 'giver of life' is the female principle. I began to ask myself if the murder of Fausta (which happened immediately after Nicaea) was not part and parcel of the same process: the bishops killed Woman as a threat to 'their' religion, the emperor killed 'his' woman as an interference with *his* god-given rule . . .?

It was said to me, in joke, that I was 'writing a play, not making a revolution'. I doubt if anyone said that to Dorothy L. Sayers. The reason for the joke was that I had asserted it was impossible to understand the history of Nicaea without first experiencing the various shifts and debates in modern feminism: and also the liberation theology in the Third World, which has revitalized so much of what Nicaea had declared 'heretical' – Christ as human-being involved with the struggles of subject-peoples of empire, Christ as bodily healer, as provider of food, as 'subversive' challenger of both military and theocratic power. This meant travel, and of course the BBC drama department had no money for that type of research: we would have to make do with books, but to find the right books and buy them cost more money than we were able to afford at the time.

But the books did not answer my questions. How can plays be written with only questions and no answers? There has to be some *story*: after all, plays are just acted stories. And the radio-form we were using gave such great scope for story-telling: the imagination could roam without boundaries. Now it so happened at about the same time there was a dramatic change in my fortunes – the Irish government had set up a scheme called Aosdána to 'honour artists' and to help them financially with their work. And I was one of the lucky ones to receive a grant. I could now buy all the books I needed, I could carry out my own creative cultural experiments with other women, and I could travel.

1981 was a crossroads year for the dispossessed and the dissidents: the Irish prisoners' campaign for political status, the growth of Solidarity in Poland, the Women's Peace Camp at the USAF base on Greenham Common, the struggles in Central America.

And then, in 1983, I was invited to go to Nicaragua. Living in Galway in the west of Ireland I was able to make contact with the local bishop, Eamonn Casey. He had been in San Salvador at Archbishop Romero's funeral, when police opened fire on the crowd of mourners. He introduced me to Sally O'Neill of the Latin American Project in *Trocaire*, the Irish Christian Aid organization; and she gave me names of people to meet in Nicaragua, including an Irish priest from the Falls Road district of Belfast who was working in Managua with the Guatemalan Church-in-exile. Not long before, Sally herself had been deported from Honduras. Soon after my return from Nicaragua, in 1984, Ronald Reagan came to Ireland, visiting Galway as part of his tour. Demonstrations against him were notable for the participation of church-people as well as secular left-wing political groups, women's peace organizations, and the Chilean refugee community. On one of these I met Fr Pat O'Brien, a 'liberation-priest', lately serving in El Salvador, and now back again in a west of Ireland parish. *The Heroes & Martyrs of the North*, a Nicaraguan musical-group representing the rural-workers' trade union, then came on their own tour of Ireland. The enthusiastic welcome they received was an ironic contrast to that given the US President. In Galway they marched gaily and openly with their music through streets which Mr Reagan could only reach by helicopter and had had to traverse in a dark-windowed 'Al Capone' limousine with armed escorts.

As for my practical feminist work: I started a series of events called 'Galway Women's Entertainment'. On our first weekend we examined ancient Greek theatre, with particular reference to Euripides' *Hippolytus*. What we found in the play was rather surprising, because it actually contained *two* plays: one of them showed, with approval, a woman (Phaedra), in tune with her sexual instincts, contrasted with the man who denied his and used up his energy against nature by hunting and killing animals. The other one presented the woman as *destroyer*: she 'goes along' with the forces of nature and the forces of nature thus turn out to be 'unnatural'. Half-way through, the play seemed to come to a stop and change its tune completely between these two themes. Euripides had enjoyed himself, first of all, with an attack on male attitudes; and then suddenly became all pompous and heavy to keep in with the patriarchal Athenian drama-adjudicators . . .

An unexpected connection between this legend and the Fausta story. One of the books I had been reading, *The Age of Martyrs, Christianity from Diocletian to Constantine*, by Fr Guiseppe Ricciotti, referred to the fact that Constantine's son Crispus had been put to death at about the same time as Fausta (his stepmother), and noted that ancient commentators who had linked the two events in a speciously romantic scandal 'may very easily have been under the influence of the myth of the incestuous love of Phaedra and Hippolytus.' If, as I now believed, the Phaedra myth itself in Euripides' version was only a cover-up for a much deeper ideological confrontation, its employment to explain Constantine's crimes was a cover-up of a cover-up, and pointed the way at once to the crucial question behind all feminist dialectic – are we totally contained within nature, or is there a part of us 'outside nature' and belonging to an external superior being? In other words: the old conflict between the idea of a mother-goddess who is *all nature inclusive*, and a father-god who has *created* nature.

It was possible for me to unravel these historical riddles because the BBC in the end gave us a small sum of money for a researcher, the scholar Geoff O'Connell of Kinvara, who found texts and references for us in the National University Library that we would never have been able to ferret out for ourselves. He discovered several important classical documents, and a most particularly helpful dynastic analysis of the third and fourth-century emperors and all their families, arranged in tabular form, from which I could place the Constantine household as a dramatist needs to – their respective ages, and backgrounds, their complicated marital arrangements, made far clearer to the understanding than in any ordinary narrative history-books. Having at last established some real facts to support the assumptions, I now had to find some way of experiencing the spirit behind the facts.

Fortunately, in Ireland, the old matriarchal rituals can still be discerned hidden under the mantle of Roman-Catholic orthodoxy. I joined various Catholic pilgrimages, which are mainly supported by women. I went to Loch Derg, a very ancient ritual, and the strangest of them all, where one goes barefoot, fasting, without sleep, for three days on an island. A number of ceremonies have to be performed, circling round and round at various points in combinations of threes and nines, inducing hallucinations by the rapid inhaling of air to fill our lungs for the repetitive chanting. All the time the priests are there to keep an eye on us and stop us from lying down on the grass, with hints that if we were so to indulge ourselves there might very well be no stopping the orgiastic fervour. Another pilgrimage was to Ballinspittle, to see the phenomenon of the 'moving statue' of the Blessed Virgin. I found that by quickly moving my head and eyes at great speed it was possible to see *anything*. I saw the statue change from the Virgin, to Padre Pio, to the Sacred Heart, and finally to a giant white-and-black cat's face (which is of course a chief symbol of the ancient mother-goddess). The night I was there, there was no religious or sacred feeling – apart from a number of pious old men trying to get us all to say the Rosary – simply one of wonder. There was a chip-van to feed us, and in the coach on the way home the women sang modern pop-songs. I discovered also that several of these women were strongly influenced by home-viewing videos on occult themes which, they said, contained secret messages about the end of the world, and rumours indeed were spreading from Connemara that this event was to take place three days after our pilgrimage.

A group of us from the Galway Women's Entertainment made a point of visiting ancient sacred sites in our own area. One of these was Knock Ma – 'The Hill of Maeve', or of 'Queen Mab' – standing isolated in a vast flat fertile plain, looking out over three counties and the Atlantic Ocean. One of my neighbours, a very old woman, told me that she would never have the courage to go up Knock Ma, because the little-people would put her eyes out – as happened to someone she'd heard of, when he saw them there preparing themselves for a visit to the town of Tuam . . . On the very top of this mountain we saw the grave of General Kirwan – he had originally wanted to be buried standing up, but the ground proved too rocky. Maeve had been the mythical Queen of Connacht, but the General was the legal landlord, and owned every inch of her hill.

I do not think that military men and military bodies have

moved very far forward from the days when the worship of Mithras, the male embodiment of the Unconquered Sun, was endemic throughout the Roman legions (its initiation open only to men). The Roman army fought only two truly religious wars – one against the intolerant male rival of their gods, Jahve of the Jews, and one against the British Goddess as incarnate in Boudicca (who can easily be identified with her Irish neighbour and kinswoman, Maeve of Connacht). Sexual superstition and sexual humiliation are still weapons of war and of coercive law-and-order. Just as Boudicca was flogged by Roman soldiers and her daughters raped, so today women are forcibly strip-searched in our gaols . . . And at the Women's Peace Camp on Greenham Common, the soldiers of the RAF Regiment and the US Air Force have been told that we are 'witches', that we 'cast spells' – their very cantonment is planted on the burial site of the last witch to be killed in that part of the world. She 'walked on water', to the horror of Oliver Cromwell's soldiers, and when they fired bullets at her she caught them in her hands and threw them back. She would not die until the troopers had tied her up and shot directly into her temple, and even the she kept on singing songs and laughing at them.

The witch's laughter and her un-masculine scorn for the bullets that make us remember her today, when the dispossessed women and the dissident women line the roads at midnight to witness the exercises of the cruise missiles going to Salisbury Plain (another sacred site): the Americans have their orders – 'Drive on, never stop, don't look, don't listen to the chants!' –

> We are the witness of your violence
> We are the victims of your violence
> And we will remember your face:
> Blood on your hands . . .

What gaps in history are being skated-over in NATO's Judaeo-Christian internal analysis of the protest? Catholics, Protestants, Anglicans, Quakers, Methodists, Presbyterians, Jews – all women who choose peace rather than war, life rather than death, free choice rather than subservience to a clerical hierarchy – linking arms with women who are opposed to the very concept of the male god. Here the Mother is held and guarded. Do the military, aware of all this, choose the precise night when the moon is at her greatest strength to flaunt their rivalry and destructive power?

Out of such experiences I began to sense what must have lain behind the Fausta story, and what must have been the male-female tensions inside the belly of early Christianity. To quote Mary Daly again: 'If you can't remember, invent.'

But what about men's structures, and the tensions inside *them*? I had two experiences to help me understand these. The first was the Irish 'Artists' Parliament', Aosdána. This was meant to be open to all artists: but I saw its democratic principles being transformed and our communal decisions transferred into the hands of a clutch of misogynist malevolent goblins hunkered over their crock of knowledge. Secondly, the BBC itself, a glorious Byzantine labyrinth, where, at the very time I was working on the plays, a series of traumatic happenings that would have done credit to Constantine's court was being revealed in the daily press as State and Media clashed, just as though it were State and Church; police entered studios and seized film, resignations were accepted, heads rolled.

I now felt I was able to read history books without being prejudiced by their authors' concepts of vital mainstreams and irrelevant eddies. The plays themselves were begun in August 1984; the first drafts of all nine were completed by March 1986: and the final text was finished in the summer of 1987. The countries I visited, thanks to my grant, were Nicaragua, Germany, Italy, China, USSR, England, Wales, Scotland, Cornwall, and the North of Ireland.

I feel strongly that the totality of Christian and post-Christian culture belongs to everyone – that the whole world for good or ill has been affected by it – and that in principle everyone should have an equal right and opportunity to voice opinions and to raise and develop issues implicit in our interpretation of the story. It was agreed with Richard Imison that a format of radio seminars should accompany the presentation of the plays. This meant that John Arden and I were released from the burden of imposed objectivity, and that we were free while writing to come to grips with our own experience, our own individual views, and to allow the gaps in *our* narrative to be filled in by other voices.

Titles in the Methuen Modern Plays
and World Dramatists series
are described on the following pages.

Methuen Modern Plays

Jean Anouilh	*Antigone*
	Becket
	The Lark
	Ring Round the Moon
John Arden	*Serjeant Musgrave's Dance*
	The Workhouse Donkey
	Armstrong's Last Goodnight
	Pearl
John Arden and	*The Royal Pardon*
Margaretta D'Arcy	*The Hero Rises Up*
	The Island of the Mighty
	Vandaleur's Folly
	Whose is the Kingdom?
Wolfgang Baur	*Shakespeare the Sadist*
Rainer Werner	
Fassbinder	*Bremen Coffee*
Peter Handke	*My Foot My Tutor*
Frank Xaver Kroetz	*Stallerhof*
Brendan Behan	*The Quare Fellow*
	The Hostage
	Richard's Cork Leg
Edward Bond	*A-A-America!* and *Stone*
	Saved
	Narrow Road to the Deep North
	The Pope's Wedding
	Lear
	The Sea
	Bingo
	The Fool and *We Come to the River*
	Theatre Poems and Songs
	The Bundle
	The Woman
	The Worlds with *The Activists Papers*
	Restoration and *The Cat*
	Summer and *Fables*

Bertolt Brecht	*Mother Courage and Her Children*
	The Caucasian Chalk Circle
	The Good Person of Szechwan
	The Life of Galileo
	The Threepenny Opera
	Saint Joan of the Stockyards
	The Resistible Rise of Arturo Ui
	The Mother
	Mr Puntila and His Man Matti
	The Measures Taken and other Lehrstücke
	The Days of the Commune
	The Messingkauf Dialogues
	Man Equals Man and *The Elephant Calf*
	The Rise and Fall of the City of Mahagonny and *The Seven Deadly Sins*
	Baal
	A Respectable Wedding and other one-act plays
	Drums in the Night
	In the Jungle of Cities
	Fear and Misery of the Third Reich and *Señora Carrar's Rifles*
	Schweyk in the Second World War and *The Visions of Simone Machard*
Brecht Weill Lane	*Happy End*
Howard Brenton	*The Churchill Play*
	Weapons of Happiness
	Epsom Downs
	The Romans in Britain
	Plays for the Poor Theatre
	Magnificence
	Revenge
	Hitler Dances
	Bloody Poetry

John Kirkmorris: *Coxcombe;* John
Peacock: *Attard in Retirement;* Olwen
Wymark: *The Child*)

Best Radio Plays of 1981 (Peter Barnes:
The Jumping Mimuses of Byzantium;
Don Haworth: *Talk of Love and War;*
Harold Pinter: *Family Voices;* David
Pownall: *Beef;* J P Rooney: *The Dead
Image;* Paul Thain: *The Biggest
Sandcastle in the World*)

Best Radio Plays of 1982 (Rhys
Adrian: *Watching the Plays Together;*
John Arden: *The Old Man Sleeps
Alone;* Harry Barton: *Hoopoe Day;*
Donald Chapman: *Invisible Writing;*
Tom Stoppard: *The Dog It Was
That Died;* William Trevor: *Autumn
Sunshine*)

Best Radio Plays of 1983 (Wally K Daly:
Time Slip; Shirley Gee: *Never in My
Lifetime;* Gerry Jones: *The Angels They
Grow Lonely;* Steve May: *No
Exceptions;* Martyn Read: *Scouting for
Boys*)

Best Radio Plays of 1984 (Stephen
Dunstone: *Who Is Sylvia?;* Don
Haworth: *Daybreak;* Robert Ferguson:
Transfigured Night; Caryl Phillips:
The Wasted Years; Christopher Russell:
Swimmer; Rose Tremain: *Temporary
Shelter*)

Best Radio Plays of 1985 (Rhys
Adrian: *Outpatient;* Barry
Collins: *King Canute;* Martin
Crimp: *The Attempted Acts;*
David Pownall: *Ploughboy
Monday;* James Saunders:
Menocchio; Michael Wall:
Hiroshima: The Movie)

World Dramatists

Collections of plays by the best-known modern playwrights in value-for-money paperbacks.

John Arden
: **PLAYS: ONE**
Serjeant Musgrave's Dance, The Workhouse Donkey, Armstrong's Last Goodnight

Brendan Behan
: **THE COMPLETE PLAYS**
The Quare Fellow, The Hostage, Richard's Cork Leg, Moving Out, A Garden Party, The Big House

Edward Bond
: **PLAYS: ONE**
Saved, Early Morning, The Pope's Wedding
PLAYS: TWO
Lear, The Sea, Narrow Road to the Deep North, Black Mass, Passion

Howard Brenton
: **PLAYS: ONE**
Christie in Love, Magnificence, The Churchill Play, Weapons of Happiness, Epsom Downs, Sore Throats

Georg Büchner
: **THE COMPLETE PLAYS**
Danton's Death, Leonce and Lena, Woyzeck with *The Hessian Courier, Lenz, On Cranial Nerves* and *Selected Letters*

Caryl Churchill
: **PLAYS: ONE**
Owners, Traps, Vinegar Tom, Light Shining in Buckinghamshire, Cloud Nine

Noël Coward
: **PLAYS: ONE**
Hay Fever, The Vortex, Fallen Angels, Easy Virtue

PLAYS: TWO
Private Lives, Bitter-Sweet, The Marquise, Post-Mortem
PLAYS: THREE
Design for Living, Cavalcade, Conversation Piece, To-night at 8.30 (Hands Across the Sea, Still Life, Fumed Oak)
PLAYS: FOUR
Blithe Spirit, Present Laughter, This Happy Breed, To-night at 8.30 (Ways and Means, The Astonished Heart, 'Red Peppers')
PLAYS: FIVE
Relative Values, Look After Lulu!, Waiting in the Wings, Suite in Three Keys

David Edgar

PLAYS: ONE
Destiny, Mary Barnes, The Jail Diary of Albie Sachs, Saigon Rose, O Fair Jerusalem

Michael Frayn

PLAYS: ONE
Alphabetical Order, Donkey's Years, Clouds, Make and Break, Noises Off

John Galsworthy

FIVE PLAYS
Strife, Justice, The Eldest Son, The Skin Game, Loyalties

Simon Gray

PLAYS: ONE
Butley, Otherwise Engaged, The Rear Column, Quartermaine's Terms, The Common Pursuit

Henrik Ibsen

PLAYS: ONE
Ghosts, The Wild Duck, The Master Builder
PLAYS: TWO
A Doll's House, An Enemy of the People, Hedda Gabler

PLAYS: THREE
Rosmersholm, The Lady from the Sea, Little Eyolf
PLAYS: FOUR
The Pillars of Society, John Gabriel Borkman, When We Dead Awaken
PLAYS: FIVE
Brand, Emperor and Galilean
PLAYS: SIX
Peer Gynt, The Pretenders

Molière
FIVE PLAYS
The School for Wives, Tartuffe, The Misanthrope, The Miser, The Hypochondriac

Clifford Odets
SIX PLAYS
Waiting for Lefty, Awake and Sing!, Till the Day I Die, Paradise Lost, Golden Boy, Rocket to the Moon

Joe Orton
THE COMPLETE PLAYS
Entertaining Mr Sloane, Loot, What the Butler Saw, The Ruffian on the Stair, The Erpingham Camp, Funeral Games, The Good and Faithful Servant

Arthur Wing Pinero
THREE PLAYS
The Magistrate, The Second Mrs Tanqueray, Trelawny of the 'Wells'

Harold Pinter
PLAYS: ONE
The Birthday Party, The Room, The Dumb Waiter, A Slight Ache, The Hothouse, A Night Out
PLAYS: TWO
The Caretaker, The Dwarfs, The Collection, The Lover, Night School, Trouble in the Works, The Black and White, Request Stop, Last to Go, Special Offer

Synge

THE COMPLETE PLAYS
The Playboy of the Western World,
The Tinker's Wedding, In the Shadow
of the Glen, Riders to the Sea, The
Well of the Saints, Deirdre of the
Sorrows

'No other playwrights have the political insight, the breadth of historical vision, the dramatic inventiveness and the sheer theatrical **knowledge** of D'Arcy and Arden.'

ALBERT HUNT, **NEW SOCIETY**

John Arden and Margaretta D'Arcy have stood out persistently for their political and artistic freedom against suffocation by the 'foam-rubber of the jumbo-jet culture' and a gathering climate of repression. This stand has forced them into many an 'awkward corner' from which, amid all the 'bumping and jumping', they have managed nevertheless to write a sheaf of fine plays among them **The Happy Haven, The Island of the Mighty** and **The Non-Stop Connolly Show,** alongside Arden's own, more personal, work including **Live Like Pigs, Serjeant Musgrave's Dance** and **Armstrong's Last Goodnight** and his Booker Prize nominated novel, **Silence Among the Weapons.**

In **Awkward Corners** they tackle two themes, broached in a previous book of essays **To Present the Pretence:** the artist's role and the 'Matter of Ireland'. Their opinions, whether describing guerrilla theatre in Galway, a trip to Nicaragua, censorship in Ireland, or D'Arcy's involvement in women's politics at Greenham, Armagh and elsewhere, are forthright, controversial and provocative. There is something here to interest followers of cultural and women's politics as well as students of Irish history. It also offers through autobiographical pieces, including an account of Arden's Yorkshire childhood and a selection of D'Arcy's poetry, a fascinating insight into a theatrical partnership which has retained its integrity despite the buffets of notoriety.

ISBN 0-413-40340-8

9 780413 403407

PRICE NET
£7.95
IN UK ONLY

COVER PHOTOGRAPH:
DAVID BLOUNT
A METHUEN PAPERBACK
THEATRE/NON-FICTION